# A Psychoanalysis for Our Time

# A Psychoanalysis for Our Time

*Exploring the Blindness of the Seeing I*

Jeffrey B. Rubin

NEW YORK UNIVERSITY PRESS

*New York and London*

NEW YORK UNIVERSITY PRESS
New York and London

© 1998 by New York University

Library of Congress Cataloging-in-Publication Data
Rubin, Jeffrey B.
A psychoanalysis for our time : exploring the blindness of the
seeing I / Jeffrey B. Rubin.
p. cm.
Includes bibliographical references and index.
ISBN 0-8147-7491-1 (alk. paper)
1. Psychoanalysis. I. Title
BF173.R76 1998
150'.195—ddc21        98-58002
                        CIP

New York University Press books are printed on acid-free paper,
and their binding materials are chosen for strength and durability.

Manufactured in the United States of America

10 9 8 7 6 5 4 3 2 1

*To George Atwood:*
*"Gladly would he learn and gladly teach"*
            —*Chaucer,* Canterbury Tales

# Contents

# Preface

Psychoanalysis is in a period of ferment, facing unprecedented challenges and opportunities. It is fashionable in our time to dismiss psychoanalysis. Polemical attacks on its theories and practices are proliferating. Confronted by challenges to its concepts and methods, one might be tempted to conclude that psychoanalysis is a relic of a bygone age.

And yet, despite these challenges, psychoanalysis continues to exert an immense influence on our collective self-consciousness. Sigmund Freud, our "dead" ancestor, is very alive in our culture. Psychoanalytic concepts such as unconscious motives, the formative role of childhood, the hidden meaning of dreams, the variability of sexuality, and the value of self-awareness have become part of our common cultural currency. We "live more than ever," notes Harold Bloom, "in the Age of Freud," who has "become a culture, our culture" (1985, p. 1). Contemporary psychoanalysts of every stripe have expanded the scope and depth of Freud's legacy; exploring new territories such as trauma, gender, race, and even spirituality.

From my vantage point as a psychoanalytic clinician, teacher, and supervisor, I believe that the circumference of Freud's legacy has yet to be drawn. What value might psychoanalysis have in our fast-paced world, with its emphasis on quick fixes and its aversion to self-investigation? Is there any place for psychoanalysis in a world in which profits are valued over people and alienation from self and other predominate?

As I ponder the recent scholarship on Freud, both the virulent attacks and the loyalist defenses, I am struck by this irony: the way psychoanalysis is typically approached by both critics and defenders has unfortunately compromised our capacity to take the full measure of Freud's complex legacy. Critics of Freud often fail to recognize the resources and potential of psychoanalysis, while its loyal defenders fail to acknowledge it problems. We need another perspective to approach psychoanalysis with critical acuity and assess both its possibilities and its perils.

This book offers an alternative perspective to current debates about the status and value of psychoanalysis. I have repeatedly witnessed—first as a patient, later as a clinician, teacher, and supervisor of other therapists—its enormous potential to enrich human lives. The integrity of human life is increasingly endangered in our age. There are pervasive encroachments on privacy, dignity, and freedom. In such times, sanctuaries for reflectiveness, emotional intimacy, and imagination are crucial, as are relationships that cherish empathy, authenticity, and self-investigation. Psychoanalysis can be such a sanctuary, offering profound tools for expanding and deepening human self-understanding and enriching relations with others.

Psychoanalysis offers a sanctuary in several ways. The special conditions of psychoanalytic treatment create an environment ideally suited for in-depth self-investigation. Conducted in a quiet, serene atmosphere, with a minimum of distractions, psychoanalysis provides a bulwark against the cognitive oversaturation and pressure toward conventionality pervading the contemporary world, which flattens human life and drains it of depth and meaning. Minimizing the manifold bombardments of daily life—telephone calls, e-mail, infomericals, and sound bites—enhances our capacity to reflect profoundly on our lives. The noncoercive, self-reflective therapeutic relationship, in which the patient is asked to speak with candor and the analyst to listen impartially and creatively, provides a haven from the frivolousness and superficiality that characterize so much of ordinary existence. The patient's subjective world is encouraged to emerge when it can be shared with another person who is deeply interested in the nature of that experience. Exploring one's hopes and fears, dreams and conflicts in such an environment fosters the discovery of hidden dimensions of one's being and the forging of new and more expansive ways of living. Such havens, in which the most profound questions about how to live can be raised and addressed, are a priceless gift to our culture. Our collective life can be infused with vitality, depth, and meaning by the sanctuary offered by psychoanalysis.

Despite the value of psychoanalysis in enriching subjectivity and decreasing alienation, its relevance for our age is compromised by its own failings, which must be addressed. Psychoanalysts are all too frequently overinvested in accepted theory and resistant to creative thinking. The institutions of psychoanalysis are also plagued by disturbing politics and insulation from fertile contact with allied humanistic and social science disciplines. Most importantly, psychoanalytic theory and practice exhibit insufficient conceptual and methodological self-awareness.

A psychoanalysis of unsuspected vitality and depth emerges when we steer a middle path between vilifying the field or uncritically defending it. Examining what is visionary about psychoanalysis while confronting what is problematic can aid it in actualizing its liberatory potential as a discipline.

# Acknowledgments

Dialogues with friends and colleagues were indispensable in the development of this book. Stephen Mitchell played a seminal role when he first encouraged me to write a book several years ago. His astute feedback on earlier drafts of several chapters significantly clarified and deepened my focus. This book was enormously enriched by Steve's input. I am deeply grateful for his ongoing intellectual generosity and support.

George Atwood was, in an important sense, a midwife to the creation of this book. Conversations with him about psychoanalysis and the human condition over the past eight years have been a source of deep intellectual nourishment. Many of the ideas arose in dialogue with him. He also read and offered enlightening feedback on each chapter. His unflagging interest, stimulation, and support were of inestimable help in completion the book. I am profoundly grateful on a personal as well as intellectual level.

Dialogues with Ken Barnes, Lou Breger, Doris Dlugacz, Bettina Edelstein, Jerry Gargiulo, Jerry Gold, James Jones, David Kastan, Paul Wyatt Kahn, Suzanne R. Kirschner, Joel Kramer, Dorthy Levinson, JoAnn Magdoff, Eugene Murphy, Steven Reisner, Alan Roland, Karen Smyers, Randy Sorenson, Christine Ware, Marc Wayne, and Leslie Wolowitz played an important role in clarifying and deepening my thinking about various aspects of psychoanalysis. Breger, Edelstein, Gargiulo, Jones, Kastan, Kahn, Magdoff, and Sorenson also took time out from their busy schedules to offer helpful feedback on several chapters. I am very appreciative of their intellectual stimulation, generosity, support, and friendship.

I would like to thank my parents, Joyce and Harris Rubin, who nourished and supported a love of learning. In addition, my father taught me to revere truth more than politics. I owe a debt of gratitude to my patients for providing me the opportunity to accompany them in their individual journeys. This book and my life have been deeply enriched by our mutual attempts to explore and understand the depths of their hopes and fears, dreams and conflicts.

I am also grateful to Dan Burston, Egon Dumler, Michael Guy Thompson, Leo Goldberger, and Timothy Bartlett for the instrumental role they played in the publication of this book. Bartlett's incisive feedback on the penultimate draft significantly enriched the manuscript. I wish to thank Jennifer Hammer for skillfully expediting the production and publication of this book. I wish to thank Dolores Metzner for her beautiful and evocative cover art. I am very grateful to Hilary de Bhál Sweeney for her generosity of spirit and creativity in making the cover design come alive. I would also like to thank David Updike for his careful and painstaking copyediting. Matthew Von Unwerth of the New York Psychoanalytic Library provided valuable bibliographical assistance.

The friendship, wisdom, love, and tireless support of Mary was indispensable in the completion of these and other projects. Sine qua non, again. My hope is that Erika and Josh and their respective generations will find the meaning and stimulation in their own lives that my forays in psychoanalysis and the humanities have afforded me in mine.

Portions of this manuscript have appeared in earlier incarnations. An earlier version of the introduction appeared in *The Death of Psychoanalysis: Murder, Suicide or Rumor Greatly Exaggerated*, edited by Robert Prince (Northvale, New Jersey: Jason Aronson, 1998). Chapter 2 will appear in the forthcoming *Provocations of Psychoanalysis*, edited by Anthony Molino and Christine Ware (San Francisco: City Lights Books). An earlier version of chapter 3 appeared in the *Journal of the American Academy of Psychoanalysis*, 25; no. 1 (1997): 15–35. An earlier version of chapter 8 appeared in *Soul on the Couch: Spirituality, Religion, and Morality in Contemporary Psychoanalysis*, edited by Charles Spezzano and Gerald Gargiulo (Hillsdale, N.J.: Analytic Press, 1997). An earlier version of chapter 9 will appear in *The European Legacy: Towards New Paradigms* (Cambridge, Mass.: MIT Press, in press). An earlier version of chapter 11 appeared in the *Journal of the American Academy of Psychoanalysis*, 24; no. 3 (1996): 457–83.

# Introduction

Looking back, at the age of sixty-nine, on the potential value of his "life's labours"—the psychoanalytic edifice he had created and developed—Sigmund Freud (1925d) remarked: "Something will come of them in the future, though I cannot myself tell whether it will be much or little. I can, however, express a hope that I have opened up a pathway for an important advance in our knowledge" (p. 70).

The letter Freud received eleven years later from Thomas Mann, Virginia Woolf, Romain Rolland, H. G. Wells, Stefan Zweig, and 192 other writers and artists on the occasion of his eightieth birthday offered an unequivocally affirmative response to the hope he had expressed. They hailed him as "the pioneer of a new and deeper knowledge of man," a "courageous seer and healer . . . a guide to hitherto undreamed-of regions of the human soul." Freud, they declared, "penetrated truths which seemed dangerous because they revealed what had been anxiously hidden, and illumined dark places. Far and wide he disclosed new problems and changed the old standards . . . his gains for knowledge cannot permanently be denied or obscured" (quoted in Jones, 1957, pp. 205–6).

Yet Freud's star—and that of psychoanalysis—seems to be waning in the late twentieth century, even as interest in it within the humanities, arts, and social sciences is increasing.[1] For many people, Freud and the eighteenth-century Enlightenment project he exemplified—achieving human emancipation and freedom through the exercise of reason—are now seen as bankrupt. Freud is thus no longer treated as the lodestar he once was in the quest to illuminate the mysteries and complexities of the self.

Psychoanalysis has a problematic standing in the contemporary world, where it confronts gnawing questions about its theoretical relevance and clinical validity. In the crowded, fragmented, competitive, and politically charged critical scene of poststructuralism, postmodernism, post-Marxism, and various feminisms, psychoanalysis, a set of discourses and practices that have potentially heuristic implications for illuminating and

1

transforming human self-understanding and conduct, has been resoundingly devalued, rejected, and marginalized.

Recent years have seen what Paul Roazen (1990) terms a "destabilization of Freud's reputation" (p. xvii) among philosophers, scientists, feminists, literary critics, and even some psychoanalysts. They have accused Freud of utilizing an epistemologically unsound methodology (Adolf Grunbaum), being a cryptobiologist (Frank Sulloway), subscribing to and perpetuating a deleterious patriarchal vision (Betty Friedan, Kate Millett, and Germaine Greer), conducting himself in an immoral manner (Frederick Crews), and retreating from psychic truths he lacked the courage to uphold (Jeffrey Masson).[2]

Much of the recent scholarship on Freud—both the virulent attacks (e.g., Crews, 1993) and the loyalist, hagiographic defenses—has impeded our capacity to discern what is valuable and what is problematic in psychoanalysis. The genuine difficulties in psychoanalytic theory and practice are sometimes neglected by apologists, who may deny the need for revision and thus neglect problems within the field. By not addressing these problems, they fail to draw fully on the liberatory possibilities of the psychoanalytic enterprise, and psychoanalysis is thus impoverished.

Critics of psychoanalysis eclipse what is valuable, often neglecting both postclassical theoretical revisions of psychoanalysis and clinical facets of the classical and post-Freudian psychoanalytic enterprise. There are at least two problems with such critics: (1) they treat the aspects of the psychoanalytic corpus that they are interested in—typically classical theory and nonclinical or nonmethodological topics—as if they are representative of the whole; and (2) by neglecting the contributions of postclassical analysts, they deny that psychoanalysis has a history and thereby critique a body of classical analytic thought that many contemporary analysts have significantly amended and moved beyond theoretically, epistemologically, and methodologically. This prevents them from fully grasping the complexity and fertility of the psychoanalytic enterprise. The theoretical landscape of psychoanalysis looks much fuller when the contributions of post-Freudian perspectives are also considered.

By foregrounding such things as the unscientific status of psychoanalytic discourse or Freud's patriarchal view of women, such critics also underplay other radical and important aspects of Freud's "multiple legacies" (Schafer, 1992, p. 152). Such studies rarely, if ever, point to the transformative context (the self-reflexive dialogue of analyst and analysand) and liberatory methodology (free association and the analysis of transference, countertransference, and defensive processes) for investigating unconscious aspects of human life that Freud offers.[3]

Both deifying and denigrating Freud or psychoanalysis—engaging in "Freud piety" (Fromm, 1959) or "Freud-bashing" (Gelfand, 1992, pp. xi–xii)—preclude the balanced perspective that is essential for reanimating psychoanalysis. Both approaches compromise our capacity to use the fertile resources of psychoanalysis and the discoveries of allied disciplines to recuperate what is useful and reformulate what is problematic.

Some questions about psychoanalysis arise because of social conditions in the United States—and perhaps elsewhere—that foster fear of and resistance to a psychoanalytic approach to life. Psychoanalysis can be a threat to a commercialized society in which a quick-fix mentality reigns and conspicuous consumption is valued over self-examination. On the therapeutic level, there is pressure from drug companies deeply invested in promoting the consumption of drugs rather than the achievement of psychological insight. In addition, there is the ubiquitous problem of managed-care organizations, many of which value profits over the psychological welfare of their clients and promote "anti-introspective treatment methods" (Gedo, 1984, p. 170) that promise short-cuts to the complex and laborious work of self-understanding. A declining standard of living in the United States has also placed economic constraints on the pool of potential analysands, contributing to a devaluation of psychoanalysis. And in a world like ours, in which individuals constantly confront a sense of impotence on many fronts, it can be profoundly unsettling to face one of the central messages of psychoanalysis, namely, that we are not even masters of our own minds (Freud, 1917b).

Perhaps some questions about the validity of psychoanalysis arise because it threatens to reveal unconscious motives on the part of critics that may be based, for example, on self-serving wishes or fears. But other doubts about the usefulness of psychoanalysis are based on genuine problems and limitations within the field. The fact that certain critiques of psychoanalysis may have selfish and reductive motives should not blind us to these very real difficulties.

That psychoanalysis is in need of revision is evident to anyone who considers the conflicts within the field about what psychoanalysis is and what it should be. Residues of phallocentrism, sexism,[4] positivism, and scientism[5] remain, as well as an "unworldliness" (Said, 1983), or the absence of an intellectually cosmopolitan vision, promoted by psychoanalysis's relative neglect of the larger social and historical world in which it is embedded. Psychoanalysts all too often operate as if people live in a vacuum; neglecting the unique sociocultural worlds in which analysands were raised and now live. Many analysts have narcissistic and dogmatic investments in inherited theory (Greenson, 1969); that is, they believe too heartily in the absolute validity of their own formulations. Others are resistant to creative theorizing in the field (Langs, 1978) and rigid and defensive about its boundaries. Intolerance toward those with different points of view has proliferated. The byzantine politics and ideological warfare within and among different schools is yet another complication, as is the marginalization of dissidents. The resistance within certain segments of the field to corrective feedback about limitations in psychoanalytic theories and practices and, most important, insufficient theoretical and methodological self-reflectiveness, compromises psychoanalysis's potential.

Freud may have discerned a fundamental difficulty in psychoanalysis in the second case in *Studies on Hysteria*. Responding to Freud's question about why she did not tell him that she loved her employer when she knew that she did, Miss Lucy R. replies, " 'I didn't know—or rather I didn't want to know. I wanted to drive it out of my head and not think of it again" (Breuer & Freud, 1895, p. 117). In a footnote to Lucy's remarks Freud says:

> I have never managed to give a better description than this of the strange state of mind in which one knows and does not know a thing at the same time. It is clearly impossible to understand it unless one has been in such a state oneself. I myself have had a very remarkable experience of this sort, which is still clearly before me. If I try to recollect what went on in my mind at the time I can get hold of very little. What happened was that I saw something which did not fit in at all with my expectation; yet I did not allow what I saw to disturb my fixed plan in the least, though the perception should have put a stop to it. I was unconscious of any contradiction in this; nor was I aware of my feelings of repulsion, which must nevertheless undoubtedly have been responsible for the perception producing no psychical effect. I was afflicted by that blindness of the seeing eye which is so astonishing in the attitude of mothers to their daughters, husbands to their wives and rulers to their favourites. (P. 117n)

A "blindness of the seeing I"[6] has afflicted Freud and many subsequent psychoanalysts—including myself—as well as mothers, husbands, and rulers. Freud's myriad contributions have been compromised deeply by an epistemological ambivalence at the heart of his life and work. A closer examination of Freud's own life in particular, and psychoanalysis in general, reveals that a conflict between a wish-to-know and a wish-*not*-to-know, or seeing and not seeing psychic truth, is a central facet of Freud's life with his family, and the subsequent history of psychoanalysis. Many aspects of psychoanalysis, including (but not limited to) Freud's self-analysis, his theory of pathogenesis, dream practice, aspects of the institutional history and politics of psychoanalysis, the analytic relationship, and even postclassical conceptions of self, embody this ambivalence about knowing. An interest in both decoding *and* concealing the truth frames and haunts both Freud's life and psychoanalysis. For example, the psychoanalytic situation and method often destabilize rigid conceptions of self and open up unforeseen possibilities for living. Yet the patient's freedom can be subverted by the tendency within psychoanalytic theories of selfhood—including post-Freudian revisionist theories such as D. W. Winnicott's "True Self" and Heinz Kohut's "bipolar self"—to fit analysands into a Procrustean conceptual bed of established psychoanalytic concepts and procedures, fostering compliance and self-imprisonment.

I have a deep love and respect for psychoanalysis. It has changed my life and the lives of many people with whom I have had the privilege to work. It is an extraordinary tool for increasing self-awareness, healing developmental arrests, resolving conflicts, heightening interpersonal sensitivity and compassion, and expanding the range of human freedom. But, as an analysand and later as an analyst and supervisor of other therapists, I have experienced how psychoanalysis can sometimes promote enslavement as well as liberation. Even as it fosters an antiauthoritarian stance toward life by questioning both established meanings and the authority humans often irrationally invest in others, it often resembles an authoritarian culture, breeding conformity and submissiveness and sapping creative thought and practice.

*A Psychoanalysis for Our Time* puts psychoanalysis "on the couch" in an effort to demonstrate that it has something rare and vital to contribute to the world, though it needs to be emended and enriched. I attempt to steer a balanced course between the Scylla of premature dismissal characteristic of anti-Freudian diatribes and the Charybdis of blind adulation often demonstrated by overzealous Freudians. Such a viewpoint recognizes that psychoanalysis serves a vital function for individuals and the world, but also acknowledges that some psychoanalytic categories and perspectives have to be questioned and in certain cases jettisoned or refined. Approaching psychoanalysis with an analytic attitude of neither defensive denigration nor unbridled reverence encourages its hidden flaws and strengths and its emancipatory potential to emerge.

For psychoanalysis to flourish, it must detect where blindness lives in its own institutions, theories, and practices. It must also develop greater historical, theoretical, and clinical self-awareness. In this book I explore various aspects of "the blindness of the seeing I" in psychoanalytic history, institutions, theories, and practices. Whether pinpointing hidden tensions in received theories, or presenting alternative narratives about marginalized figures in psychoanalysis's past, or highlighting key omissions in analytic practices, each chapter in this book suggests ways to increase psychoanalysis's self-awareness. What emerges is a psychoanalysis that has great relevance for our time. Freud's work in particular and contemporary psychoanalysis in general offer a way of thinking about the nature of the self that challenges the narrow terms of contemporary debates.

The nature of the self is hotly contested in contemporary thought. Views of the self obviously have enormous implications for the ways we define and treat such issues as the nature of human nature, psychological health, morality, and relationships. Two traditions dominate current discourse on subjectivity: the traditional Western humanist conception of the self—Descartes's "master and proprietor of nature"—a sovereign, autonomous, unified subject who engages in rational reflection, exercises choice, and experiences freedom; and the poststructuralist, antihumanist view of a subject that is decentered and enslaved, divided within itself with no organizing center, and completely controlled and shaped by language and history.[7]

Freud and psychoanalysis avoid both the naive humanist, Cartesian conceptions of an autonomous, rationalistic self, and the nihilistic, antihumanist, poststructuralist notions of a fragmented self lacking the capacity for agency or freedom. By acknowledging psychic determinism without disavowing the possibility of human freedom, and by delineating the shaping power of unconsciousness without devaluing the power of reason, what I would term Freud's *posthumanist* self challenges the reductive terms that frame the issues in the humanist-antihumanist debate and thereby has something important to contribute to this stalled conversation.[8] Freud's posthumanist self and practice are explored in more detail in chapter 9.

Humanism is an embattled concept in contemporary discourse (Dallmayr, 1984). It has come under increasing attack in recent years from critics representing a multitude of perspectives who claim, among other things, that the Enlightenment project has culminated, in the twentieth century, in totalitarianism and nihilism.[9] The viability and even the existence of the Cartesian humanist conception of the self, arguably our secular god, has been challenged by French philosophers (Jacques Derrida) and psychoanalysts (Jacques Lacan), artists (Francis Bacon), and literary theorists (Paul de Man), among others, who herald the dissolution and "death of the subject" and assert that humans are puppets of language and history.

Antihumanist perspectives on self in turn have been challenged by critics (e.g., Waugh, 1989) who point out that the view of the self as a linguistic illusion interferes with the notion of human agency and thus inhibits political engagement. If there is no subject, then there is no one who is alienated or oppressed, no evil to challenge, and no one to contest it.[10]

Both humanist and antihumanist perspectives on self, in my view, have something valuable to offer contemporary understanding of human beings. Introspection, reason, agency, choice, and freedom, as humanists recognize, exist and are crucial to human beings. Human self-blindness and servitude (to language), as antihumanists realize, are also central facets of human life. However, by taking a particular facet of subjectivity, such as reason or the disunity of the self, to be the whole of it, we allow other central aspects of selfhood to be eclipsed, and we neglect crucial dimensions of self-experience. Both the humanist evasion of self-unconsciousness and the antihumanist neglect of freedom and responsibility foster an incomplete and impoverished perspective on selfhood.

Neither humanist nor antihumanist discourse provides a sufficient perspective for understanding self-experience. Both the rationalistic, egocentric individualism of humanism and the unfree, decentered self of poststructuralism make it difficult to develop adequate accounts of the complexity of subjects. People, after all, are shaped by multiple internal and external factors, including the physical and the cultural, as they attempt to navigate the complex and ever-changing waters of our multidimensional world.

Furthermore, by positing false and disabling dichotomies—sovereign self or illusory self, human agency or human imprisonment, freedom or determinism—the humanist-antihumanist debate creates an intellectual dead end in contemporary discourse that impedes an understanding of self-experience. It is difficult if not impossible to apprehend the complexity that is the self when human experience is artificially divided into false dualities. To address clearly the psychological complexity and fluidity of our world, we must recognize that experiences of self-assertion and communion, the exercise of will and the experience of enslavement, coexist and interweave within an individual. We are neither totally free nor completely determined, neither unitary nor dispersed, neither powerless nor masterful. We are all of these. Freud and psychoanalysis offer resources for escaping the intellectual cul-de-sac that social science and humanist discourses on subjectivity have generated. Such resources are essential for survival in our world.

For psychoanalysis to reach its radical potential and be of real benefit in our world, it must develop a capacity for a more thorough self-reflexivity that was not practiced by Freud and his contemporaries but is available to us. Reflexivity, from the Latin root *re-flectere*, means "to bend back." Self-reflection, like self-analysis, is beset by a common difficulty: the examination of one's self or perspective inevitably occurs within the limiting and limited horizon of that very perspective. Since we cannot transcend our subjectivity, reflecting on the partiality of our own perspective cannot help us eliminate it. But understanding the impact of this partial perspective on our thought can sometimes aid in revealing alternative conceptions of self and world.

"All worlds have halfsight," writes e. e. cummings (1972), "any world must always half perceive . . . / Only whose vision can create the whole . . . / he's free into the beauty of the truth" (p. 845). It seems true that "all worlds have [only] halfsight." But there is no "vision that can create the whole." Psychoanalysis and psychoanalysts are not alone in the "blindness of the seeing I": It seems to be a key aspect of the human condition. All humans thus confront the dilemma Søren Kierkegaard (1843) pinpointed when he said, "Life must be understood backward . . . [but] it must be lived forward" (p. 111).

Because blindness constitutes our very historical being, the crucial challenge for psychoanalysis and psychoanalysts is not how to eliminate self-blindness—which is impossible—but how to cultivate greater self-reflexivity. We have to pursue knowledge of the human condition while retaining an awareness of both its complexity and its inevitable incompleteness (Stephen Mitchell, personal communication). This reflexivity can take various forms. In this book I focus on developing greater historical, theoretical, and clinical reflexivity in psychoanalysis. The book is thus divided into three parts: "Psychoanalytic History and Institutions," "Psychoanalytic Theory," and "Psychoanalytic Practice."

Part 1 explores various aspects of psychoanalytic history and organizations, including the hidden impact of Freud's relationship with his mother on his life and work; censorship and the politics of early psychoanalysis as embodied in the Secret Committee and its treatment of Sandor Ferenczi; and the rigid nature of psychoanalytic groups, including the way they promote conformity and impede innovation.

Ranging across diverse theoretical terrain, including Freudian, Winnicottian, and Kohutian conceptions of selfhood, part 2 looks at aspects of analytic theory, such as unconscious omissions in psychoanalytic conceptions of self; the patient's role in constructing an identity; the idols psychoanalysts worship; and the impact of spirituality on self-experience.

Part 3 examines clinical facets of psychoanalysis, including unproblematized (and thus problematic) conceptions of how analysts represent the complexity of the therapeutic process in case reports; hidden inequalities and modes of domination in the analytic relationship; and the liberatory implications of Freud's analytic method and his "deterministic psychology of freedom" (Gay, 1990, p. 89).

The disparate strategies and tools I draw on in examining these topics are gleaned from a range of sources, including psychoanalysis and allied nonpsychoanalytic disciplines such as the deconstructionism associated with Derrida, the genealogical approach to history advocated by Foucault, feminist accounts of the politics of knowledge as it relates to the process of representing subjects (Hutcheon, 1989), and anthropological strategies that attempt to represent subjects in a nonsubjugated manner (Clifford & Marcus, 1986). Whether detecting the internal contradictions and evasions in apparently coherent analytic theories, offering a "counterhistory" to conventional narratives about the psychoanalytic past, or exploring topics that are normally neglected in psychoanalysis, the following chapters seek to contribute to the development of a methodology through which psychoanalysis might become more essentially and continually self-reflective and thereby more relevant to our age.

Psychoanalytic texts are generally devoid of self-reflexivity.[11] It is easier to advocate reflexivity than to practice it. And it is hardest to practice it on one's own work. This creates an interesting tension in the texts of those—like me—who suggest that no theories, including psychoanalytic ones, are final; that all are partial, essentially contestable, and potentially in need of revision. When theoretical claims in such texts are treated without skepticism—which is what usually happens in the generally unreflexive discourse of most psychoanalysts—then these claims are granted an unchallenged authority that invalidates the author's claims about the partiality of all viewpoints. It is as if one is saying: all perspectives are partial—except my own.

In thinking about this tension, which I realized could neither be transcended nor avoided, I decided that it fit with the spirit of reflexivity that I was theoretically recommending for psychoanalysis in general to depart from psychoanalytic conventions and more fully problematize my own perspectives in this text. To do this will at times necessitate different forms and styles of exposition than might ordinarily appear in psychoanalytic writings.

My reflexivity about my own work takes various forms. I reflect on my own theoretical omissions, attempt to notice where my own desires and confusion are smoothed over and where unsolved problems inhabit my discourse, present alternative interpretations to my own favored constructions, and envision perspectives that may not yet exist, but perhaps need to be imagined.

I employ a nontraditional, self-consciously experimental format with some trepidation because it questions conventional analytic modes of explication underwritten by scientific assumptions of realism, truth, and rationality, which may be central to the self-image of the reader as well as the discipline of analysis as a whole.[12] My hope is that by attempting to embody the perspective I am advocating, I will give the reader an intensified *experience* of reflexivity, as well as a sense of how it might be fostered.

Because immaculate perception and objective theorizing are impossible, my work will undoubtedly exemplify the dual status that Linda Hutcheon (1989) terms "complicity" and "critique", blindness and insight. My hope is that readers from different theoretical and personal vantage points will engage my text and, in reflecting on it, perhaps formulate their own questions and critique. In that way, other blind spots and possibilities within both my work in particular and psychoanalysis in general might emerge. The willingness to recognize the contingent nature of even our most cherished formulations and continually explore and play with alternatives is essential to promoting the vitality of psychoanalysis.

# PART I

# Psychoanalytic History
# and Institutions

# 1

# To See or Not to See?

## That Was Freud's Dilemma

This book chronicles the tension between seeing and not-seeing, or the "blindness of the seeing I," in psychoanalytic history, institutions, theories, and practices. Although the explicit purpose of our discipline is to remove censorship and increase self-awareness, mystifications, omissions, and self-deceptions are built into the fabric of psychoanalytic theory and practice in ways that compromise and obscure its radical potential. The first and cardinal example of the blindness of the seeing I emerges in the life and work of the creator of psychoanalysis, Sigmund Freud. This chapter explores the genesis of this phenomena in his relationship with his mother, as well as several salient manifestations of this theme in his life and work.

Emphasizing the importance of an author's life has low prestige in our current intellectual climate. There is a general skepticism about psychobiography in psychoanalysis and a tendency in poststructuralist discourse to diminish the significance of the author by focusing on language rather than the one who writes it.

When one examines Freud and his life in a *Freudian* light—namely, without uncritically accepting traditional accounts, and with an interest in the importance of what is *not* said and what is said symbolically and derivatively—extant biographical information, letters, and Freud's own theoretical writings yield new and provocative questions and important hypotheses. In contrast to the vast majority of investigators, who follow Freud's defensive lead and focus on the impact of his father, I argue that the hidden impact of Freud's mother was also crucial to his development and his theories, leading to both a wish to know and a fear of knowing. In doing this I am attempting to specify more concretely the problematic relationship he had with his mother that is alluded to by Peter Gay (1988) and Paul Roazen (1971). The former speaks of "Freud's evasion of his complicated feelings about Amalie Freud" (p. 335), while the latter maintains that Freud was the victim of an "obscure [emotional] deprivation" (p. 41).

Freud was, as he himself said, a *"conquistador,"* an intrepid explorer of the hidden regions of the psyche. Throughout his life he was passionately interested in unraveling riddles and searching for the truth: "In my youth I felt an overpowering need to understand something of the riddles of the world in which we live and perhaps even to contribute something to their solution" (1926b, p. 253). "Truth," Freud wrote to Sandor Ferenczi in 1910, "is the absolute goal of science" (Freud & Ferenczi, 1993, p. 122).

But psychoanalysis is also shadowed by an opposite tendency, which emerges in the first case in its epoch-making founding document, *Studies on Hysteria* (Breuer & Freud, 1895). On May 1, 1889, Freud began treatment of Emmy von N.

> I took on the case of a lady about forty years of age. . . . She was a hysteric and could be put into a state of somnambulism with the greatest ease. . . . I decided that I would make use of Breuer's technique of investigation under hypnosis. . . . This was my first attempt at handling that therapeutic method. (P. 48)

Freud employed hypnosis to help Emmy von N. recall and describe traumatic, buried experiences from her past. But Freud's approach to the case also deviated from the "therapeutic method" of "catharsis"—the abreaction or discharge of strangulated, traumatic affects by means of verbalization—in his use of the antianalytic technique of expunging and burial. Freud used hypnosis to discover what event in her life had produced the most lasting effect on her and appeared most frequently in her memory. She indicated that it was her husband's death. Freud had her describe this event to him in detail, which she did with deep emotion. Notes Freud:

> My therapy consists in wiping away these pictures, so that she is no longer able to see them before her. . . . I remembered that she had already mentioned this experience this morning, and, as an experiment, I asked her on what other occasions this "seizing hold" [seized by terror] had happened. To my agreeable surprise she made a long pause this time before answering and then asked doubtfully, "My little girl?" She was quite unable to recall the other two occasions. My prohibition—my expunging of her memories—had therefore been effective. . . . I made it impossible for her to see any of these melancholy things again, not only by wiping out her

memories of them in their *plastic* form but by removing her whole recollection of them, as though they had never been present in her mind. (Pp. 53, 58–59, 60–61)

It is instructive to juxtapose Freud's description of his work with Emmy von N. with his account of her apparently incidental recall of two words that she had difficulty remembering.

> Another time, when she was feeling in good health, she told me of a visit she had paid to the Roman Catacombs, but could not recall two technical terms; nor could I help her with them. Immediately afterwards I asked her under hypnosis which words she had in mind. But she did not know them in hypnosis either. So I said to her: "Don't bother about them any more now, but when you are in the garden to-morrow between five and six in the afternoon—nearer six than five—they will suddenly occur to you." Next evening, while we were talking about something which had no connection with catacombs, she suddenly burst out: "Crypt," doctor, and "Columbarium." (P. 98)

A "crypt" is, among other things, an underground cell, a chamber or vault, especially when used as a burial place or a secret hiding place. "Columbarium" is a pigeonhole or a subterranean sepulchre. Is it possible that Emmy von N. is uncannily describing her experience of Freud, whose technique of cure-through-expunging ultimately makes *him* a crypt—the site, if you will, where Emmy von N.'s traumatic past had been secretly buried?[1]

Freud regarded his viewpoints in these early studies, as he indicated in the preface to the second edition of the *Studies on Hysteria*, "not as errors but as valuable first approximations to knowledge which could only be fully acquired after long and continuous efforts" (Breuer & Freud 1895, p. xxxi). The official history of psychoanalysis is that Freud's subsequent refinements of psychoanalytic theory and technique—particularly the replacement of hypnosis and catharsis with interpretation of free associations leading to insight—render his method of expunging with Emmy von N. an aberration based on a prepsychoanalytic understanding and formulation. In other words, his approach to Emmy von N. is a momentary detour on the path to psychoanalytic truth that is superseded by a more properly psychoanalytic understanding and practice. From this perspective, Freud's encrypting should be dismissed as an artifact of his inchoate attempts at finding and formulating what would eventually become a revolutionary therapeutic treatment.

The story is more complex. As Freud listened to his patients and pursued his own self-analysis, his understanding of unconscious processes deepened. His discovery and understanding of resistance and transference did generate fundamental changes and advances in his conception of the therapeutic process. Psychoanalytic theory and practice evolved; hypnosis and catharsis fell by the wayside. But encrypting never left Freud or psychoanalysis. In fact, it remained encrypted. In the next section, I attempt to show the familial roots of Freud's simultaneous wish-to-know and wish-*not*-to-know about psychic truth.

## Freud's Family: The Hidden Fault(line) of the Mother

Freud's family life is difficult to fathom, as there is very little known about it. Freud suppressed vital information about himself. The "veil of disguise" Freud (1910a) detected in dreams is mirrored by a veil surrounding his family. The very information that would help us gain a more complete understanding of his family is often missing from Freud's writing. In his *Autobiographical Study* (1925d) there is scant mention of his parents or his childhood. In a letter to his fiancée in April 1885 he wrote: "I have destroyed all my notes of the last fourteen years as well as letters, scientific extracts, and manuscripts of my works. Among letters, only family letters have been spared. Let the biographers labor and toil, we won't make it too easy for them" (quoted in Gay, 1988, p. xv). This gesture of concealment was repeated more than once in later years. In 1907 he again burned his papers. And in the spring of 1938, as he was readying to leave Austria for England, Anna Freud and Marie Bonaparte reclaimed papers he had thrown in a wastebasket (ibid.).

Freud mentions his father much more frequently than his mother in his autobiographical writings. His mother has thus remained more enigmatic than his father (e.g., Roazen, 1971, p. 39). Jacob Freud is depicted as a kind, decent, gentle, likable, passive, placid man. As Jacob neared the end of his life and experienced illness and marked physical deterioration, Sigmund saw his father as weak and decrepit and dwelled on the lack of courage of the "paralytic old man" (Freud, 1900, pp. 216–17).

The available portrayals of Freud's mother are not flattering. Ruth Abraham (1982–83) emphasizes Amalie Freud's "predatory, emotionally consuming nature" (p. 444) and describes her as "possessive and demanding" (p. 450). Paul Roazen (1971) describes her as "domineering" (p. 48) and "imperious." He notes that

> many in the family suffered from her authoritarian character. According to family lore, her middle daughter, Dolphi, was not allowed to have a life of her own; she gave herself up to taking care of her mother, who even as an old woman was "a tornado." For Dolphi, as Freud's son Martin related it, "Constant attendance on Amalie had suppressed her personality into a condition of dependence from which she never recovered." (P. 45)

Martin's depiction of his grandmother concurs: "My father's mother, Amalie, whom I knew very well, was a typical Polish Jewess, with all the shortcomings that implies, she was certainly not what we would call a 'lady,' had a lively temper and was impatient, self-willed, sharp-witted" (M. Freud, 1967, pp. 201–3). Freud's niece, Judith Bernays Heller, who in her youth spent much time with her maternal grandmother, concurred with her cousin's assessment and added: "she was charming and smiling when strangers were about, but I, at least, always felt that with familiars she was a tyrant, and a *selfish* one" (Heller, 1973, p. 338). "There is every indication," as Roazen (1971) aptly notes, "that Amalie Freud was—to use her son's vulture imagery in his study of Leonardo—a tough old bird" (ibid.).

Drawing on Alexander Grinstein's (1990) research concerning "novels and other literary works to which Freud alluded in associations to his dreams and in his letters to Fliess, as well as [Freud's] list of 10 'good books,' " Robert Holt (1992) notes the "striking similarities" Grinstein found in the "depictions of mother figures and other women that seemed to have impressed Freud." These works repeatedly present " 'the women as an aggressive, threatening, and nongiving figure' (Grinstein, 1990, p. 400). Mothers are usually harsh, cold, and dominating" (Holt, 1992, p. 10). Elizabeth Zetzel (1966) detected a striking discrepancy between Freud's published account of the Rat Man (1909b) and his clinical notes. In the published case, "the father was seen as an important real object— one who interfered with or threatened his son's instinctual impulses. . . . The patient's mother . . . was only mentioned in six brief, essentially unrevealing statements" (Zetzel 1966, p. 220). Yet Zetzel noted "more than forty references to a highly ambivalent mother-son relationship in the original clinical notes" (ibid.).

Freud was his mother's first-born and supposedly her undisputed favorite: "A man who has been the indisputable favorite of his mother keeps for life the feeling of a conqueror, that confidence of success which often induces real success" (E. Jones, 1953, p. 5). According to Ernest Jones, Freud's mother referred to him as "*mein goldener Sigi*" (p. 3). Freud describes his relationship with his mother in idealized terms: the relationship between mother and son is "altogether the most perfect, the most free from ambivalence of all human relationships" (Freud, 1933b, p. 133).

In my view, Freud's idealized portrait of the mother-son relationship reflects a defensive process that conceals her negative and disappointing qualities and thus protects Freud from the anguish of confronting the shattering truth about their relationship.

Freud's description of the psychosexual development of the girl offers important clues as to his actual experience of his mother (e.g., Tomkins, 1963; Stolorow & Atwood, 1979). Discussing the girl's transition from the pre-Oedipal phallic stage to the Oedipal period when the powerful attachment to the mother ends, Freud (1933b) wrote:

> The *turning away from the mother is accomplished by hostility*; the attachment to the mother ends in hate. A hate of that kind may become very striking and last all through life; it may be *carefully overcompensated* later on; *as a rule one part of it is overcome while another part persists.* (Pp. 122–23)

The reproaches against the mother, according to Freud, include that she gave the child too little milk, which is experienced as lack of love, and that she gave birth to other siblings.

> But what the child grudges the unwanted intruder and rival is not only the suckling but all the other signs of maternal care. It feels that it has been *dethroned, despoiled, prejudiced in its own rights*; it casts a jealous hatred upon the new baby and develops a grievance against the *faithless* mother. . . . We rarely form a correct idea of the strength of these jealous impulses, of the tenacity with which they persist and of the magnitude of their influence on later development. Especially as this jealously is constantly receiving *fresh nourishment* in the later years of childhood and the whole *shock* is repeated with the *birth of each new brother or sister*. Nor does it make much difference if the child happens to remain the mother's *preferred favorite*. A child's demands for love are immoderate, they make exclusive claims and tolerate no sharing. (P. 127, italics added)

The references to (1) the mother's "preferred favourite" (e.g., "mein goldener Sigi") who is "dethroned," "despoiled," and "prejudiced in its own rights" by the repeated births of new siblings; (2) the "carefully over-compensated" repressed hostility; and (3) the self-blame encoded in the description of the child's "immoderate" and "exclusive claims" for love that "tolerate no sharing," which exculpates the "faithless" mother who has traumatically disappointed the child, all suggest that Freud's description of "female" development is, in fact, a depiction of the negative aspects of his own experience with his mother. In these descriptions of "female" development are embedded unconscious derivatives of Freud's narcissistic rage at his own "faithless" mother, who traumatically "dethroned" and "despoiled" him—supposedly her "preferred favourite"—by giving birth to seven siblings in ten years.

Freud's account of why the girl becomes alienated from the mother while the boy does not offers further autobiographical information:

> Girls hold their mother responsible for their lack of a penis and do not forgive her for their being thus put at a disadvantage. . . . With the discovery that her mother is castrated it becomes possible to drop her as an object, so that the motives for hostility which have long been accumulating, gain the upper hand. This means, therefore, that as a result of the discovery of women's lack of a penis they are debased in value for girls just as they are for boys and later perhaps for men. (Pp. 124–127)

This account is problematic. Why does the boy also not devalue and drop the mother as a love object because she has no penis?

These contrasting accounts of psychosexual development for the boy and the girl suggest a "defensive splitting of the maternal imago" (Stolorow & Atwood, 1979, p. 67). The idealized image of the mother is preserved in Freud's account of the boy's Oedipal development. The "faithless" mother who deprived and disappointed him tends to emerge in his account of the girl's psychosexual development, where it was more sequestered and thus provided less opportunity for the repressed rage to emerge. Further, as noted by Silvan Tomkins (1963), the despised attributes of the repressed, split-off image of Freud's mother reappear in his idea that the inevitable outcome of female development is a deficient sense of justice.

The same sort of displacement of blame and exculpation is at work in Freud's depiction of *parents* in his Oedipal formulations. The available evidence suggests, as mentioned earlier, that Freud experienced his father as passive and weak. It is thus difficult to imagine a less likely candidate for the menacing "paternal" figure of the Oedipal drama than Jacob

Freud. Since there is such a remarkable discrepancy between the strong and punitive figure of the Oedipal *theory* and his own placid and decrepit father, one is forced to wonder about the identity of the powerful and dangerous figure to which Freud's theory refers. In "Female Sexuality," Freud (1931a) mentions the girl's "dread of being killed (? devoured) by the mother" (p. 227). While this is sometimes a projection of the girl's own hostility, Freud also attributes it to "a dread which on its side justifies the death wish against her. . . . It is impossible to say how often this dread of the mother draws countenance from an unconscious hostility on [the mother's] part, which the child divines" (p. 237). In men the dread of being eaten refers to the father, "but is probably the result of the transformation of oral aggressive tendencies directed upon the mother. The person the child wants to devour is the mother who nourished him" (ibid.). Freud, as Abraham (1979) aptly notes, "does not mention the possibility of the mother's hostility directed onto a son (only onto a daughter), but it seems just as likely that the boy may divine a hostile intent in his mother, to which he may respond and with which he may identify" (p. 74). This may be one reason why Freud (1930) places such emphasis on the protective function of the father: "I cannot think of any need in childhood as strong as the need for a father's protection" (p. 72). Is it conceivable that the terrifying and castrating figure of Freud's Oedipal theory is a displaced image of his mother, who is experienced by Freud as devouring and depleting (e.g., Abraham, 1979; 1982–83)?

Freud (1931a) himself provides evidence for the claim that hostility toward the mother is projected onto the father: "How is it that boys succeed in keeping intact their attachment to the mother, which is certainly no less strong than the girl's? . . . Because boys are able to deal with their ambivalent feelings toward her by transferring all their hostility to the father" (p. 235). Freud seems to enact this process in his theoretical formulation of the Oedipus complex.

Additional evidence of a hidden negative dimension to the mother can be found in Freud's (1900) discussion of anxiety dreams in *The Interpretation of Dreams*. This account casts doubt on Freud's idyllic, ambivalence-free characterization of his relationship with his mother and suggests that it may have been hate, rather than love, that Freud concealed:

> It is dozens of years since I myself had a true anxiety dream. But I remember one from my seventh or eighth year, which I submitted to interpretation

some thirty years later. It was a very vivid one, and in it I saw *my beloved mother, with a* peculiarly peaceful, sleeping expression on her features, being carried into the room by two (or three) people with *birds' beaks and laid upon the bed.* I awoke in tears and screaming, and interrupted my parents' sleep. (P. 583)

Freud's associations to the dream included the idea that the bird-beaked figures derived from "an ancient Egyptian funerary relief" and that "the expression on my mother's features . . . was copied from the view I had of my grandfather a few days before his death as he lay snoring in a coma. The interpretation carried out in the dream by the 'secondary revision' must therefore have been that my mother was dying" (ibid.).

It is worthwhile to view the dream in the context of a section in *The Interpretation of Dreams* called "Dreams of the Death of Persons of Whom the Dreamer Is Fond," in which Freud discusses dreams involving "the death of some loved relative—for instance, of a parent" (p. 248). Freud distinguishes two classes of such dreams—"those in which the dreamer is unaffected by grief . . . and those in which the dreamer feels deeply pained by the death and may even weep bitterly in his sleep" (ibid.). Speaking of the latter, he says: "The meaning of such dreams, as their content indicates, is a wish that the person in question may die" (p. 249). Freud's dream about his mother illustrates the second class, yet his discussions of it emphasize that the image of his dying mother conceals sexual rather than aggressive wishes. This constitutes further evidence of the way in which Freud segregated hostile feelings from his account of his relationship with his mother and maintained an idealized, ambivalence-free image of her (e.g., Stolorow & Atwood, 1979, p. 54).

Why did Freud have such hostility toward his mother? One explanation is that he felt betrayed by her. By giving birth to seven babies in ten years, she dramatically undermined her special relationship with him as he was repeatedly abandoned for his new siblings. But there is, in my view, another important reason: he also felt exploited and depleted by his mother. His disavowal of his negative feelings, conscious idealization of his mother, and reticence to provide more data on this topic make this claim less immediately apparent and also difficult to prove. A perusal of his theoretical remarks on man's "dread" of women, the narcissism of parental "love," and the depleting nature of love in general may, however, enable us to circumvent Freud's censorship and gain a more nuanced portrait of this troubled relationship.

Freud encourages the use of theory-as-autobiography in his discussion in the *Psychopathology of Everyday Life* (1901b) of his inability to recall a patient's name: "There thus runs through my thoughts a continuous current of 'personal reference', of which I generally have no inkling, but which betrays itself" (p. 24). In what follows, I examine and interweave "theoretical" and biographical/autobiographical material in an attempt to illuminate the subtle and disavowed experiences that seem to have deeply haunted and shaped Freud's life and work.

It is difficult to jibe Freud's (1916–17) idyllic, ambivalence-free account of the relation between mothers and sons, which "provides the purest examples of an unchangeable affection, unimpaired by egoistic considerations" (p. 206), with his claim that parents are narcissistic: "If we look at the attitude of fond parents towards their children, we cannot but perceive it as a revival and reproduction of their own, long since abandoned narcissism. . . . [The child] is to fulfill those dreams and wishes of his parents which they never carried out" (1914d, pp. 90–91). "A mother," claims Freud (1933b), "can transfer to her son the ambition which she has been obliged to suppress in herself" (p. 133).

Is Freud's claim about the narcissism inherent in parenting autobiographical, an expression of his own experience with a narcissistic mother? Freud seems to acknowledge this in a brief footnote in *Group Psychology and the Analysis of the Ego* (1921). I will reinsert the footnote into its proper place in the passage (and italicize it) so that Freud's claim can be read as a continuous statement and grasped in its entirety: "almost every intimate relation between two people which lasts for some time—marriage, friendship, the relations between parents and children—*perhaps with the solitary exception of the relation of a mother to her son, which is based on narcissism* . . . contains a sediment of feelings of aversion and hostility, which only escapes perception as a result of repression" (p. 101).

One wonders, with Holt (1992), if Amalie Freud exemplified the narcissistic women Freud (1914d) wrote about in *On Narcissism*:

> Strictly speaking, it is only themselves that such women love with an intensity comparable to that of the man's love for them. . . . Such women have the greatest fascination for men, not only for aesthetic reasons . . . another person's narcissism has a great attraction for those who renounced part of their own narcissism and are in search of object-love. . . . The great charm of narcissistic women has, however, its reverse side; a large part of the lover's dissatisfaction, of his doubts of the woman's love, of his complaints of her enigmatic nature, has its roots in this incongruity between the types of object-choice. (P. 89)

That Freud may have been on the receiving end of the dark side of narcissism is suggested by the "bitter thought" revealed in his analysis of the central wish in the specimen dream in *On Dreams*. Freud stops short of explicating the dream, failing to draw closer together "the threads in the material revealed by the analysis, and show[ing] that they converge upon a single nodal point." He claimed that "concerns of a personal and not of a scientific nature prevent . . . my doing so in public. . . . I should be obliged to betray many things which had better remain my secret, for on my way to discovering the solution of the dream all kinds of things were revealed which I was unwilling to admit even to myself" (1901a, p. 640). The central wish in the specimen dream is "I wish I might for once experience love that cost me nothing" (p. 672).

Let us reflect once more on Amalie Freud's description of her son, "mein goldener Sigi." Are these words an expression of unconditional love, or of ownership of an idealized possession that is valued for what it might vicariously offer in terms of borrowed self-esteem? By this I mean that he may have been asked to "fulfill those dreams and wishes of his parents which they never carried out," in particular, the "ambition" that his mother had been "obliged to suppress in herself." Freud's family was poor. When he was born, they occupied a "single rented room in a modest house" (Gay, 1988, p. 7). There is some evidence that during Sigmund's boyhood and youth Jacob Freud's business was declining and that this "impecunious wool merchant" (Gay, 1988, p. 4) needed to be supported by his wife's family and others. The family's poverty may have been painful or at least difficult for the ambitious Amalie, who was raising seven children in cramped quarters. Could it be that she felt deprived and disappointed about her life and sought some sort of vicarious vindication through her intellectually gifted son? Freud may have been his mother's favorite, but the cost of her narcissistic "love" was high: he had to give her what she wanted, rather than get what he needed emotionally.

In this light, Freud's strange and counterintuitive depiction of women as having a less-developed conscience and sense of justice and their debilitating effect on men becomes less perplexing. Speaking of women, Freud (1925d) claims that "they show less sense of justice than men, that they are less ready to submit to the great necessities of life, that they are more often influenced in their judgements by feelings of affection and hostility" (pp. 257–58). Freud's conscious rationale for why women do not develop the same strong super-ego as men is that they follow a different course in the Oedipus complex. According to Freud, women, unlike men, do not give up the Oedipus complex completely because they have no castration to fear. With the absence of this fear, girls do not renounce Oedipal longings or internalize sexual prohibitions. Thus, the super-ego, which forms and develops as the heir to the Oedipus complex, fails in women to "attain the strength and independence which give it its cultural significance" (p. 129).

There is no clinical evidence within psychoanalysis for this dubious claim. In fact, psychoanalysts, sexologists, and biologists have "raised damaging doubts" (Gay 1988, p. 519) about its veracity. Freud (1918) claimed that men "dread" women and that women deplete men. Speaking of primitive man, Freud said: "man fears that his strength will be taken from him by woman, dreads being infected with her femininity and then proving himself a weakling. The effect of coitus in discharging tensions and inducing flaccidity may be a prototype of what these fears represent. . . . There is nothing in all this which is extinct, which is not still alive in the heart of man to-day" (pp. 198–99).[2]

Enrichment, as well as depletion, occurs in human relationships. While depletion may be a periodic feature of men's experience of women, Freud posits it as a universal dimension of human relationships. It is reasonable to assume that this was Freud's experience with a mother whose emotional abandonments and narcissistic exploitation enervated him. The son of such a mother might well dread women and anticipate—based on previous experience—that women would deplete him. When Marie Bonaparte once commented, "Man is afraid of women," Freud replied, "He's right" (Gay, 1988, p. 522). In this context, Freud's infamous question, "What do women want?" might be rephrased: "What does my mother want from me?"

If Freud lacked clinical data demonstrating gender differences in the development of conscience and a sense of justice, then what is the source of his dubious claims about women's supposed ethical inferiority? Freud, in my view, reifies his own painful experience of maternal abandonment, betrayal, and psychic depletion caused by his own enmeshed relationship with his mother into a universal lacuna in women, a deficient sense of morality.

Freud's claim about the perfection of the mother-son relationship appears to have been more of a wish than a clinical observation. There is no evidence that Freud's self-analysis investigated this crucial relationship or that he ever worked through its impact on him.

Freud attributed his own pathology to his Czech nanny. That his mother's influence was defensively denied is strongly reflected in Freud's one-sided assessment of the origins of his difficulties, in which his mother is mentioned only briefly. Describing his attempts in his self-analysis to understand the causative influences in his own neurosis, Freud (1985) writes to Wilhelm Fliess on March 10, 1897:

> my "primary originator" [of neurosis] was an ugly but clever women who told me a great deal about god and hell, and gave me a high opinion of my own capacities; that later (between the ages of two and two-and-a-half) libido toward *matrem* was aroused; the occasion must have been the journey with her from Leipzig to Vienna, during which we spent a night together and I must have had the opportunity of seeing her *nudam* . . . and that I welcomed my one-year younger brother (who died within a few months) with ill wishes and real infantile jealousy, and that his death left the germ of guilt in me. (P. 219)

Freud recognizes the incompleteness of his explanation. In the same letter, he writes: "I still have not got to the scenes which lie at the bottom of all this" (ibid.). In his analysis of a dream in the postscript to this letter, he supposedly provides the missing pieces:

> She was my instructress in sexual matters, and chided me for being clumsy and not being able to do anything . . . she encouraged me to steal "Zehners" (ten-Kreuzer pieces) to give to her. . . . The dream can be summed up as "bad treatment." (Pp. 220–21)

It is instructive to juxtapose the issue of "bad treatment"—which Freud ascribes to the Czech nanny—with an autobiographical remark and some theoretical reflections by Freud on ambivalence and splitting. In *The Interpretation of Dreams*, Freud (1900) admits: "my emotional life has always insisted that I should have an intimate friend and a hated enemy. I have always been able to provide myself afresh with both" (p. 483).

Freud (1912–13) maintained that "ambivalence," the "simultaneous existence of love and hate towards the same object" (p. 157), is present in everyone. Furthermore, "the feelings which are aroused in . . . relations between parents and children . . . are not only of a positive or affectionate kind but also of a negative or hostile one" (1910a, p. 47). We need to recognize that "at a very early age . . . the two opposites should have been split apart and one of them, usually the hatred, have been repressed" (1909b, p. 239).

Writing about one of his patients, Little Hans, Freud says, in words that may well represent the defensive operations he performed in relation to his mother and nanny: "The conflict due to ambivalence is not dealt with in relation to one and the same person; it is circumvented . . . by one of the pair of conflicting impulses [hostility] being directed to another person [the nanny] as a substitutive object" [for the mother] (1926a, p. 103).

Given Freud's propensity for splitting—his tendency to "circumvent" the conflict of ambivalence by making someone the hated enemy and someone else the all-good friend—it would not be prudent to accept his own conscious assessment of the nanny's culpability and the mother's innocence at face value. His nurse—who Freud says gave him "a high opinion of my capabilities" and "provided me at such an early age with the means of living and surviving"—is designated as the "hated enemy," which exculpates his mother and thus enables him to protect and preserve an idealized image of her.

Amalie Freud died on September 12, 1930. On September 15, Freud wrote to Ernest Jones (1957): "I will not disguise the fact that my reaction to this event . . . has been a curious one . . . I can detect . . . an increase in personal freedom . . . No grief otherwise . . . I was not at the funeral . . . (p. 152). In a letter to Sandor Ferenczi he wrote that his mother's death "has affected me in a peculiar way, this great event. No pain, no grief . . . at the same time a feeling of liberation, of release" (Freud, 1960, p. 400). If Freud loved her so much—if the mother's bond with the son is "altogether the most perfect, the most free from ambivalence of all human relationships"—then is it not odd and symptomatic that he had no emotional reaction to her death? The "feeling of liberation, of release" and the "increase of personal freedom" suggest that Freud was imprisoned by his relationship with his mother.

Freud (1910b) claims that the adult's scientific curiosity is a sublimation of infantile curiosity about questions that one "does not ask" (p. 78). The curiosity is aroused, in Freud's view, by "some event—by the actual birth of a little brother or sister . . . in which the child perceives a threat to his selfish interests" (ibid.).

"One must suppose," claims Jones (1955), "that in Freud's earliest years there had been extremely strong motives for concealing some important phase of his development—perhaps even from himself" (p. 409). Jones speculates that it was his deep love for his mother" (ibid.). The evidence suggests that the reason was far more complex, involving a complicated pattern of ambivalence, idealization, and denial.[3]

Freud's adult scientific curiosity and passion for truth may have been fueled, at least in part, by questions he dared not ask about his family and himself. Could it be that traumatic experiences in Freud's family, particularly the psychic captivity he experienced by the idealized mother who traumatically abandoned him and narcissistically deprived and exploited him, generated in him a powerful conflict, a simultaneous wish-to-know and a wish-*not*-to-know what happened/happens? And that is why *knowing* about psychic truth—including his experience in his family—might promise, for Freud, a mixed reward: freedom from the mystifying, traumatically disappointing and enervating world of his family *and* the danger of starkly confronting the disturbing truth about his mother's emotional betrayal and his own psychic enslavement. Knowledge simultaneously may have represented unfettered, unalienated subjective life—living without mystification, deceit, restriction, or self-alienation—and a confrontation with the emotional exploitation and deprivation he experienced in his family. For Freud, then, to face this reality would be to escape the enervating prison of his home *and* to lose forever the idealized picture of his mother and their ambivalence-free relationship. Decoding concealment could mean both escaping psychological enslavement and confronting shattering emotional pain and loss, including experiencing and confronting emotional deprivation that he had spent his entire life defensively denying and disavowing.

## Ambivalence about Knowing in Freud's Self-Analysis

The theme of ambivalence about knowing is also manifest in Freud's own practice of self-analysis, which dramatically illustrates the conflict over seeing and not-seeing. In the late 1890s Freud had begun an intensive self-examination of various conscious and unconscious aspects of his own life. The method he employed was his own free association to, and analysis of, his dreams, parapraxes, and so forth. He associated to his own dreams and traced "idea and affect in the . . . manifest dream—both to recent and to indifferent material from the preceding twenty-four hours—the day residue or the dream day and memories of early events" (Lansky, 1992b, p. 9). Freud's insights and formulations were not based on participation in the analytic process (e.g., Lansky, 1992a). He employed a prepsychoanalytic methodology, by which I mean that he analyzed his own dreams using the associative method, without the advantage of engaging in a psychoanalytic relationship devoted to the illumination of resistance, transference, and countertransference. Freud maintained that being analyzed by someone else is markedly superior to self-analysis as a path to self-knowledge (e.g. Gay, 1988, p. 97). And yet, despite the fact that those members of the first generation of analysts who had not been analyzed were, according to Freud, never proud of it (e.g., Gay, 1988, p. 97f), he only participated in an insulated self-analysis.

As the founder of psychoanalysis Freud was in a unique and inherently isolating position, with no one initially available for him to go to for analysis. This was not the case as the field developed. Even with the availability of psychoanalysts and the subsequent development of the concept of transference, Freud continued to use only self-analysis.

Without the opportunity to track and illuminate the vicissitudes of his resistances and transferences, some of his habitual and restrictive ways of perceiving, thinking, feeling, fantasizing, and relating remained unconscious. Furthermore, Freud's initial self-investigations occurred, as Melvin Lansky (1992b) and Erik Erikson (1954), among others, recognize, in the context of an intense, unacknowledged, and unanalyzed transference to Fliess.

The closest Freud ever came to an analytic experience—albeit deeply modified—was his mutual dream analysis with Carl Jung during a seven-week trip to the United States in 1909. In Jung's (1971) account:

> From the beginning of our trip . . . we started to analyze each other's dreams. Freud had some dreams that bothered him very much. The dreams were about the triangle—Freud, his wife, and his wife's younger sister. . . . When Freud told me about the dream in which his wife and her sister played important parts, I asked him to tell me some of his personal associations to the dream. He looked at me with bitterness and said, "I could tell you more, but I cannot risk my authority." (P. xviii)

Freud's letters to Fliess suggest that his self-investigation was arduous work, both exhilarating and deeply unsettling. Despite the breathtaking discoveries—dream mentation, elaborate unconscious strategies of self-deception, infantile sexuality, unconscious guilt—Freud admitted to Fliess on August 14, 1897, that "this [analysis] is harder than any other" (Freud 1950, p. 214).

It became increasingly clear to Freud that self-analysis was often incomplete and insufficient. In "self-analysis the danger of incompleteness is particularly great. One is too easily satisfied with a part explanation behind which resistance may easily be keeping back something that is of more importance perhaps" (1936a, p. 234). By 1912 he recommended a training analysis that expedites "learning to know what is hidden in one's own mind" (1912a, p. 117). In "Analysis Terminable and Interminable" (1937), Freud extends his earlier recommendations about training analysis and suggests that analysts should reenter analysis approximately every five years. Without such a renewed commitment to exploring oneself, there is the danger of countertransference-induced projection of one's own blindnesses into "the field of science, as a theory having universal validity" (1912a, p. 117).

The absence of a psychoanalytic relationship focused on the systematic illumination of the unconscious subjective world of the analysand deeply compromises the results of even the most perspicacious self-analysis. A solitary, transferenceless self-analysis could never detect, let alone work through, one's transferences and resistances. Self-blindness and blindness about self-blindness necessarily pervade a self-analysis.

The very concept of self-analysis exemplifies Freud's conflict about wishing-to-know and wishing-*not*-to-know. His revolutionary tool for investigating subjective life—self-analysis—revealed *and* concealed certain crucial facets of his own life in particular and human subjectivity in general. On the one hand, his self-analysis profoundly enriched his (and our) understanding of various aspects of human subjectivity; on the other hand, it completely closed off certain crucial avenues for unveiling the mystifications of his childhood that might have been available if he was in an analytic relationship devoted to understanding his transferences.

The risk to his "authority" was not the only reason Freud censored his own associations and did not avail himself of a formal analytic experience. His avoidance of the analytic relationship served at least two other important functions. Examining himself in the isolated, self-sufficient context of his self-analysis protected Freud from the threat of finding in anyone to whom he would turn for his own psychoanalytic treatment a potentially exploitative and treacherous other. It also shielded Freud from both the dreaded experience of perceiving his mother and other family members in a more negative light, and experiencing a shattering deidealization of his image of his mother.

That the closeness of a therapeutic relationship might have been deeply dangerous for Freud—stirring up fears of exploitation or betrayal—is hinted at both in a telling remark to Karl Abraham about friendships and his troubled history of emotional intimacy. He informed Abraham: "I have always sought for friends who would not first exploit and then betray me" (quoted in Jones, 1955, p. 419). His relationships with loved ones and colleagues were often characterized by initial idealization, subsequent bitter disappointment, and eventual withdrawal or acrimony. Freud's heroic, insulated quest for self-understanding served as a self-protective and incomplete substitute for an emotionally intimate therapeutic relationship in which his core issues and conflicts might emerge and be worked through.

Describing the effect on analysts of self-unconsciousness, Freud (1912a) emphasizes that "every unresolved repression in him constitutes what has been aptly described by Stekel as a 'blind spot' in his analytic perception" (p. 116). "No analyst," claims Freud (1910c), "goes further than his own complexes and internal resistances permit" (p. 145).

This may be why Freud was an incompletely emancipated visionary, whose work opened up breathtakingly innovative vistas even as it enshrined conventional presuppositions and prejudices. Freud oscillated between an admixture of "progressive-critical" and "regressive-conventional theorizing," notes Louis Breger, (1981, p. 57). "Freud is continually moving forward in radical directions and retreating to safe conventional ground, first revealing material that raises the most critical questions about his society's values and practices and then slipping back to side with those very values against society's victims" (p. 8). Much of Freud's work, including his metapsychology, his case studies, his theories of sexuality, neurosis, and anxiety, and his conceptions of masculinity and femininity, exemplify this unresolved conflict.

## Not-Knowing in Freud's Theory of Pathogenesis

Examples of the tension between the wish-to-know and the wish-*not*-to-know can be found in Freud's theory of pathogenesis. Freudian perspectives on pathogenesis simultaneously illuminate and inhibit our understanding of human psychopathology. I focus on two particular aspects of this vast topic, the genetic perspective on pathology and the seduction theory, to highlight my thesis.

"Infantilism," the centrality of infancy on subsequent development, was a central tenet of Freudian psychoanalysis. "There are two positions which I have never abandoned," claims Freud (1906), "the importance of sexuality and of infantilism" (pp. 277–78). The genetic perspective was never explicitly mentioned in Freud's metapsychology, although its existence is implicit, as the following passage suggests:

Not every analysis of psychological phenomena deserves the name of psychoanalysis. The latter implies more than the mere analysis of composite phenomena into simpler ones. It consists in tracing back one psychical structure to another which preceded it in time and out of which it developed. Medical psychoanalytic procedure was not able to eliminate a symptom until it had traced that symptom's origin and development. Thus from the very first psychoanalysis was directed towards tracing developmental processes. It began by discovering the genesis of neurotic symptoms, and was led, as time went on, to turn its attention to other psychical structures and to construct a genetic psychology which would apply to them. (1913b, pp. 182–83)

Genetic considerations, as Alex Holder (1970) notes, underlie many if not all psychoanalytic conceptualizations: "The whole theory of infantile sexuality, the postulation of specific phases of libidinal development, the assumption of fixation points . . . and many further analytic concepts emphasize the genetic roots in any disturbance" (p. 43).

Freud (1909a) stresses the importance of the genetic perspective: "when an adult neurotic patient comes to us for psychoanalytic treatment . . . we find regularly that his neurosis has as its point of departure an infantile anxiety . . . and is in fact a continuation of it; so that, as it were, a continuous and undisturbed thread of psychical activity, taking its start from the conflicts of his childhood, has been spun through his life" (p. 143). The importance of early childhood also emerges in Freud's (1940) assertions that "the aetiology of the disorders which we study is to be looked for in the individual's developmental history—that is to say, in his early life" (p. 156) and "neuroses are acquired only in early childhood . . . even though their symptoms may not make their appearance till much later. . . . In every case the later neurotic illness links up with the prelude in childhood" (p. 184).

Freud originally explained adult psychopathology in terms of trauma caused by childhood parental seduction. In section I of the "Neuro-Psychoses of Defense" and section II of "The Aetiology of Hysteria," Freud maintained that seduction by adults is one of the commonest causes of hysteria. In a letter to Fliess on September 21, 1897, Freud wrote: "in all cases, the *father*, not excluding my own, had to be blamed as a pervert" (Freud, 1985, p. 264). One's illness—in Freud's two-person model of mind and development—was caused by the deeds of others.

As is well known, Freud revised the seduction theory. Referring to his previous clinical work, he wrote:

> At that time [1897] my material was still scanty, and it happened by chance to include a disproportionately large number of cases in which sexual seduction by an adult or by older children played the chief part in the history of the patient's childhood. I thus overestimated the frequency of such events (though in other respects they were not open to doubt). (1905c, p. 274)

Beginning in 1897 Freud's explanation of pathogenesis shifted from an "interpersonal theory of infantile seduction" to a "drive theory of infantile sexuality" (Mitchell, 1993b, p. 472), in which the fantasies within one's mind, not the conduct of others, cause psychopathology. This is illustrated by Freud's claim that "if hysterical subjects trace their symptoms to traumas that are fictitious, then the new fact which emerges is precisely that they create such scenes in *phantasy*" (1914c, p. 17). Pathology arises, in this one-person conception, not from traumatic interpersonal experiences, but from the child's difficulty managing drive energies arising from within.

Although Freud revised his first seduction theory, he never gave up his earlier theory of pathogenesis. That Freud never completely abandoned the seduction theory—although the relative influence of actual experience probably declined compared to other factors such as fantasy—is suggested by his warning, even after presenting the Oedipal theory, that "you must not suppose . . . that sexual abuse of a child by its nearest male relatives belongs entirely to the realm of phantasy. Most analysts will have treated cases in which such events were real and could be unimpeachably established" (Freud, 1916–17, p. 370). It is also suggested by his (1933d) claim that the mother's care is the universal basis for the child's seduction and sexual development. Freud's remarks at the Vienna Psychoanalytic Society on January 24, 1912, suggest that he retained a conception of psychopathology that acknowledged the importance of actual experience. Speaking of the girl's fantasy of seduction, he says: "the grain of truth contained in this fantasy lies in the fact that the father, by way of his innocent caresses in earliest childhood, has actually awakened the little girl's sexuality (the same thing applies to the little boy and his mother). . . . This fantasy, which often dominates a women's entire life . . . [remains] one part truth, one part gratification of love, and one part revenge" (Nunberg & Federn, 1975, pp. 24–25). Freud did not rule out that such things as abuse were implicated in pathogenesis, but he viewed sexual seduction as one of several causal factors, including fantasies. He aptly noted that

> in scientific matters people are very fond of selecting one portion of the truth, putting it in the place of the whole and of then disputing the rest, which is no less true, in favour of this one portion. . . . Are neuroses exogenous or endogenous illnesses? . . . This dilemma seems to me no more sensible on the whole than another that I might put to you: does a baby come about through being begotten by its father or conceived by its mother? Both determinants are equally indispensable, as you will justly reply. In the matter of the causation of the neuroses the relation, if not precisely the same, is very similar. (1916–17, pp. 346–47)

Symptoms and pathology were, as Freud was fond of saying, *overdetermined*. Fantasies and reality stand in a "complemental series" (1916–17, p. 360) to each other. Freud (1914c) claimed that dispositions and experience are "linked up in an indissoluble aetiological unity" (pp. 17–18). Hysterical symptoms, for example, might be caused by fantasies or reality factors, individually or in some combination.

Freud's nod to theoretical complementarity and his concept of the super-ego (with its explicit recognition of the way the values and ideals of significant others and the culture deeply shape our own standards and judgments) suggest that he recognized the importance of objects and interpersonal relations. The notion of the object appears throughout Freud's work (Tyson & Tyson, 1990). In *Group Psychology and the Analysis of the Ego* (1921), for example, Freud wrote that identification early in life involves an emotional tie with another person. In *Mourning and Melancholia* (1917a), he described the ego as the repository of abandoned objects: "the shadow of the object fell upon the ego" (p. 249). These passages offer clear evidence that Freud did not omit interpersonal relations—as is sometimes charged—although he did not provide a fully elaborated account of them, either. Object relations were viewed by Freud in terms of "drive expression" rather than "a developmental progression of evolving object relations independent of the drives" (Tyson & Tyson, 1990, p. 69). Freud admitted that he had little understanding of pre-Oedipal objects. D. W. Winnicott (1960b) noted that although "it would seem that a great deal of psychoanalytic theory is about early childhood and infancy," in one sense "Freud can be said to have neglected infancy as a state" (p. 586).

The complementarity Freud claims for interpersonal experience and fantasy in pathogenesis is belied by his tendency to place greater *explan-atory* emphasis and weight on fantasy. Actual interactions and experiences are not always granted a fully complementary role with fantasy in practice. After his revision of the seduction theory, Freud did tend to adopt a nonrelationally oriented, monadic view of mind and pathology.[4]

There is some evidence that Freud knew about but censored the impact of noxious relational influences on human development. James Strachey notes in a footnote to Freud's "On Femininity" (1933b) that "in some additional footnotes written in 1924 for the Gesammelte Schriften reprint of *Studies on Hysteria*, Freud admitted having on two occasions suppressed the fact of the father's responsibility" in the patient's belief in having been seduced (pp. 120–121; see, e.g., Freud 1985, pp. 134 n. 2, 170 n. 1).

From my reading of Freud's experience in his family, he needed to censor malevolent relational experiences and to *deemphasize* the reality of human influence because of the traumatic interpersonal experiences with his mother that he had spent a lifetime attempting to deny. To emphasize in a more central way the role of actual experiences with others as a causative force in generating psychopathology might be to confront dreaded truths of his own formative years.

Pathology does not occur in interpersonal isolation as "encapsulated intrapsychic formations" (Langs, 1978, p. 481). It arises, not within a "closed intrapsychic system" (ibid.), but as a result of both interactive and intrapsychic processes (e.g., Mitchell, 1988). Freud's relative neglect of certain facets of the interactive dimensions of pathology tends to turn his explanatory model of pathogenesis away from the actual traumatic experience of children. The psychological consequences are not trivial. "To attribute the affective chaos or schizoid withdrawal of patients who were abused as children to 'fantasy,' " as Robert Stolorow and George Atwood (1992) note, "is tantamount to blaming the victim and, in so doing, reproduces features of the original trauma" (p. 56). In subscribing to an incomplete view of the aetiology of psychopathology, Freud and psychoanalysts holding similar views contribute to what Edgar Levenson (1983) has termed a "mystification process" (p. 21).

Freud's theory of pathogenesis is yet another example of the simultaneous wish-to-know and wish-*not*-to-know.[5] With its focus on the way the past shapes the psychic present, the genetic perspective on psychopathology revolutionized understanding of the vicissitudes of human subjectivity. The one-person fantasy model of pathogenesis neglects the actual sources of trauma in childhood or postchildhood experiences with others. Freud illuminates the importance of childhood in human development even as he eclipses the actual *experience* of children.[6]

## To See or Not to See in Psychoanalysis

The original fault line in psychoanalysis—the "blindness of the seeing I"—began, I believe, with Freud. His attempt to come to terms with his disturbing and confusing relationship with his mother led to a wish to know combined with a fear of knowing, which created a blind spot from which psychoanalysis is still recovering. The "blindness of the seeing I" is itself encrypted. It is encoded symptomatically in the classical psychoanalytic theory of pathogenesis and Freud's self-analysis. It might be argued, and I suspect many people still believe, that the blindness of the seeing I exists, but only in "them"—that is, in classical analysts. But no school of psychoanalysis has either cornered the market on Truth or avoided self-blindness.

Countertransference-based distortions in theory and practice, as Heinrich Racker (1957) notes, are passed from analyst to analysand and teacher to student. The field of psychoanalysis is thus permeated with Freud's conflict over knowing. Psychoanalysis detects censorship and discovers buried psychological realities; yet blind spots and self-deceptions haunt the field and compromise its liberatory potential.

The blindness of the seeing I has had a powerful influence on subsequent psychoanalytic history, institutions, politics, theories, and clinical procedures. It has deeply shaped psychoanalytic models of human development and of mind, fostering a one-person model of emotional development and psychopathology that locates pathology within the individual. Interactional influences on the individual and the reality of interpersonally induced trauma are neglected. The analyst's influence on the treatment and the patient's transference are insufficiently delineated. The analyst is set up all too often as the one-who-knows, which fosters excessive certainty and dogmatism. This can promote hidden authoritarianism in clinical practices. It can also breed a rigid and sectarian institutional environment in which those who question analytic orthodoxy are pathologized and marginalized. Analytic innovators are not encouraged to trust their ideas. Their creativity is compromised and their capacity for visionary work stifled. Psychoanalysis is then predisposed to be a religious clerisy rather than an intellectual hothouse.

It is vital to the psychic health of psychoanalysis that the burials and blind spots permeating the field be detected. The subsequent chapters of this book will explore various blind spots in psychoanalytic theory, organizations, politics, and practice. In making conscious what was formerly buried, perhaps we can lessen the self-induced blindness that has afflicted us and regain the lost potential encrypted within psychoanalysis itself.

Freud's reflections on his own interpretation of *Hamlet* in *The Interpretation of Dreams* (1900) alerts us to my own partiality in my interpretation of the relationship between Freud's life and work:

> But just as all neurotic symptoms, and, for that matter dreams, are capable of being "overinterpreted" and indeed need to be, if they are to be fully understood, so all genuinely creative writings are the product of more than a single motive and more than a single impulse in the poet's mind, and are open to more than a single interpretation. In what I have written I have only attempted to interpret the deepest layer of impulses in the mind of the creative writer. (p. 266).

Despite the fact that authentic, creative writing (such as Shakespeare's or Freud's work) is produced by "more than a single motive and more than a single impulse," Freud treats his interpretation of *Hamlet*—which is inevitably only a "single interpretation"—as if it enjoys a foundational status. My interpretation of Freud also embodies this tension between what might be termed the multiplicity of meaning and the singularity of theorizing. I focus on only one corner of that personal and theoretical mansion that is Freud's life and work: the way Freud's disappointing and mystifying experience with a mother he consciously idealized generated a wish to know and a fear of knowing. While this version of Freud sheds some light on disparate facets of his life and work, the multitude of alternative interpretations and perspectives that can be generated about him dwarfs any singular interpretation I or anybody else might offer. My reading is thus only one version of Freud. Other versions are inevitable and necessary.

The Way that can be Named, as Lao Tzu notes, is not the way. Psychoanalysts have tended to adopt one of three positions in relation to their own theorizing: (1) granting it unquestioned (and unearned) validity;

(2) evincing skepticism about theory—viewing it as an impediment to elucidating the analytic material—which eclipses its unconscious impact on what is "discovered"; and (3) seeing it as indissolubly shaping the analytic encounter.

The theoretical middle way for psychoanalysis between the dangers of interpretive dogmatism and interpretive agnosticism might be to recognize that theory can never be forsaken, should never be absolutized, and must always be analytically scrutinized and understood. My theorizing in this chapter focuses on not-seeing in Freud. My own partiality emerges in the word *or* in the title of this chapter: "To See or Not to See." Another way of thinking about blindness and insight in psychoanalysis and in this chapter is to frame the topic, not in terms of *or*, but of *and*: "To See *and* Not to See." Blindness *and* insight, seeing *and* not-seeing both coexist in Freud, in this text, and in psychoanalysis. From that perspective, the crucial task in reforming psychoanalysis is not removing blindness—which, as I suggested in the introduction, seems quixotic—but increasing self-reflexivity. The remaining chapters in this book explore how that might be done from various perspectives.

# 2

# Politics and Censorship
# in Psychoanalysis
### Sandor Ferenczi and the Secret Committee

> I wonder when all us dispersed members of an unpolitical com-
> munity will meet again and whether it will turn out that politics
> has corrupted us. I cannot be an optimist and I believe I differ
> from the pessimists only in so far as wicked, stupid, senseless
> things don't upset me because I have accepted them from the be-
> ginning as part of what the world is composed of.
>
> Sigmund Freud to Lou Andreas-Salomé, July 30, 1915

The tension between the wish to see and the wish-*not*-to-see
is dramatically enacted in the politics and institutional structure of early
psychoanalysis. On an organizational level, psychoanalysis embodies
Freud's ambivalence about knowing. On the one hand, psychoanalytic
organizations contribute to the transmission of knowledge and accumu-
lated wisdom. On the other hand, psychoanalytic institutions are all too
often unconscious about their own internal politics. This chapter is about
a striking example in which censorship by the early institutional organization of psychoanalysis created within the profession an unconsciousness
like that depicted in Freudian dream theory.

## Sandor Ferenczi and the Secret Committee

In July 1912 Ernest Jones proposed to Sandor Ferenczi that an "Old
Guard' or secret society" be established to protect psychoanalysis against
dissenters who might be disruptive to Freud's ideas and the psychoanalytic movement (Rand & Torok, 1987, p. 281). Jones hoped to form a

ring of men around Freud who would deal with the opposition while Freud focused on his work. Freud responded to Jones's proposal in a letter dated August 1, 1912:

> What took hold of my imagination immediately is your idea of a secret council composed of the best and most trustworthy among our men to take care of the further development of psychoanalysis and defend the cause against personalities and accidents when I am no more . . . I know there is a boyish and perhaps romantic element too in this conception, but perhaps it could be adapted to meet the necessities of reality. I will give my fancy free play and leave to you the part of censor. . . . The committee would have to be *strictly secret* in its existence and its actions. . . . I had better be left outside of your conditions and pledges; to be sure I will keep the utmost secrecy and be thankful for all you communicate. (Jones, 1955, pp. 153–54)

The "Secret Committee," composed of Freud, Ferenczi, Jones, Otto Rank, Hanns Sachs, and Karl Abraham, was created to conserve and consolidate the psychoanalytic movement. (Max Eitingon later became a member). Jones recommended that they discuss any theories that seemed "to depart from any of the fundamental tenets of psychoanalytical theory" before publicly presenting them (p. 152). The committee met for the first time in May 1913. Freud dissolved the group in April 1924, reestablished it at the end of 1924, and finally disbanded it in 1927.

The committee members' reaction to Sandor Ferenczi's classic paper, "Confusion of Tongues between Adults and the Child" (1933), illuminates the workings of the secret society and the way it used the repressive processes detailed in Freudian dream theory and censored certain disturbing theoretical and clinical reflections of Ferenczi. This is a telling example of an institutional manifestation of the fear of knowing.

Ferenczi occupied a unique place in the psychoanalytic pantheon. He had been a greatly esteemed psychoanalytic clinician (treating various analysts, including Melanie Klein, Michael Balint, and Clara Thompson), as well as Freud's cherished pupil, valued colleague, and analysand. Freud's respect for Ferenczi's theoretical sophistication and clinical acumen emerges in their correspondence (e.g., Hoffer, 1991, p. 465) and in Freud's behavior toward him and public assessments of him. In a January 4, 1928 letter Freud speaks of the "pre-eminent maturity you have acquired during past years and which remained unequaled" (Grubich-Simitis, 1986, p. 271). Freud sent Ferenczi his new manuscripts to read and comment on and was touched by Ferenczi's offer to come to Vienna to analyze him in 1926 (Jones, 1957, p. 120). In his obituary of Ferenczi, Freud (1933c) claimed that Ferenczi's writings "made all analysts into his pupils" (p. 228). On Ferenczi's fiftieth birthday, Freud (1923c) had this to say about his former analysand and beloved colleague:

> Ferenczi's scientific achievement is impressive above all from its many-sidedness. Besides well-chosen case histories and acutely observed clinical communications . . . we find exemplary critical writings. . . . But besides all these, there are the papers upon which Ferenczi's fame principally rests, in which his originality, his wealth of ideas and his command over a well-directed scientific imagination find such happy expression, and with which he has enlarged important sections of psycho-analytic theory and has promoted the discovery of fundamental situations in mental life. (Pp. 268–69)

At the end of his life, Ferenczi was investigating and illuminating theoretical and clinical issues that are currently at the forefront of psychoanalytic debates, such as the intersubjective nature of human development and the psychoanalytic process, the role of reality in pathogenesis, the analyst's contribution to the patient's transference, the role of noninterpretive factors in the therapeutic action of psychoanalysis, and the constructive utilization of countertransference in treatment.

In "Confusion of Tongues between Adults and the Child" what Freud termed Ferenczi's "acutely observed clinical communications . . . his wealth of ideas and his command over a well-directed scientific imagination," are perhaps most apparent. In this paper, Ferenczi reiterates and extends Freud's 1896 claim, which Freud largely disavowed in 1897, that sexual seductions of children by parents or parental surrogates cause neurosis. A central dimension of this paper is Ferenczi's illumination of the phenomenology of self-submission and subordination. He enriches Freud's earlier work by delineating the defensive strategies employed by the abused child, such as self-invalidation and identification with the aggressor,[1] and the psychic cost of abuse—including self-fragmentation and nullification, impaired sexual functioning, and a consequent difficulty in loving. Ferenczi also criticizes the defensive and countertransferential stance of analysts who view their patients as inferior and do not believe their patient's reports of childhood abuse, which he believed retraumatized the patient and contributed to the patient's self-invalidation (e.g. Grosskurth, 1991, p. 213).

Let us briefly examine Ferenczi's account of the psychology of traumatization. Sexually frustrated parents or adults in the child's life (aunts, uncles, grandparents, household help, tutors) seek substitute sexual satisfaction and sexually abuse the child. The "perpetrator" denies what she or he has done. Attempts by the child to seek the help of the other caregiver are usually "refused by her as nonsensical" (Ferenczi, 1933, p. 163). The child is thereby traumatized: "These children feel physically and morally helpless, their personalities are not sufficiently consolidated in order to be able to protest, even if only in thought" (p. 162). This leads to the *"introjection of the guilt feeling of the adult"* (ibid.). Fear causes children to "subordinate themselves like automata to the will of the aggressor, to divine each of his desires and to gratify these; completely oblivious of themselves they identify themselves with the aggressor" (ibid.). The seeds of self-mistrust and self-invalidation are planted. The child "feels enormously confused, in fact, split—innocent and culpable at the same time" (ibid.). The child's "confidence in the testimony of his own senses is broken" (ibid.). Tormented by guilt, the behavior of the abusive adult becomes harsher, which makes the child feel even greater guilt and shame. Crippled self-trust leads to self-submission. The submissiveness and identification with the aggressor profoundly arrests and warps self-development. The abused child either "changes into a mechanically obedient automaton or becomes defiant, but is unable to account for the reasons of his defiance . . . his sexual life remains undeveloped or assumes perverted forms" (p. 163).

Ferenczi ends his paper by recommending that psychoanalysts and parents take more seriously "the way of thinking and speaking of your children, patients, and pupils and to loosen, as it were, their tongues" (p. 166). "Behind the submissiveness or even the adoration, just as behind the transference of love, of our children, patients, and pupils," suggests Ferenczi, "there lies hidden an ardent desire to get rid of this oppressive love. If we can help the child, the patient or the pupil to give up the reaction of identification, and to ward off the over-burdening transference, then we may be said to have reached the goal of raising the personality to a higher level" (p. 164).

One comes away from an encounter with this paper with greater clarity about the psychological impact of psychic trauma and the conscious and unconscious strategies employed by the abused to lessen self-vulnerability, maintain connectedness to the abuser, and retain some hope of change.

In Freud's obituary of Ferenczi in 1933, one year after the presentation of "Confusion of Tongues between Adults and the Child," he sounds a less enthusiastic note than he did eleven years earlier: "It is impossible to believe that the history of our science will ever forget him" (1933, p. 229). This is worlds away from the unequivocally positive praise of his 1922 assessment of Ferenczi. Freud's straining prose and more equivocal tone signal an important shift in his assessment of Ferenczi.

Aware of the general tenor of Ferenczi's paper, Freud wished it to be suppressed. Ferenczi, however, intended to deliver the paper at the Twelfth International Psycho-Analytic Congress at Wiesbaden in September 1932. On August 29, Freud wrote to fellow Secret Committee member Eitingon:

> He must not be allowed to give the paper. Either another one or none. He does not seem disinclined now to be chosen as president [of the International Psycho-Analytical Association]. Whether he can still be chosen by all of you after these revelations is another question. Our behavior will depend, in the first place, on whether he agrees to the postponement [of the paper] as well as on the impression that he makes on all of you [the committee] in Wiesbaden. (Unpublished telegram from Freud to Eitingon, September 2, 1932, quoted in Sylwan, 1984, p. 109).

Eitingon also wished to suppress this paper (Jones, 1957, p. 173).

Ferenczi visited Freud en route to the Congress and read him the paper on September 1. The following day, Freud sent Eitingon a telegram: "Ferenczi read me his paper. Harmless and dumb. . . . The impression was unfavorable" (quoted in Masson, 1984, p. 170).

In spite of the efforts of Freud and the others, in early September 1932 Ferenczi presented "Confusion of Tongues" at the Congress in Wiesbaden. From the ad hominem judgments about his character that pervaded the committee members' response, as well as the absence of dialogue about the theoretical and clinical claims in his work, one is left with an unmistakable impression that no one engaged the *content* of the paper. Rather, the committee speculated about Ferenczi's character and his supposed pathology.

Ferenczi's claims about the trauma inflicted on children by sexually abusive adults were treated by members of the committee as symptoms of his own pathology, particularly delusionality, hostility, and paranoia (e.g., Grosskurth, 1991, p. 217). In a letter about Ferenczi to Jones on May 29, 1933, Freud wrote: "She [a patient of Ferenczi's] seems to have produced [in him] a *pseudologia phantastica*; he credited her with the oddest childhood traumas, which he then defended against us. In this confusion his once so brilliant intelligence was extinguished. But let us keep his sad end as a secret among us" (Jones & Freud, 1993, p. 721). The German medical dictionary *Psychyrembel* defines *pseudologia phantastica* as the "invention of experiences that are just fairy-tales' " (Masson, 1984, p. 182). Freud gives no indication as to how he "knew" that Ferenczi's patient's reports of childhood traumas, and Ferenczi's belief in their validity, were fairy-tales.

Jones wrote to Freud about Ferenczi after the Congress on September 9, 1932: "His exceptionally deep need of being loved, together with the repressed sadism, are plainly behind the tendency to ideas of persecution" (Jones, 1993, p. 706). Jones (1957) later wrote to Freud of Ferenczi's "latent psychotic trends" (p. 176) and his "delusions about Freud's supposed hostility. Toward the end came violent paranoia and even homicidal outbursts" (p. 178). No proof is ever offered by Jones for this powerful assertion, and there is no independent confirmation for his claims (e.g., Roazen, 1971, p. 69). Available accounts all invalidate Jones's allegations. Clara Thompson, a student, friend, and analysand of Ferenczi who had contact with him from 1932 until his death in 1933, states: "except for the symptoms of his physical illness, there was nothing psychotic in his reactions which I observed. I visited him regularly, and talked with him, and there was not a single incident, aside from memory difficulties, which would substantiate Jones' picture of Ferenczi's psychosis or homicidal mood" (quoted in Fromm, 1955, p. 132). In a personal communication to Erich Fromm, Michael Balint offers a similar perspective, noting that despite Ferenczi's affliction with a "very serious neurological condition his mind remained clear till the end and I can vouch for that from personal experience, as I saw him frequently during his last months, practically once or twice a week" (ibid.). Fromm further indicates that "Ferenczi's stepdaughter, Mrs. Elma Lauvrik, who was with Ferenczi until his death, wrote me a statement, entirely confirming Dr. Thompson's and Dr. Balint's descriptions" (ibid.). The lack of evidence for Jones's assertions suggests that his account was, as Paul Roazen (1971) puts it, "a travesty of truth" (p. 371).[2]

Freud's denial of responsibility for Ferenczi's condition is evident from a letter he wrote to the latter on November 1, 1933: "When today I have to conjure all this [Ferenczi's experiences with, and growing estrangement from, Freud and the committee] from memory the sole consolation I have is the certainty that I contributed remarkably little to the transformation. Some psychological fate has brought it about in you" (quoted in Jones, 1957, p. 177).[3] By attributing Ferenczi's struggles to psychological phenomena arising solely within Ferenczi's mind, Freud denied his negative treatment of Ferenczi and invalidated Ferenczi's experience of traumatization. This perpetuated Ferenczi's sense of self-mistrust and kept him "tongue-tied" about his childhood traumas and his subordinated stance in relation to Freud. He was then left with pathological self-blame, guilt, and a sense of unworthiness.

Ferenczi's crippled self-trust is illustrated by the pathological self-assessment and the grave clinical self-doubt he voiced toward the end of his life about the efficacy of his highly venerated clinical work. He claimed, for example, that he was schizophrenic: "Psychoanalytical insights into my own emotional emptiness, which was shrouded by psychosis led to a diagnosis of *schizophrenia*" (Ferenczi, 1932, p. 160). His doubts about his clinical work are illustrated by his reflections on his treatment with R.N., the last entry in his clinical diaries: "Sadism. Disregard for patient's sufferings. . . . *Theories* invalid. Blinded. . . . These are imposed on patients. . . . There must be punishment" (pp. 214–15).

Ferenczi's pathological self-blame and his identification with the aggressor (Freud) precluded his ability to work through his self-mistrust and submissiveness. Thus Ferenczi remained a prisoner of his childhood traumas and never fully gave up "the reaction of identification" with the persecutor or the "burdensome transferences"—involving a self-nullifying submission to an idealized other (Freud), who is let off the hook for any reprehensible treatment—which would have raised his personality "to a higher level" (Ferenczi, 1933, p. 164).

After Ferenczi's death, Jones broke his promise to Ferenczi to publish "Confusion of Tongues" in English. Jones wrote to the American analyst A. A. Brill on June 20, 1933: "To please him [Ferenczi] I had already printed his congress paper, which appeared in the Zeitschrift, for the July number of the *Journal*, but now, after consultation with Freud, have decided not to publish it. It would certainly not have done his reputation any good" (quoted in Masson, 1984, p. 153). Here Jones enacts and rationalizes his role as the committee's censor: burying Ferenczi's ideas that he and other committee members found disturbing. The proofs of the paper were destroyed; it remained, if you will, encrypted in the political unconscious of psychoanalysis until Michael Balint rescued it from potential oblivion and had it published in English sixteen years later in the *International Journal of Psycho-Analysis* (Masson, 1984, p. 153).[4]

From all available evidence, Ferenczi, the theorist par excellence of self-subjugation, was himself subjugated. He succumbed to the negative description of his antagonists, which caused him to deny the reality of their persecution of him and to incorporate into himself the pathological features of his colleagues' defensively negative assessments.

Ferenczi's life and theory enact the self-subjugation he was not able to illuminate more fully theoretically. His failure to work these issues through on a personal and theoretical level kept him psychically captive and constrained and impeded the further development and refinement of his innovative insights and discoveries. He did develop (but did not fully work out) what Freud termed a "new variety of analysis," which maintained that caregivers have a formative influence on human development and that analysts play a central role in the therapeutic process including the patient's transference. He emphasized the importance of the analyst's self-reflectiveness and pioneered the use of countertransference as a tool in understanding the patient and fueling the therapeutic process.[5] But he did not fully embrace or codify his most innovative discoveries. His visionary theoretical and clinical alternative to Freudian psychoanalysis remained in the form of disparate theoretical insights and technical recommendations rather than a coherent system or school of thought that could be transmitted to the next generation.

Psychoanalysis was impoverished by his failure to complete the enormously suggestive work he initiated. An enriched psychoanalysis might have pursued some of the questions Ferenczi's corpus and example invite us to raise: Are psychoanalytic theories ever complicit with the traumas they were developed to heal? What is the cost of unresolved transferences to analytic theories, institutions, and analysts? Are there ways of making the analytic process more self-reflective and less asymmetrical? It might have led to a more self-reflective, relational, humanistic, and dynamic psychoanalysis, one that did not neglect countertransference until the 1950s; that reflected more actively on its own presuppositions and blind spots; that looked at the analyst's impact on the analytic environment and relationship; that explored unresolved transferences to analytic institutions, theories, supervisors, and analytic pioneers; and that strove to value therapeutic mutuality even as it explored the inevitable asymmetries and hidden operations of power in analytic relationships and institutions.

Neither the "wise baby" (Ferenczi, 1932, pp. 81–82) nor the "*enfant terrible*" of psychoanalysis (Ferenczi, 1931, p. 127), Ferenczi was a divided adult whose life and work oscillated between self-assertion and self-subordination, creativity and compliance. He profoundly illuminated subtle recesses of self-submission even as he valiantly and incompletely struggled to achieve psychic liberation.[6]

The growing respect in contemporary psychoanalysis for Ferenczi's pioneering work has been achieved despite the Secret Committee's attempts to stifle him and actively negate his most vital psychoanalytic contributions. The members of the committee would have benefited from heeding Ferenczi's cautionary warning to Jones on January 6, 1930: "Perhaps we should draw the lesson . . . that psychoanalysts in particular, more than has been the case until now, should not allow scientific and scientific-technique differences of opinion to degenerate into personal attacks" (quoted in Masson, 1984, pp. 231–33).

## Censorship and Psychoanalytic Organizations

The early institutional structure of psychoanalysis embodies the processes leading to censorship and unconsciousness described in Freudian dream theory, which portrays the conflict between the dreamer's wishes pressing for expression and the censoring forces that conceal them. Dreams, according to Freud, are the product of two opposing factors, infantile wishes striving for expression and *censorship* of these wishes. A dream, in Freud's view, is the attempt to gratify an unconscious wish under the constraint of censorship. Censorship attempts to prevent the dreamer from recognizing the conflict between adult values and the infantile wishes pressing for gratification (1900, p. 144). The wishful impulses are kept out of consciousness because they conflict with conscious ideals and values and would generate unpleasurable feelings such as shame, guilt, disgust, or anxiety: "We can thus plainly see the purpose for which the censorship exercises its office and brings about the distortion of dreams: it does so *in order to prevent the generation of anxiety or other forms of distressing affect*" (p. 267).

The case of Ferenczi reveals how an organization of a few men, functioning precisely like the censor in Freudian dream theory, controlled and systematically limited what analytic insights and theories were permitted expression. Clinical reflections and discoveries that clashed with the values and ideals of the members of the secret committee—and thus generated anxiety or other forms of distressing affect, like the forbidden wishes in the latent content of the dream—were inhibited and suppressed. This process of censorship, like the censorship in dreams, was kept secret. Can it be merely a coincidence that the content of Ferenczi's censored paper corresponded precisely to Freud's own deepest conflicts concerning parental culpability in the genesis of psychopathology as discussed in chapter 1?

One major formal difference between the institutional structure of psychoanalysis, with its Secret Committee and censor, and Freudian dream theory and interpretation is that in the latter what is censored and repressed is decoded by the collaborative interpretative work of the analysand and the analyst, without which the dream's latent content and meaning remain unconscious. The Secret Committee had a censor (Jones) but no decoder. Since censorship without decoding results in unconsciousness, the existence of the Secret Committee suggests that, ironically, a movement devoted to the unraveling of censorship and self-deception itself promoted concealment and myopia. More importantly, it provides a further dramatic illustration of the tension in psychoanalysis between the wish-to-see and the wish-*not*-to-see.

The creation of the Secret Committee was not an isolated, inconsequential act. Even now there is ongoing "institutional censorship" (Rand & Torok, 1987, p. 279) of various primary source documents in psychoanalysis, such as Freud's letters. Investigators of psychoanalysis, as Phyllis Grosskurth (1991) points out, "have been hindered in their investigations by the absurd restrictions imposed by the Sigmund Freud Archives on the material in the Library of Congress. . . . Only by the publication of these letters and the removal of all the restrictions at the Library of Congress will we be able to acquire a fuller knowledge of the history of psychoanalysis" (p. 222). In his own research on Freud, Peter Gay (1988) experienced "the restrictive policy of Freud's guardians, either denying or slowing down access to important materials . . . the protective way that Freud's family and adorers have withheld some of the most intriguing material or sought to 'correct' his image for posterity" (pp. 753, 744).

It might be argued that concern for Freud's reputation and the ultimate survival of the psychoanalytic movement justified establishing the Secret Committee and restricting public access to psychoanalytic documents. Secrecy can serve a positive function, creating a protective space for countercultural groups such as antifascist organizations (e.g., Simmel, 1950). "Freud's apprehensions for the safety of his psychoanalytic system," Nicholas Rand and Maria Torok (1987) astutely note, "may seem perfectly reasonable. But historical documents were being suppressed in 1957 [and still are in 1998!]—a time, when, at least in the West, all threats to eradicate the psychoanalytic movement had vanished" (p. 282). The censorship embodied in the repression of various psychoanalytic documents and the creation of the Secret Committee—seen in a *Freudian* light—is symptomatic rather than accidental.

This censorship is symptomatic of several things. Psychoanalysis all too often *promotes* as well as detects unconsciousness, the very phenomenon it explicitly seeks to master. Ironically, concealment is at work in a movement that focuses so extensively on openness and disclosure. Organizationally, psychoanalysis has neglected its own seminal insights about censorship in individual psychology—namely, that censorship signals buried anxiety and or distressing affect, which creates pockets of unconsciousness if it remains undetected. This unconsciousness undermines group as well as individual functioning. The censorship that pervades psychoanalysis also suggests that psychoanalytic scapegoats such as Ferenczi may screen and hide secrets about and blind spots in analytic history, theories, and practices.[7]

Freud taught us that censorship is instituted to lessen anxiety and other disturbing affects. Psychoanalysis itself, no less than individual patients, may more readily reach its developmental maturity and potential when it analytically explores and attempts to come to terms with anxiety generated by innovative and disturbing formulations, rather than disavowing and concealing the secrets haunting its past and present. Studying the *conflicts* in psychoanalysis—rather than censoring or marginalizing dissident thinkers—can reveal alternative perspectives to unquestioned analytic ideologies.

The dramatic replication of censorship in the institutional structure of psychoanalysis is a troubling phenomenon. Whether secret politics and censorship of difference and alternative theories—rather than an open, impartial search for truth—persist in contemporary psychoanalysis is a question that is, or at least ought to be, open to further examination. The fact that so few people are pursuing this sort of inquiry embodies the collective blindness of the seeing I and offers a testament to the way the field is still held captive by ambivalence about knowing.

# 3

# Fostering Tolerance and Creativity in the Culture of Psychoanalysis

One has to allow for a certain multiplicity of views, even an alloy with such-and-such percent nonsense.
—Sigmund Freud to Sandor Ferenczi, June 22, 1914

Psychoanalysis as a therapeutic method consciously values candor, rationality, tolerance, and freer associations. Psychoanalysis as a culture is permeated by censorship of innovative ideas, pettiness, intellectual sectarianism and intolerance, and hidden authoritarianism. This chapter reflects on the disparity between the two and suggests ways in which psychoanalysis could foster a culture more congenial to tolerance, experimentation, and creativity. Whereas psychoanalysis could have been a facilitative environment, a kind of Winnicottian potential space that fostered constructive dissent and playing with inherited languages and theories, it has become leery of risk and innovation and pervaded by intolerance of difference ever since Sandor Ferenczi was scapegoated and censored by the Secret Committee.

I first focus on the impact of the Secret Committee members' treatment of Ferenczi on psychoanalysis. Offering a revisionist reading of psychoanalysis in the years 1932–50, I highlight the trauma to *psychoanalysis* of the way Ferenczi was treated, especially many subsequent analysts' fear of being accused of not being Freudian. I then focus on some of the reasons for the theoretical fundamentalism permeating psychoanalytic institutions. Finally, I recommend a psychoanalysis that encourages greater tolerance, experimentation, and creativity within its own ranks and thereby more readily reaches its developmental potential.

The internal politics of analysis, as well as the polis as a sphere of analytic investigation, is neglected, relative to sexuality, in psychoanalysis.[1] For example, inquiry into the political nature of the reception of innovative analytic ideas, the choice of analytic curricula, and the appointment of training analysts receives very little attention. Ironically, the "political" (rather than the sexual) may now be the unconscious of psychoanalysis.[2] Psychoanalysts have not adequately explored the impact the Secret Committee's treatment of Ferenczi had on their profession. This is one of the places where the political unconscious of psychoanalysis lives.

## The Trauma to Psychoanalysis of the Scapegoating of Ferenczi

The Secret Committee pathologized, ostracized, and marginalized Ferenczi after he presented his controversial and visionary paper, "The Confusion of Tongues between Adults and the Child," at the International Psycho-Analytic Congress at Wiesbaden in 1932. Members of the Secret Committee, for example, labeled him "mad" and "paranoid" (Jones, 1957, pp. 45, 176, 178) after he presented the paper. The absence of corroborating evidence for the committee's diagnosis of Ferenczi (e.g., Fromm, 1955; Roazen, 1971) suggests that *political* (as well as psychological and theoretical) issues were at play.

Michael Balint (1968) claims that the Freud-Ferenczi conflict discussed in the previous chapter was a "trauma" to psychoanalysis: "The impact of this event was so painful that the first reaction of the analytic movement to it was denial and silence, broken only in recent years" (pp. 152, 149). A schism developed among analysts concerning the relative importance of fantasy versus trauma in the aetiology of psychopathology, the curative impact of recollection or repetition in treatment, and whether the psychoanalytic method should be restricted to neurosis or extended to borderline disorders and psychosis.[3] The Freud-Ferenczi conflict, in Balint's view, generated a silence that inhibited confronting these controversial issues. Perhaps by tacit consent, discussions of technique and countertransference were constrained. The dearth of literature on countertransference during the twenty-year hiatus between Ferenczi's seminal work in the late 1920s and early 1930s on the analyst's contribution to the treatment, and the related work of Harold Searles (1949), Paula Heimann (1950), and Margaret Little (1951) support Balint's claim.[4] Psychoanalytic inquiry, notes Freud (1914b), is "accustomed to divine secret and concealed things from despised or unnoticed features, from the rubbish-heap, as it were, of our observations" (p. 222). I want to suggest a revisionist reading of psychoanalytic history in which this lacuna in the analytic literature is viewed as an unconsciously symptomatic gap rather than a merely contingent omission. One of the "secret and concealed things" that could be divined from this "unnoticed" feature of psychoanalytic history—the nearly twenty-year absence of writings on countertransference (1932–49)—is that analysts by tacit consent decided to stay away from subjects that had generated the conflict between Freud and Ferenczi. Psychoanalysis itself, as well as Ferenczi, was divided and ultimately undermined by the Secret Committee's treatment of Ferenczi.

The committee's reaction to Ferenczi not only "considerably delayed the development of our analytic technique" (Balint, 1968, p. 52), it also established a corrosive precedent within psychoanalysis: a fear of *not being Freudian.* This fear had other motivations besides that of avoiding Ferenczi's fate, including a desire to keep alive the hope of a vital tie to Freud, who had been the analyst of various analysts (e.g., Ferenczi, Ernest Jones, and Helene Deutsch). Whatever the origins of this fear, it discouraged analysts from dissenting from orthodoxy.[5]

Although divergent viewpoints have proliferated throughout the history of psychoanalysis, there has been a pervasive intolerance of innovation and a penchant—even within revisionist movements—for orthodoxy and dogmatism. Anyone who believes that orthodoxy only lives in classical psychoanalysis need only observe the defensiveness among many followers of D. W. Winnicott, Heinz Kohut, or Harry Stack Sullivan when their theories or practices are questioned.

Intellectual intolerance has compromised the capacity of psychoanalysis to become what Winnicott calls a "potential space" (1971, p. 107)—that is, an imaginatively generative environment that provides the emotional safety and encouragement to use imaginatively, play creatively with, and alter inherited psychoanalytic languages, theories, and practices so as to expand the theoretical and clinical possibilities within the field.[6] Instead, the seeds were sown for what Winnicott might term an *un*facilitative environment, one not conducive to risk, innovation, and creativity. This deeply restricted and sometimes even foreclosed the possibilities within psychoanalysis to disagree with Freud or explore innovative and alternative theories and practices. Subsequent analysts may have become gun-shy about deviating from received psychoanalytic truths.

Analysts who questioned the established psychoanalytic faiths had at least six options: (1) pursue innovations and be treated as a heretic (like Ferenczi); (2) secede (like Jung) and become alienated from mainstream psychoanalysis, which deprives both the dissenter and the field of psychoanalysis of potentially corrective feedback; (3) stifle dissent and comply with received views; (4) smuggle in innovations under the cloak of "parameters" or "model-mixing" (e.g. Mitchell, 1988) based on diagnostic or developmental considerations;[7] (5) secretly pursue innovations; and (6) engage in deviations from mainstream analysis while utilizing traditional terminology that feigns allegiance to a paradigm from which one has deviated. Winnicott (1960a), for example, developed a radically new way of thinking about health and self—the authentic and alive True Self—only to claim erroneously that his novel formulations were merely outgrowths of Freud's ego, id, and super-ego. Winnicott maintained that his formulations regarding the True Self "can be discerned in the early formulations of Freud. In particular I link what I divide into a True and a False Self with Freud's division of the self into a part that is central and powered by the instincts (or by what Freud called sexuality, pregenital and genital), and a part that is turned outwards and is related to the world" (p. 140). In fact, Winnicott's concepts were completely unrelated to Freud's formulations.

## The Impact on Psychoanalysis of the Fear of Not Being Freudian

The fear of not being Freudian has, in my view, promoted an unhealthy tradition of polarization rather than cross-pollination within psychoanalysis. Psychoanalytic history is permeated by an "intolerance of diversity" and numerous schisms (Eisold, 1994, p. 785). Marianne Eckhardt (1978) notes schisms in psychoanalytic organizations in Germany, Austria, France, Sweden, and Norway. Frances Gitelson (1983) records them in Spain, Brazil, Mexico, Argentina, Venezuela, and the United States. Jacob Arlow (1972) mentions half a dozen splits in the American Psychoanalytic Association as well as splits in Colombia and Australia.

The intolerance of diverse points of view in psychoanalytic institutes ranges from "automatic dismissal of differences, on the one hand, to schismatic annihilation on the other" (Eisold, 1994, p. 787). Writing about the conflict that surfaced at a Los Angeles psychoanalytic institute, Joan Fleming (1976) noted the "unrelenting hostility and distrust among various groups and individuals, whatever their theoretical orientation. There was no single discernible basis for the presence of so much bad feeling" (p. 911). Innovative thinking that challenged the reigning orthodoxy was largely forced to go underground instead of being integrated into the field. The writings of Otto Rank and Carl Jung illustrate this phenomenon.

Contemporary psychoanalysis seems more receptive to divergent viewpoints. The heightened emphasis in recent years on the value of theoretical pluralism and multiple models in accounts of how treatments work suggests that fertile *diversity*, not sectarianism, characterizes contemporary psychoanalysis. That this diversity is often a kind of pseudopluralism is suggested by two works on single psychoanalytic treatments, in which each treatment is examined by analysts representing perspectives ranging from classical analysis to self psychology (Rothstein, 1985; Pulver et al., 1987). Theoretical ecumenicalism is recommended but not often practiced: divergent viewpoints coexist rather than cross-fertilize. The perspectives of other schools are not fully engaged or viewed empathetically. The interpretation of each school rarely reflects the insights of other traditions. Détente, rather than mutual influence, reigns.

The development of separate and insular "schools" of thought, each with its own theoretical and clinical presuppositions, further illustrates this pseudopluralism in analysis. However, the existence of separate schools has had both negative and positive effects on the field. Separate schools provide environments in which different perspectives can grow and develop. But the theories of each school tend to fossilize and become immutable Truths, resistant toward corrective feedback and transformation, which precludes openness and tolerance to alternatives. Separate schools may generate a "fundamentalist attitude," notes Ralph Greenson (1969). "Followers of a school react to new ideas from a different school as though they were a danger, a threat to the very foundation of their professional beliefs" (p. 355). This has occurred in psychoanalytic institutions whenever a "new" theory—whether interpersonal psychoanalysis, object relations theory, or self psychology—challenged the assumptions of the reigning paradigm. The ideas of one's own school are overestimated while alternatives from "rival" schools often are not adequately considered. The curricula of many training institutes illustrate Greenson's claim by failing to integrate the work of thinkers from other schools of thought. Each institute defines itself in terms of its founder— a single great man—and the curriculum centers around the theories of that person. Heinz Kohut is neglected at Jungian institutes, Harry Stack Sullivan is minimized at self psychology–oriented institutes, and so forth. Controversial new ideas are rarely, if ever, given a fair hearing. Students all too often are not exposed to seminal thinkers such as Ferenczi, although this has been changing in recent years.

The literature on psychoanalytic training paints a disturbing picture of excessive orthodoxy, idealization, and intimidation (Eisold, 1994, p. 786). Michael Balint's (1948) account of candidates' "submissiveness to dogmatic and authoritative treatment without much protest and too respectful behavior" (p. 167) seems an apt description of a generalized trend. Such training contributes to a rigid psychoanalytic culture. Placing an adult, who may be in a highly responsible position in other facets of his or her life, in the inherently submissive stance of an analytic *student* can be unsettling. This stress is heightened when the candidate is asked to perform analysis without highly developed theoretical or clinical tools. One important way that analytic candidates handle this tension is to comply with the demands of their training institution, hide vulnerability, bury theoretical disagreements, and inhibit risk and creativity. Fitting in with the institutional ethos—including minimizing self-vulnerability—enables trainees to solidify their precarious status. Embracing the theories of the school with which one identifies offers a sense of intellectual and emotional comfort. It serves as a map that guides and orients the analyst through the analytic process. It also gives one a stable identity and a sense of belonging.

The trainee's unresolved submissive and/or idealizing transferences toward the analyst, supervisor, or the founder of the school of therapy with which he or she identifies seem not to be worked through in most analyses (e.g., Roustang, 1982). The therapist's own psychic individuation and authenticity—as embodied in the therapeutic risks and experiments he or she engages in—may thus be experienced as psychologically dangerous or destabilizing. Although Freud established interminable questioning as an indispensable facet of psychoanalytic inquiry, his tendency to discourage coworkers from being colleagues with independent viewpoints fostered dependent followers who were reluctant to question his party line (James Jones, personal communication). Analysts often may experience guilt or shame over therapeutic interpretations or interventions that deviate from the dictums of whatever figure(s) they idealize. This is true of non-Freudians as well as Freudians.

The complex living experience of the therapeutic relationship and process is unwittingly converted, in such a situation, into what Arnold Gold-berg (1990) terms a "prisonhouse" of confining formulas and rules. Being intellectually straitjacketed can restrict the analyst's capacity to under-stand and to freely and completely respond to the exigencies of the ther-apeutic process. The analyst listens *for* confirmation of his or her pre-ferred theories, rather than listening *to* the client's ideographic material. This impairs clinical effectiveness and often generates a sense of staleness and boredom. It is difficult to feel engaged when one is intellectually imprisoned within a restrictive theoretical framework.

The authoritarianism that persists in the structure of psychoanalytic institutes and in psychoanalytic education—discernible, for example, in candidates not being more involved in questioning how analytic pedagogy and curricula might be different—often both disempowers candidates and tacitly if not explicitly discourages the flowering of their psycholog-ical and intellectual self-trust. The passivity of candidates that regularly permeates psychoanalytic classrooms may be a testament to the way an-alytic students have been disempowered.

Speaking of her survey of different training methods in European in-stitutes, Anne-Marie Sandler (1990) offers an unusually frank description of her personal struggles with what may be a more general problem in psychoanalysis: "I found myself wanting to deride those methods which were different from those I was accustomed to, and it took some time to overcome my culture shock and to accept, at an emotional level, the re-ality that there were outstanding analysts who have followed a different training route" (p. 49). Psychoanalysis will be more true to its basic spirit—its fascination with the complexity and mystery of human beings and human life—when it realizes that the greatest danger is dogma, not diversity, difference, or dissidence.

Two phenomena typical of most groups, including psychoanalytic ones, also compromise psychoanalysis's capacity to encourage diversity and dissidence. The "routinization of charisma" is the tendency of the second generation of a movement to codify, institutionalize, bureaucra-tize, and routinize the vital, alive, and unformalized insights of the first generation (Weber, 1946). The first generation of psychoanalysts often questioned inherited viewpoints about such things as human conduct, motivation, and psychopathology; forged new intellectual vistas; and di-rectly experienced something novel about human psychology. Many psy-choanalytic concepts and practices, however, became static and ossified in succeeding generations. In the hands of Freud's successors, for example, his improvisational practices and provisional "recommendations" for conducting psychoanalytic treatment all too often became ritualized and rigidified into inviolable ground rules that were treated as commandments. This is not to deny that the first generation was not immune to these trends, as the conduct of the Secret Committee toward Ferenczi suggests. And later generations of analysts have also enriched psychoanalysis (as well as routinized it) by jettisoning antiquated theories and extending inchoate concepts.

Wilfred Bion's (1970) account of the psychology of groups highlights a second crucial factor that compromises the capacity of psychoanalysis as a culture to be more self-reflective and open to self-transformation. Bion, like Freud (1921), illuminated the inherently conservative and conformist nature of groups—including psychoanalytic organizations and institutions—which impedes risk and innovativeness. The psychoanalytic group has an established order, which is evident in its attempt to preserve its identity and cohesiveness through shared language, beliefs, conventions, law, and culture. This group is invested in its own cohesion and perpetuation. It thus eschews any individual who threatens the prevailing ideology and power arrangements it has established. This may promote rigid doctrines and antiquated theories, eventually leading to ossification. Innovations can be narcissistically destabilizing (Greenson, 1969) and may generate envy or resistance toward the innovator (Langs, 1978).

Those "exceptional individuals" Bion (1970) terms "mystics"—such as the Socratic gadfly, innovative scientists, or visionary analysts—challenge and threaten group identity. The word *mystic* is sometimes used as a term of reproach toward someone who is said to be self-delusive, confused, or clinging to irrational beliefs. There is nothing inherently mystical (or mystifying) about mysticism, as William Haas (1956) notes, if one has engaged in a transformative self-investigative practice such as meditation for an extended period of time under the tutelage of an experienced teacher. Bion's "mystic" refers, I suspect, to an innovator or visionary, not to someone committed to the occult or involved in mystifying behavior. She or he is what Georg Simmel (1950) termed a "stranger," someone—like Freud (e.g., Loewenberg, 1995)—who is both inside and outside the culture. Not aligning solely with the group affords a critical distance from its mores and a greater capacity to question and sometimes challenge taken-for-granted facets of group norms, values, and goals.

The mystic, in Bion's view, is both essential and dangerous to the health and stability of the group. By introducing new ideas and change, the mystic unsettles the prevailing order of the group and ensures that it avoids intellectual sclerosis even as she also triggers profound anxiety. The group needs to provide for the mystic if it is to stay viable and not get mired in ossified beliefs or become a secular cult. The mystic keeps the group honest, but the group also wants to eliminate her. Psychoanalysis after Ferenczi seems to have become a discipline in which the balance was heavily weighted toward nullifying rather than nurturing the mystic. Regenerative possibilities that only the mystic might foster and nourish thus were much less likely to arise.

One potentially vital "mystical" impulse in psychoanalysis was the group of esteemed second-generation European analysts (e.g. Otto Fenichel, Edith Jacobson, and Annie Reich) whom Russell Jacoby (1983) termed the "political Freudians." They debated sexual and social codes and explored the relationship of psychoanalysis to social and political issues. They reflected, for example, on such issues as the relationship of psychoanalysis to Marxism and how psychoanalysis could illuminate culture. Unfortunately, this group ended when Nazism and Fascism forced its members to leave the cosmopolitan intellectual climate of Europe and relocate to the insular and medically conservative United States at a time when McCarthyism was rampant. Expelled from continental Europe, on the run from Fascism and Nazism, refugees in the more insular world of American psychoanalysis, political Freudians like Fenichel hid their radical allegiances, transmitted nothing of their political heritage to younger colleagues, and settled for survival. Their potential legacy died with them and remained buried in the political unconscious of psychoanalysis until Jacoby's pioneering research uncovered the details of this neglected tradition.

In addition to its internal orthodoxy, psychoanalysis traditionally has been insulated from potentially enriching dialogues with other humanistic and social science disciplines. The encounter between psychoanalysis and allied disciplines is usually a one-way affair, a kind of intellectual imperialism in which the emphasis is on what *psychoanalysis* offers history (or literature, anthropology, feminism, philosophy, or sociology). What these disciplines might offer psychoanalysis is rarely explored. Frank Sulloway (1992) aptly notes how the insularity of the professional organization of psychoanalysis has hindered the dissemination of psychoanalytic knowledge outside the specialized confines of the field, which mitigates against nonanalysts critically examining its epistemological doctrines and problems. By segregating itself from potentially enriching cross-pollination with other disciplines, and by marginalizing psychoanalytic visionaries, psychoanalysis deprived itself of two sources of corrective feedback.

## Psychoanalysis as a Facilitating Environment

The fear of not being Freudian, the subsequent marginalization of psychoanalytic dissidents, the submissiveness fostered by psychoanalytic education, and the proliferation of separate and insular analytic schools have ensured that psychoanalysis has not become a "mystical" group. Three cautions are necessary. First, blatant opposition to Freud's teachings should be avoided because it may insulate one from what Freud has to offer. Second, since dissent is not monolithically constructive—it may, for example, be fueled by defensive motives—we need to champion theoretical contestation of outmoded doctrines even as we realize that too much dissent can inhibit the full development of specific points of view. To pursue a particular point of view in depth and develop its full implications may, at times, necessitate foreclosing other perspectives. Third, heterogeneity may sometimes promote divisiveness rather than fertile diversity: the separate languages of each school may create a psychoanalytic tower of babel.

How, then, can we facilitate a psychoanalytic climate that is more congenial to diversity and change? Guidelines for nourishing psychoanalytic "mysticism" cannot be definitely established, but concrete things can be done. There are at least two components to this process: (1) detecting where psychoanalysis is closed, and (2) creating a psychoanalytic culture that fosters greater self-awareness, risk, and creativity.

Questions that cannot be asked about psychoanalytic theory or practice—the kind of questions that Ferenczi asked—or questions that are answered too quickly may signal areas of closure within the field. The members of the Secret Committee would have been truer to the spirit of psychoanalysis if they had been curious about their negative reaction to Ferenczi's innovative ideas, rather than condemning them. Unquestioned assumptions or conclusions are immune to critical scrutiny and potential modification. Theoretical and clinical "certainty" often hides and rests on a foundation of buried doubt, ambiguity, and contradictions.

Attending to what Freud (1906) termed "indirect representation" can help us detect areas of premature closure in the field:

The only way in which a carefully guarded secret betrays itself is by subtle, or at most ambiguous, allusions. In the end the patient becomes accustomed to disclose to us by means of what is known as "indirect representation", all that we require in order to uncover the complex. (P. 110)

Because of the tradition of censorship, intolerance, and political infighting bequeathed by the Secret Committee, dissenters from psychoanalytic orthodoxy—such as Ferenczi—are usually devalued and consigned to the periphery of the field, rather than utilized to cross-fertilize and emend traditional psychoanalytic formulations. They often play bit parts in standardized versions of psychoanalytic history. But the marginalized theories of certain psychoanalytic dissidents, as well as the allusions of patients, may also sometimes offer an "indirect representation" of buried aspects of psychoanalysis—as appears, for example, to be the case with the neglected contributions of Ferenczi. Psychoanalysis would greatly benefit from what Foucault termed "counter-histories" of analysis, like Russell Jacoby's *The Repression of Psychoanalysis*, in which neglected and marginalized voices are highlighted and elaborated.

Theory is Janus-faced: it is stabilizing as well as potentially inhibiting for the analyst (Friedman, 1988). It may mitigate the complexity and anxiety of analytic work as it orients clinicians in relation to their patients and connects them to a tradition and colleagues. It may also impede creative thinking and practice as it sometimes funnels analysands into the Procrustean bed of established meanings and concepts.

Dialogue, not dogma, characterizes a progressive psychoanalysis. Keeping alive what Thomas Kuhn (1978)—speaking of healthy science—termed an "essential tension" between the stasis of inherited doctrines and the changes and transformation generated by innovations is central to creating a psychoanalytic climate that fosters creativity and inventiveness. Psychoanalysis, like a successful jazz group, athletic team, or intimate relationship, needs "grounded openness" (Ralston, 1994, p. 6), a balanced blend of openness and flexibility and groundedness and structure. Inflexibility generates a sterile intellectual environment and inhibits the discovery of new theories and practices. Ironically, our clinical successes can promote inflexibility. Questions often recede as success increases. Risk and experimentation is discouraged, and our capacity for growth and creativity is inhibited, when we remain entrapped within the potential prison of what has already worked. This impedes exploration and the birth of the new.

And yet, while flexibility can be a psychoanalytic virtue, too much openness and exploration can be experienced as anarchic or chaotic. It can be psychologically confusing and unsettling, for example, to remain open to a multitude of analytic perspectives, each of which adopts antithetical assumptions about human nature, the aetiology of pathology, and the analytic relationship and process. By balancing openness and groundedness, and thus promoting equilibrium and diversity, psychoanalysis may preserve what it has discovered while remaining open to revision.

Psychoanalysts need a less narcissistic, more fluid relationship to their own theories, a topic I address in the last three chapters of this book. By this I mean we need to value our theories without being enslaved by them. We need to hold them lightly rather than tightly, so that they are treated as provisional guides that can be dispensed with or transformed when necessary. This will help us "utilize all ways and be bound by none . . . absorb what is useful, reject what is useless, and add what is specifically our own" (Lee, 1975).

Psychoanalytic education has to become more liberatory for analysts to be able to do this. The focus has to shift from the socialization to the emancipation of analytic candidates. I have come to feel that analytic teachers most honor their students when they help them to grow beyond a defensive, submissive stand toward the teacher, to question what they are learning and make it their own. My own experiments in encouraging this have recently led me to attempt to make the teaching experience a "practice of freedom" (hooks, 1994, p. 51) that aids analytic candidates in becoming more active, empowered learners rather than passive, deferential consumers. For example, I asked each of the candidates in a course I taught on human development to reflect on and write about either a personal or clinical experience of gender that challenged or amended traditional psychoanalytic conceptions. Each student discussed a topic that had either been neglected or insufficiently elaborated in previous writings on gender. One student, for example, shared how pregnancy had been a time in which she felt great power, generativity, and intuitiveness. This led to suggestive reflections in class about the inadequacies of traditional analytic conceptions of woman-as-deficient-man[8] and the way the concept of penis envy may defend against what *men* might envy in *women* as well as capture an important experience for some women. The consensus of the candidates was that this exercise empowered them and helped them see their own experience as a greater resource in understanding their patients and themselves.

Challenging or modifying psychoanalytic theory when the data call for it will make it easier to listen *to* what patients (and students) are attempting to teach us, rather than to listen *for* confirmation of what we already know. When the freedom of candidates plays a more central role in psychoanalytic education, then the field may be more saturated with practitioners who are comfortable with reflective and disciplined transgression of either orthodox *or* revisionist shibboleths. Crucial questions about the partiality of one's favored analytic theories and the secondary gains such partiality might serve more readily emerge in such a climate. The potential value in schools of psychoanalytic thought that one has not been personally exposed to in analytic training may then be more evident.

I have often been struck by the conspicuous difference between the interest analysts demonstrate toward unfamiliar elements of their patients' narratives and the relative absence of such curiosity and tolerance toward alien aspects of the theories of colleagues. Andre Green (1993) notes the irony that "analysts listen more easily to their patients than they can to each other" (p. 221). Too often, theories that seem foreign are rejected out of hand rather than engaged. John Gedo (1986) has termed "empathic scholarship" (p. 105), Heinz Kohut's (1973) suggestion that the empathic stance of attempting to understand a psychological phenomenon from within its own frame of reference be applied to social and historical phenomena.[9] Greenson (1969) offers two ways of doing this: he recommends making the curricula more "flexible and heterogeneous" and studying "seriously the views of those we disagree with" by exchanging views openly based on "clinical material described in detail" (p. 357). The trend to bring together analysts from diverse perspectives to discuss the "same" clinical material suggests that contemporary psychoanalysis is moving in this direction. But what also eventually needs to occur is a dialogue in which the claims of otherness are more fully engaged and one's own fundamental assumptions are more deeply put at risk. In his discussion of the hermeneutical philosopher Hans-Georg Gadamer, philosopher Richard Bernstein (1992) points to the sort of attitude that psychoanalysis needs. Understanding demands that one is willing to "test and risk one's convictions and prejudgments in and through an encounter with what is radically 'other' and alien" (p. 4). One needs to open oneself "to the full power of what the 'other' is saying" (ibid.). Opening "does not entail agreement but rather the to-and-fro play of dialogue" (ibid.). Without dialogue there is only a "self-deceptive monologue where one never risks testing one's prejudgments" (ibid.).

Kohut's "Two Analyses of Mr Z." and the more recent work of Merton Gill, among others, illustrates the willingness to put one's theories at risk—and the capacity for theoretical self-transformation—that psychoanalysis tends to lack. Kohut's and Gill's theoretical and clinical paradigms were dramatically transformed through an encounter with alternative perspectives. This capacity is essential to the health and vitality of psychoanalysis.

Investigating the theoretical and clinical perspectives of dissidents or schools of thought different than our own with the kind of empathic attunement usually reserved only for analysands could lessen the destructive intellectual insularity, polarization, and xenophobia pervading our field. It could also enrich our own perspectives, or at least spur us to further delineate and articulate our own concepts and practices. Then the psychoanalytic visionary/mystic might be seen as a potentially valuable resource, rather than as a misguided heretic who deserves to be consigned to the political unconscious of psychoanalysis.

A psychoanalytic culture that fostered creativity would be an open structure amenable to corrective feedback and change, rather than a closed one dedicated only to its own survival. Such a culture would be more focused on learning and growth than self-perpetuation and self-inflation. The leadership of this kind of open organization would be self-reflective. It would examine the unconscious attractions of discipleship and attempt to foster colleagues rather than followers. It would strive to keep destructive envy and competitiveness in its ranks in check (e.g., Loewenberg, 1995). It would value diversity and constructive disloyalty rather than the removal of opposition. Organizationally, it might resemble improvisational jazz "in which no one is totally in charge, in which people play off each other's strengths, in which anyone picks it up, and in which there are different voices that are respectful of differences" (Levinson, 1994, p. 245). Both individual competence—the capacity to play "solo"—and sensitivity to the needs of group life are crucial.

In such a psychoanalytic culture, conflicts over theories and practices could be utilized to illuminate the essential presuppositions and unconscious organizing metaphors of divergent viewpoints, rather than evaded through fiat or premature resolution. Since disputes about theory, as Gedo (1984) recognized, often "reflect underlying value judgments" (p. 158), which themselves cannot be absolutely justified, a mystical psychoanalytic culture might, in the sense popularized by Richard Rorty (1979), replace the urge to discover timeless Truth with an interest in generating stimulating conversations. Such conversations will probably lead not to consensus, but to what Thomas Ogden (1991) terms the "uneasy coexistence of a multiplicity of epistemologies" (p. 369).

Orthodoxy (whether of a traditional or revisionist variety) often breeds despotism. Humility, suspicions about certainty, openness to surprise and discovery, and perhaps a sense of humor about the contingency and provisionality of one's most hallowed viewpoints might characterize the psychoanalytic climate I am pointing toward. D. W. Winnicott illustrated this spirit when, as an eminent seventy-three-year-old psychoanalyst with an international reputation, he reversed roles at a psychoanalytic conference in 1969, gave up his authority, and let a younger junior colleague (Ishak Ramzy) supervise him (Kahr, 1996). Winnicott, like the Oxford Clerk in Chaucer's *Canterbury Tales*, "would gladly learn and gladly teach."

In such a psychoanalytic culture, candidates would be supported by faculty when they transgressed orthodox thinking of whatever stripe when it was outdated; analysands would be encouraged by their analysts to transcend their own limitations; and analytic conferences and journals might celebrate a thousand psychoanalytic models blooming.

We will know that psychoanalysis is no longer an unfacilitative, unmystical group when the "experimentation with disloyalties" that Winnicott (1986b, p. 138) recognized in healthy families would be more important in psychoanalytic groups and institutions than blind fidelity to inherited doctrines and fear of not espousing politically correct psychoanalytic viewpoints. The internal conflicts, defensive processes, and latent possibilities of analytic institutions and policies would be the object of analytic scrutiny in such a culture (e.g. Eisold, 1994, p. 797). Candidates might play a more active role in shaping their education, and analytic conferences and journals would be more tolerant of dissenting viewpoints. Until such time, the path of fundamental transformation and reformation largely lies with individual psychoanalysts who recognize that psychoanalysis is a living and elastic art (Ferenczi, 1928, p. 99) and are committed to discovering where blindness lives in their own theoretical beliefs, clinical practices, and institutional allegiances.

Our beliefs, ideals, and theories play a central role in our identity and our sense of self-stability. Because we tenaciously protect and defend these aspects of our identity, it is a highly difficult task to challenge or alter them. We psychoanalysts have perhaps had an easier time looking at others than at ourselves. Because character changes slowly, it is worth reconsidering Freud's (1937) reflections on the "interminable" nature of analysis and self-understanding and his recommendations for ongoing work on oneself. Building ongoing self-analysis into our practices seems crucial.

In a psychoanalytic universe that was more congenial to self-analysis, dissent, and the insights of other humanistic and social science disciplines, politics *and* sexuality, Ferenczi *and* Freud, traditional and revisionist theories might all be seen as part of an interanimating conversation about the complexity and heterogeneity of human life.[10]

PART 2

# Psychoanalytic Theory

It is tempting to conclude, from the censorship of Sandor Ferenczi by Sigmund Freud and the Secret Committee and the rigidity and intolerance in analytic institutions discussed in the previous chapters, that the blindness of the seeing I existed only in classical psychoanalysis, embedded in its history and organizations. But this blindness also lives in the theories, social organization, and practices of contemporary analysis.

This section focuses on a crucial aspect of analytic theories, namely, conceptions of selfhood. Theories about the self are a cornerstone of the analytic enterprise. The nature of self-experience is of central concern to psychoanalysis, which has elucidated subtle and important facets of selfhood. In fact, psychoanalysis is arguably the most interesting discourse on selfhood in the twentieth century, illuminating the complexity and multidimensionality of self-development, human motivation, and self-structuralization with clarity and precision. Postmodern discourse also demonstrates an exemplary attunement to self-complexity. By depicting the heterogeneity of the self, it has usefully challenged the notion of a unitary, singular self. But postmodern writings all too frequently posit a "negative identity"—the "death of the subject"—throwing out the baby of subjectivity in the act of draining the bath water of self-singularity. Psychoanalysis, unlike postmodern discourse, appreciates the multidimensionality of self-experience without ushering in a disabling nihilism.

Although psychoanalysis can contribute to a greater understanding of the nature of selfhood, it displays a curious and symptomatic ambivalence about human individuality. On the one hand, successful therapy fosters the emergence of the analysand's individuality. On the other hand, when analysts subscribe too rigidly to preset, normative narratives of development and the nature of self, an analysand's individuality can be unwittingly compromised as it is assimilated into someone else's a priori version of the good life.

This tension between what might be termed the *liberating* and *con-*

*straining* views of selfhood in psychoanalysis is exemplified by the innovative and highly influential writings of D. W. Winnicott and Heinz Kohut, two of the most central and esteemed postclassical theorists. Their respective theories of self-experience—Winnicott's True Self waiting to be discovered and actualized and Kohut's bipolar self composed of ambitions and ideals and striving toward self-cohesion—offer important revisions and expansions of classical psychoanalytic theories of self and motivation. Each evinces exemplary clinical sensitivity to crucial dimensions of self-experience.

But there is another aspect to their theories in particular (and to psychoanalytic theories of self-experience in general), which seems not to have been sufficiently recognized. Winnicott's and Kohut's theories both partake of the blindness of the seeing I, simultaneously revealing and obscuring the complexity and heterogeneity of self-experience. Their theories theoretically reduce, as well as elucidate, the multidimensionality of selfhood that their clinical practices attempt to liberate. Winnicott illuminates a crucial facet of self-experience—namely, authenticity and psychological deadness—but he pays insufficient attention in his theories and practice to the patient's role in self-creation. Kohut's theory of self-development illuminates self-experience, but the exclusion of gender-specific theorizing eclipses the experience of women and does not adequately recognize the different priorities that may characterize the ways in which women, and some men, organize their experience.

The five chapters in part 2 each in their own way explore a different dimension of the blindness of the seeing I in relation to psychoanalytic theories in general and visions of self-experience in particular. Chapter 4 focuses on the hidden religiosity in psychoanalysis that constricts analytic theorizing in general and its accounts of self-experience in particular. I argue that psychoanalysis needs to work through its religiosity in order to experience a more meaningful spirituality, which would improve psychoanalytic theorizing and organizations. Chapter 5 explores unacknowledged tensions and gaps in Winnicott's conception of selfhood arising out of the way his theories are embedded in, and circumscribed by, his own life. Chapter 6 explicates some of the constricting aspects of the search for an essential, preexistent True Self. In place of such a singular construct, I offer a more multidimensional conception of self-experience. Chapter 7 elucidates blind spots in Kohut's account of self-experience, including androcentric biases in his conception of selfhood.

From Freud's archeological search for the origins of psychopathology to Winnicott's attempt to discover (and actualize) the buried, antecedent True Self, psychoanalysis has skillfully highlighted the historical as opposed to the emergent, or immanent and evolving, facets of self-experience—who the self *was* rather than what it *might be*. Chapters 6 and 7 stress the formative role that the patient's current self-creative efforts play in the construction of identity. In other words, we need to build a meaningful life in the present as well as discover hidden dimensions of ourselves from the past. If cleaving to a unitary sense of self is problematic—disavowing our psychological complexity and thus limiting our behavioral repertoire—then the Kohutian emphasis on self-cohesion is a necessary, albeit insufficient, facet of mental health. Chapter 7 also illuminates pathological facets of self-cohesion and creative aspects of self-unintegration. Chapter 8 addresses unconscious egocentricity in psychoanalytic accounts of self-experience and the cost of psychoanalysis's neglect of the spiritual, including impoverished accounts of intimacy and morality.

We live in difficult and confusing times. There is widespread psychological alienation, cognitive oversaturation, and emotional disconnection and depletion. It is my hope that exploring hidden blind spots and gaps in analytic theories of selfhood will clear away illusions about self-experience that have held us captive, and will aid analysts in conceiving of self-experience in novel and fresh ways. This would enhance our capacity to cope with the unique challenges confronting besieged individuals in the late twentieth century.

# 4

# Psychoanalysts and Their Gods

Psychoanalysis has always been a religion in which you are not
allowed to believe in God.     —Adam Phillips, *On Flirtation*

Psychoanalysis, like the science it emulated, prided itself on its
rationality, its capacity to detect illusions and renounce comforting and
erroneous beliefs. One of the reasons for its antipathy toward religion
was that the latter was presumed by Freud, as an heir of the Age of the
Enlightenment, to be based on illusory consolations and false salvations,
rather than the clear-eyed, stoical rationality of psychoanalysis. In my
view, an unacknowledged religiosity permeates psychoanalysis, very
much to the detriment of the field. In this chapter I examine some of the
manifestations and consequences of this and suggest that psychoanalysis
needs to work through its religiosity to find a more meaningful spirituality.

The blindness of the seeing I lives in psychoanalysis in its hidden religiosity, which embodies an important and disabling tension in psychoanalysis and constricts the field as a whole in a variety of ways. On the
one hand, psychoanalysis offers powerful tools for detecting and working
through illusions, self-deceptions, and submissiveness to authorities, and
for promoting greater tolerance and compassion toward different ways
of being and living. On the other hand, the religiosity that haunts psychoanalytic theory and practice fosters idolatry, deference to authorities,
and intolerance of difference.

Since its inception psychoanalysis has been, for the most part, ada-
mantly *antireligious*; traditionally, psychoanalysts, following Freud's
lead, have pathologized and dismissed religious experience. Religion, for
Freud and the vast majority of subsequent psychoanalysts, was an illusion; a universal obsessional neurosis (1927, p. 43); a childhood neurosis
(1927, p. 53); a form of masochism (1930); a reaction formation against

unacceptable impulses (1927); a "delusion" (1927, p. 31); a remnant of prescientific thinking adopted by the psychologically neurotic and immature.[1]

Because of the psychoanalytic animus against religion, psychoanalysis and religion appear to have no common ground. And yet, both psychoanalytic critics (e.g., Sulloway, 1979; Webster, 1995)[2] and loyalists (Holt, 1996) have noted important resemblances between the two: ancestor worship, creeds, dogmas, taboos, rituals, priestly classes, and totemism[3] are common to the social organization of both religions and psychoanalysis. Psychoanalysis includes the worship of authorities—such as Freud (or the originator of the particular analytic school of thought to which one feels allegiance)—as well as adherence to theories and practices. The theories of those who are worshiped become inviolable creeds and rituals that are followed dogmatically, and thus often become dogmas. Psychoanalysis also includes an exclusive and hierarchically stratified organization with strict rules for inclusion based on kinship through the common totemic affiliation of the correct analytic pedigree. As we have seen, psychoanalysts who question or deviate from the orthodoxy of tradition—such as Sandor Ferenczi, Carl Jung, Alfred Adler, and Otto Rank—are too often treated as "heretics" (e.g., Roazen, 1971, p. 224).[4]

## Ancestor Worship

The founder of each school of psychoanalysis (Freud, Jung, Melanie Klein, Jacques Lacan, Harry Stack Sullivan, D. W. Winnicott, Heinz Kohut, etc.) has been worshiped with a godlike reverence. Psychoanalyst Wilhelm Stekel stated it directly when he said: "I was the apostle of Freud who was my Christ" (Stekel, 1950, p. 106.). Worship may also take the form of hagiographical accounts of the founder's life—such as Ernest Jones's biography of Freud—and uncritical examinations of his work. If one is skeptical about the pervasiveness of the idolatry of psychoanalytic pioneers, it might be helpful to reflect on the powerfully negative reactions to dissenters discussed in the previous chapter. Why are certain dissenters in psychoanalysis "excommunicated" and vilified unless one is laboring under the illusion that someone, namely oneself or the founder of the school of thought to which one feels the greatest allegiance, possesses the Truth. Dissenters would not be heretics without some orthodoxy that the founder or the disciple treated as received Truth.

The founder may or may not foster this sort of behavior, and may even warn about its dangers or actively discourage it. Freud, at least in some instances, discouraged efforts to deify him. In a letter to Ferenczi on October 6, 1910, he wrote he was "not that psychoanalytic superman whom we have constructed, and I also haven't overcome the countertransference" (Freud & Ferenczi, 1993, p. 221). Freud wrote to Jung that "a transference on a religious basis would strike me as most disastrous; it could only end in apostasy, thanks to the universal human tendency to keep making new prints of the clichés we bear within us. I shall do my best to show you that I am unfit to be an object of worship" (Freud, 1974, p. 98).

Unfortunately, unconscious deference frequently exists on the part of devotees and rarely seems to be worked through. Even a psychoanalytic revisionist such as Winnicott, who exemplified psychoanalytic originality, struggled to free himself from the grip of an unconscious deference to Freud, as I discuss in more detail in chapter 5. Winnicott both denied his uniqueness and originality and claimed a spurious allegiance to and continuity with his theoretical predecessors (Freud) and colleagues (Klein) that hid, and allowed him to disavow, some of his theoretical innovativeness. One might even argue that Kohut, who was also a psychoanalytic revisionist, put the new wine of some of his insights about narcissism into the old bottle of traditional analytic drive theory in order to demonstrate his allegiance to traditional psychoanalysis and Freud.[5]

The idealization of a psychoanalytic pioneer—like idealization in general—can stifle creativity in the follower and inhibit revisions of the former's theories. Unconscious worship often inhibits the emergence of a thinker's own more radical insights. The failure to individuate from whomever one deifies undermines one's self-trust, promotes self-disempowerment, and stifles critical engagement with the concepts or practices of the deified figure. Inconsistencies and omissions in the pioneer's corpus are thus more difficult to detect and necessary revisions are compromised. This may be part of the reason why, as Robert Wallerstein (1988) noted, we have yet to mourn Freud. Freud is like a ghost whose presence haunts us, rather than an ancestor who influenced us but whose legacy we have made our own (Loewald, 1980).

## Psychoanalytic Creeds and Dogmas

When the founder's doctrines become dogmas that are treated as items of faith and assumed to have an absolute truth, it may then be considered blasphemous or heretical to challenge them (Bakan, 1966, p. 8). Those who did not accept the psychoanalytic creeds were often excommunicated. Freud's remark to Jung is one of innumerable examples that could be cited in the history of psychoanalysis: "My dear Jung, promise me never to abandon the sexual theory. That is the most essential thing of all. You see, we must make a dogma of it, an unshakable bulwark" (Jung, 1965, p. 150).

Psychoanalysts often universalize the validity of the particular psychoanalytic theories, beliefs, and creeds they inherit (and dogmas they construct)—whether classical or postclassical—instead of making them their own. Examples of this abound in every school of psychoanalysis from Freud to the present. Psychoanalytic conceptions of human nature and development are illustrative. Let us take Erik Erikson's sensitive work on the psychosocial dimensions of identity as one of many possible examples.

Erikson's formulations, as Alan Roland (1988) notes, are "completely based on the data of Western personality. Strivings for autonomy and initiative in young children, or the identity crises, moratoria, and syntheses of adolescence and young adulthood may be central to American, and even Western development, but they certainly are not to Indian and Japanese development" (p. 314). Erikson's account both superimposes concerns that may be more salient to males in the United States onto men and women from India and Japan and neglects what seems central to Indian and Japanese children, such as the "child's reactions to the active encouragement of dependency needs in the earlier phases of childhood, and the child's negotiation of the severe crackdown on behavior in familial hierarchical relationships from ages four or five through adolescence" (ibid.).

But conceptions of the self are not, as many analysts seems to assume, universal, transcultural, or transhistorical. Different societies construe selfhood in different ways.[6] Studies of foreign culture demonstrate that conceptions of the self are culturally variable. For example, Bradd Shore's (1982) ethnographic work in Samoa challenges the universal pretensions of the Western humanist conception of an autonomous subject concerned primarily with self-knowledge, freedom, and individuation: the "Samoan language," Shore informs us, "has no term corresponding to 'personality, self, character'; instead of our Socratic 'know thyself,' Samoans say 'take care of the relationship' " (p. 65).

Roland's (1988) experiences with non-Western patients in psychoanalytic treatment convinced him of the unconscious "Western-centric" bias underlying psychoanalytic formulations about human personality. Through treating Indian patients and supervising the clinical work of Indian and Japanese psychoanalysts and mental health professionals, he found that the psychological makeup of persons in India and Japan is qualitatively different from that of northern Europeans and Americans due to fundamental differences in cultural principles and the social patterns and child rearing that these principles shape and delimit. What Roland terms the "familial self," which is rooted in and attuned to the subtle emotional and hierarchical relationships of the family, predominates in Indian and Japanese people and contrasts sharply with the Western individualized self, which arises out of contractual, egalitarian relationships geared toward individualism.[7] Psychoanalysis, in my view, needs to be skeptical rather than worshipful toward theories that are made into universal creeds.

## Psychoanalytic Idolatry

Analytic universalism often fosters *idolatry*, which, as theologian Reinhold Neibuhr suggested, occurs when one absolutizes the relative (Jones, 1991). Let me briefly mention two examples in psychoanalysis.

The generic, ungendered, unracialized human subject—white and male—seems to be a psychoanalytic idol. The generic use of "man" has pervaded the history of psychoanalysis from Freud until the present.[8] Unconscious androcentric assumptions exist even in revisionist conceptions of the self. Lynn Layton (1990), for example, has pointed out the unacknowledged androcentric assumptions in Kohut's bipolar self, which I discuss in greater detail in chapter 7.

When culture-specific psychoanalytic categories that seem to be rooted in the experiences of white, middle- and upper-middle class heterosexual men are applied universally to the experience of people from radically different sociocultural, racial, gendered, and historical backgrounds— women, African-Americans, homosexuals, and so forth—both within and outside Western culture,[9] the experience of these people tends to be misapprehended and seen as "inferior or psychopathological" (Roland, 1988, p. xvi).

Psychoanalysts often treat science as an idol. Freud, notes Jones (1953), believed in "Science with a capital [S]" (p. 40). From its inception, psychoanalysis has aspired to the status of science. In *New Introductory Lectures on Psycho-Analysis*, Freud (1933d) makes this explicit, asserting that science is psychoanalysis's Weltanschauung. Those who doubt that the worship of science still pervades psychoanalysis might consider how frequently those who *defend* psychoanalysis against critics such as Adolf Grünbaum, who criticize it for being unscientific, accept the basic premise of these critics—namely, that psychoanalysis is not a valid enterprise unless it apes the canons of scientific method.

Science has established itself as the supreme form of legitimate knowledge and authority in our world, largely by means of the claim that its "truth" is based on rigorous methods of experimentation and proof. Looking to science as the final court of epistemological appeal rests on a misunderstanding and is the seedbed of illusion. Its claims to authority notwithstanding, science is not a neutral, objective epistemological activity devoid of personal, social, and historical influences. Like all human enterprises, it arises out of specific settings, involves complex psychological motivations, and is shaped and delimited by linguistic, historical, and sociocultural conventions. Feminist critiques of science (Keller, 1985) and neopragmatist (Rorty, 1979, 1982) and hermeneutical examinations of interpretation and theorizing (Gadamer, 1976) suggest that the very terms of the debate about whether psychoanalysis is a science are problematic and reductionist. Science itself is not the methodologically neutral and epistemologically apodictic enterprise we often imagine; in practice, it is much less "scientific" than we assume. The quest for a neutral framework of investigation or interpretation is quixotic because there can be no objective, neutral observation and theorizing (Rorty, 1979, 1982).

Science can be a useful servant, but it is a poor master. When judiciously invoked, it can be heuristic. But it is not the royal road to truth. Its status and prestige have no firmer basis than the prevalence of social and intellectual conventions that members of a specific "disciplinary matrix" and community agree to follow (e.g., Kuhn, 1970). Thus, the crucial question is not whether psychoanalysis is "scientific," but rather why science is fetishized and deified by many psychoanalysts. The absence of *justification* for why psychoanalysis's validity should rest on the procedures of a different discipline with different goals and methods is striking and telling.[10]

## Priestly Classes, Taboos, and Rituals in Psychoanalysis

Psychoanalytic institutions are organized around both the universal validity of the founder's thought and fidelity to the founder himself, which generates notions of analytic purity and impurity and establishes boundaries demarcating the priestly class from the heretics. The Secret Committee illustrates the existence in the early days of psychoanalysis of a priestly class who had a privileged status and influence. The monopoly trade practice of the American Psychoanalytical Association is a more recent example. In psychoanalysis in the United States, medical doctors trained in psychiatry have traditionally been the priestly class while analytically trained psychologists (and social workers) were outside the psychoanalytic Church. Candid admissions during the discovery phase of the suit by psychologists against the American Psychoanalytic Association revealed "economic motives in discriminating against psychologists about admission to training programmes" (Kirsner, 1990, p. 90).

Psychoanalytic thinking that is consistent with the beliefs of the founder and/or the priestly class is viewed as natural, official, and correct; alternatives are viewed as deviations and "heresy." Boundaries are then established between the elite, those who are members of the priesthood, and those who are outside. Membership in the priesthood all too often entails exclusive allegiance to the theories, practices, and dogmas of the select. This leads to a policing of allegiances, resulting in the censorship without decoding discussed in chapter 2. Dissent is marginalized.

Organizations, like cultures, are built on the twin pillars of what they *exclude* as well as what they include. What Julia Kristeva (1982) terms the "abject," that which we find loathsome and other, may be a central part of what is excluded. From its place of "banishment" it exerts an uncanny significance and force. Whatever one renounces and treats as foreign and alien still influences one's consciousness and conduct. Members of fundamentalist organizations and hate groups illustrate this principle in a particularly disturbing manner. Their whole identity revolves around attacking or removing whatever they despise. The abject is "what I permanently thrust aside in order to live" (Kristeva, 1982, p. 2). It is as if we say "that is not me, I am not that." Organizational as well as individual identity rests upon whatever we disavow. It is "something rejected from which one does not part" (p. 4), "the place where I am not and which permits me to be" (p. 3).

Each school of analysis usefully highlights a neglected facet of human development and the therapeutic process. For example, psychic complexity and conflict are illuminated by classical analysis and contemporary Freudians. Internalized object relations are clearer because of object relations theorists. Interpersonal analysts have elucidated interpersonal reenactments in the therapeutic relationship, and self psychology has clarified the importance of caregivers providing selfobject functions in the vicissitudes of self-development. In highlighting particular aspects of human nature and development and psychoanalytic treatment, each school also inevitably neglects other facets of people and the therapeutic relationship and process. The language of analytic purity and impurity that all too frequently appears in psychoanalytic discourse signals that theories that lie outside the paradigm of the founder of a school may inadvertently be treated as *abject* and *taboo*. Taboo knowledge is knowledge that is excluded or forbidden from use or mention by a group for its own protection because of social custom or emotional aversion. For example, in much classical analysis, the stress on the role of fantasy and asocial, endogenously arising drives in human behavior may render taboo discussion of the relational influences on thought and conduct. Self psychology and object relations theory, in highlighting the way the other is central to the fate of the self, may make the complexity of the other and its status as a *subject* a taboo topic. In elucidating the irreducibly relational nature of treatment, interpersonal analysis may make taboo the importance of states of solitariness and isolation.

Freud described a clinical example of taboos in an unpublished letter to Ferenczi on January 4, 1928. Speaking of the way many analysts deferentially submitted to the ground rules he had established, Freud wrote: "But what I achieved in so doing was that the obedient ones didn't take notice of these dissuasions and subjected themselves to them as if they were taboos"[11] (Freud & Ferenczi, forthcoming).

Rituals can become a way of keeping out the abject and enforcing orthodox creeds and practices. That psychoanalysis is all too often ritualistic is suggested by the way many analysts view ground rules and resistance. I discuss the former in greater detail in chapter 11. Suffice it to say here that ground rules are often viewed not as facilitating conditions for conducting treatment, but as standardized structures with a priori validity that all patients must fit into and submit to. Writing to Oskar Pfister about the analytic precepts on October 22, 1927, Freud (1963) said: "You know the human propensity to take precepts literally or exaggerate them. I know very well that in the manner of analytic passivity that is what some of my pupils do" (p. 113).

When the patient challenges or deviates from the analyst's ground rules, he or she is often reflexively accused of "resistance." It is tautological for the analyst to devise the ground rules beforehand without the patient's input and then adhere to them in spite of any problems the patient may have with them.

## Beyond Religiosity in Psychoanalysis

Moving beyond religiosity necessitates both understanding the functions that it serves *and* being able to handle a psychoanalytic universe that is not religious. Freud and Kohut give us a running start.

Freud's interest in religion is evident throughout his work. Several recurrent themes dominate his disparate reflections on the subject. Freud saw himself as a destroyer of illusions. In a letter to the poet Romain Rolland, a student of the renowned Indian saint Ramakrishna, Freud wrote that "a great part of my life's work . . . has been spent [trying to] destroy illusions of my own and those of mankind" (Freud, 1963, p. 341). An "illusion," for Freud (1927), is an unrealistic belief that contradicts experience and reason (p. 30). It is not an *error*, but a "wish-fulfillment" (pp. 30–31). While he points out that an illusion is not necessarily "false" and that "the truth-value" of religious doctrines does not lie within the scope of psychoanalytic inquiry (p. 33), he nonetheless precedes to condemn religion as comparable to a "childhood neurosis" (p. 53).

Two childhood wishes or psychological needs lead people to construct religious beliefs: the necessity of coming to terms with the complicated emotions of a child's relation to his or her father, and the child's sense of helplessness in the face of the danger of the inner and outer worlds. Helplessness arouses the need for protection. Religious ideas, according to Freud, are born of the need to make tolerable the human sense of helplessness. They are designed to offer compensation, consolation, and protection for our existential vulnerability. Religion "allays our fear of the dangers of life" (1927, p. 33).

Freud believed however, that all sorts of "crimes" (p. 32) were committed in the name of religion: "when questions of religion are concerned, people are guilty of every possible sort of dishonesty and intellectual misdemeanor" (ibid.). He hoped that humankind would surmount this "neurotic phase" and attain an "education to reality" (p. 49). Like the Roman poet Lucretius, he wished to awaken humankind from the enchantment in which the priests held it captive (Gay, 1987). But Freud believed, to borrow a metaphor he used in contrasting psychotherapy with psychoanalysis, that only a select few are capable of replacing the superficial salve of religious illusions with the "pure gold" of psychoanalysis.

In his account of a form of idealization involving enthrallment with an idealized Other, Kohut enlarges on Freud's reflections on the self-protective aspects of idol worship. One does not have to subscribe to Kohut's aetiological explanation (of a self-defect caused by the mother's failure to serve as a proper stimulus barrier, supply tension-relieving gratifications, and soothe her child; or the analogy he fashions between reliance on an idealized Other and addictive substances) to be edified by his claim that one can have an idealized relation to one's analyst or supervisor (e.g., 1971, p. 46), an ideological system of thought, or a psychoanalytic theory. The idealized relationship might replace something vital that is missing from one's self or shore up one's sense of personal vulnerability or insecurity by offering the possibility of feeling connected to and protected by someone or something larger and more powerful.

The implication of Kohut's insights about idealization is that it is central to self-stability and it is thereby threatening to question or let go of it. De-idealization, as Arnold Goldberg (1990) notes, may be fraught with fear:

> We seem unable to remain alone in our ideas for too long and inevitably gravitate to points of rest that beckon to us with comfort and sureness. . . .
> It is one thing to complain about the shackles that bind the prisoner . . . to psychological isolation, but it is quite another to set him free. Fear of freedom is not an idle anxiety; the comforts of restraints must be replaced by some sort of guidelines or set of controls. One reason that psychoanalysts cling to rules and heroes is the realization that without them they would be set adrift. (P. 68)

Drawing on the reflections of Freud, Kohut, and Goldberg, we might speculate that the religiosity in psychoanalysis is an attempt on the part of psychoanalysts to allay either an existential feeling of helplessness or a sense of self-vulnerability. We attempt to shore up our selves by clinging to our illusions or idealized relations to analytic figures, creeds, or rituals so that we might replace something vital that is missing within ourselves. I wonder if religiosity exists and persists in psychoanalysis because it is also an attempt at self-cure for an "illness" caused by psychoanalysis itself.

It was his fate, claimed Freud (1914c), to "agitate the sleep of the world" (p. 21). Psychoanalysis, in Freud's (1917b) now infamous claim, struck a blow to humankind's narcissism by demonstrating that we are not even masters of our own minds. Psychoanalysis demystified taken-for-granted views of self, meaning, and understanding—teaching us that all aspects of emotional life have multiple, and often unconscious, meanings and purposes. In profoundly destabilizing ordinary, quotidian conceptions of self and world, psychoanalysis has left us psychologically homeless as well as challenged our collective narcissism.

A world in which familiar faiths and beliefs are more problematic than comforting unwittingly fosters self-mistrust, self-doubt, and self-vertigo. Perhaps we seek the foundational certainties Goldberg alluded to because the world psychoanalysis has bequeathed to us is as deeply threatening as it is exhilarating to our inherited ways of thinking about self and world.

Religiosity in such a universe, whether in the form of ancestor worship, totems, dogmas, idolatry, or rituals, allows us an escape from the dangers of an unruly freedom and uncertainty. It may be a self-cure for the terrors of unbridled inquisitiveness and aliveness in a universe of resolute complexity. If we did not assume the existence of and seek some sort of unassailable, foundational certainty for our theories and practices, could we eschew religiosity without ushering in either a disabling uncertainty or a nihilistic chaos?

Let me briefly reflect on what a psychoanalysis with less religiosity might look like. In ancestor worship, one person—whether Freud, Klein, Sullivan, Winnicott, Lacan, or Kohut—possesses the Truth. This person's writings serve as master texts or gospels. The existence of a single master narrative—whether classical or revisionist—leads to what Roy Schafer (1992) terms a "common ground" of theory, which flattens complexity and turns attention away from the "creative and progressive aspects of the struggles between different systems of thought and practice" (p. 191). In a psychoanalysis without ancestor worship or a priestly class, we would have less idealized and more nuanced portraits of our ancestors. This would make it easier to mourn, work through, and integrate their complex legacies. It might lead to an egalitarian community of psychoanalysts who treated each other with a sense of mutual respect and greater civility and celebrated a diversity of viewpoints. It would problematize the power wielded by the gatekeepers. Detecting unexamined presuppositions, gaps, or tensions in our theories would be easier when psychoanalytic wisdom was available to members of the community rather than treated as the province of single individuals.

"Sacred" psychoanalytic theories would then be more open to disconfirmation and emendation, rather than worshiped as unassailable creeds. Psychoanalytic rituals would be viewed more as contingent practices that continually need to be reassessed, rather than as static rules to be unthinkingly followed. A psychoanalysis that de-absolutized the relative rather than idolized it would be more intellectually cosmopolitan. The boundaries separating psychoanalysis from mutually enriching cross-fertilization with allied humanistic and social science disciplines would be more permeable.

In a psychoanalysis in which religiosity was less unconscious, analysts might wonder more about what we attempt to ward off by its presence and less about whether we were deviating from orthodoxy. Psychoanalytic creeds and rituals would not enjoy so much authority. Rigidity and intolerance would be viewed as a greater danger than dissent and provisionality. A spirit of questioning and tolerance, rather than piety and intolerance, might be a virtue. Civility rather than power politics might reign. Independent thinking might more readily flourish and theories and practices might be, in Winnicott's sense, *created* as well as found (Gargiulo, 1989). Fashioning a variety of local narratives about selves might be more highly valued—even if it did not lead to the Truth about Man—than positing timeless, universal Truths.[12]

One of the monographs of the Freud Museum in London is titled *Is Psychoanalysis Another Religion?* (Ward, 1993). From the perspective I have offered in this chapter, the answer seems to be, "In certain ways, yes." But that answer begs a more important question: What is the impact of religiosity on psychoanalysis? The "gods" that psychoanalysts still worship impede their understanding of their patients and the world and inhibit creativity and development in the field. When we have a psychoanalysis with less religiosity and more spirituality, both analysts and analysands will be enriched.

# 5

# The Wish to Be Seen and the Dread of Being Found

## A Psychobiographical Study of D. W. Winnicott

Psycho-analytic research is perhaps always to some extent an attempt on the part of an analyst to carry the work of his own analysis further than the point to which his own analyst could get him.  —D. W. Winnicott, "Hate in the Countertransference"

D. W. Winnicott was an early and significant figure in the search for a new, more emancipatory vision of psychoanalysis. He liberated psychoanalysis from the confines of certain dimensions of the classical analysis he deeply respected and also served as a bridge between classical psychoanalysis and the relational revolution in contemporary psychoanalysis. Relational analysis refers to the increased concern in a variety of schools of analysis—including object relations theory, interpersonal psychoanalysis, self psychology, and intersubjectivity theory—with the impact of actual and fantasied relationships with caregivers and significant others on the development and structuralization of the self. Relational theorists have expanded psychoanalytic understanding of human development and the causes of psychopathology and greatly enriched clinical approaches to a range of patients and clinical disorders.

And yet, despite Winnicott's seminal importance in freeing psychoanalysis from viewpoints that held it captive, his theorizing on selfhood, arguably the central dimension of his work, is afflicted with the blindness of the seeing I. Winnicott, like Freud and Kohut, is often idealized by his followers. His theories enjoy a "landmark" status, making it very difficult to critique them constructively. Insufficient attention is devoted to ascertaining their limitations. Identifying the tensions and gaps in Winnicott's theories of selfhood opens up the possibility of crafting alternative accounts of what it means to be an individual, which is essential in a historical age in which human beings feel increasingly limited by available conceptions of self.

This chapter explores blind spots in Winnicott's venerated views of self generated by their embeddedness in personal conflicts. I examine the theoretical tension between Winnicott's two conceptions of selfhood: the buried, authentic self, which must be found: and the vulnerable, hidden core of our being, which must never be found. Drawing on autobiographical and biographical material on Winnicott, as well as selected aspects of his own theoretical corpus viewed psychobiographically, I trace the theoretical inconsistency of certain of Winnicott's ideas about human selfhood to his own unconscious conflicts about authenticity and relatedness. These conflicts arose from his own experience with a depressed, emotionally unavailable mother, whom he lived to take care of; an absent and puritanical father, who deeply impinged on his autonomy; and two analysts who failed to make contact with him at a deep psychological level. His contradictory theory of subjectivity is a symbolic encapsulation of two frightening dangers in his life: (1) conforming, being inauthentic, feeling unknown and constricted; and (2) being found and swallowed up in the demands of others.

The data for this chapter have been gleaned from diaries, letters, interviews, memoirs, and theoretical writings, reflections on recurrent modes of thought and conduct in Winnicott's life, contemporary testimony about him from colleagues (e.g., Thompson, 1996, p. 155), and attention to the range of thoughts, feelings, and fantasies evoked in me by immersion in Winnicott's life and thought. Five psychoanalytic perspectives have deepened my reflections on this data. From classical psychoanalysis I have utilized the genetic perspective and the attention to defensive processes. Intersubjectivity theory has sensitized me to the irreducibly relational nature of human development and the therapeutic process. Self psychology and object relations theory have refined my attention to issues related to self and other and the formative influence of caregivers on development. My perspective has also been enriched by the focus in interpersonal psychoanalysis on the therapeutic value of interpersonal reenactments and on one's own subjective reactions as a potentially useful source of data.

The subjective roots of Winnicott's theory do not invalidate his reflections on human subjectivity, but they do shape and delimit its horizon and the scope of its applicability. By delineating the subjective origins of Winnicott's theory of subjectivity, my aim is to foreground certain subtle underlying assumptions and illuminate the particular scope of his project on subjectivity. Because I believe that without Winnicott's pioneering insights psychoanalysis and the humanities would be impoverished, my critique is meant in the spirit of enriching emendation.

Winnicott was a seminal figure in the history of psychoanalysis, as well as one of the key figures in British object relations theory. His clinically astute observations and innovative concepts have immeasurably enriched the theoretical and clinical landscape of psychoanalysis. His work on "primary maternal preoccupation," the "facilitating environment," the "True and False Self," and "transitional objects," for example, has expanded psychoanalytic understanding of parenting, human development, psychopathology, the psychoanalytic setting and relationship, and the cultural sphere, including art and religion. The numerous references to his theories and clinical insights in psychoanalytic articles and books attest to his seminal status and enduring influence within psychoanalysis. Literary and feminist critics, religious thinkers, and aestheticians, among others, have also found his insights suggestive and heuristic. Many would agree with his wife Clare's posthumous assessment that "his findings . . . recognised by many as having implications beyond the immediate area of study . . . throw light on all areas of living" (Grolnick et al., 1978, p. 18).

Winnicott was intrigued by the nature of self-experience and in particular those experiences that thwart and facilitate its development. He maintained that authentic and vital selfhood is a universal human concern: "the search for the self and a way of feeling real, and of living from the true rather than from the false self, is a task that belongs not only to schizophrenics; it also belongs to a large proportion of the human race" (1989, p. 491).

His concept of the True Self is usually considered the heart of this work. This concept conveyed his view of the familial and therapeutic conditions that facilitate or interfere with the development of the self. Winnicott (1963) also presented a second, less recognized theory of self in his writings on the vulnerable core of the self that is constantly in danger of being violated by contact with the outside world and must remain hidden and permanently unknown by others. When these two theories are considered together, a theoretical inconsistency emerges. This inconsistency is most evident in his assertion of two opposing things: (1)

that the True Self is the authentic core of the person that needs to be found and expressed, and (2) that the self is *"an isolate, permanently non-communicating, permanently unknown* . . . incommunicado element" (p. 187) that must not be found.

Winnicott's account of the artist—which is paradigmatic for all human subjectivity—explicitly illustrates this conflict: "In the artist of all kinds I think one can detect an inherent dilemma, which belongs to the co-existence of two trends, the urgent need to communicate and the still more urgent need not to be found" (1963, p. 185). The urgency of not being found arises from the anticipated dangers to self-integrity. "Starting from no fixed place," he writes, "I soon came, while preparing this paper for a foreign society, to staking a claim, to my surprise, to the right not to communicate. This was a protest from the core of me to the frightening fantasy of being infinitely exploited. In another language this would be the fantasy of being eaten or swallowed up. In the language of this paper it is *the fantasy of being found"* (p. 179).[1]

A critic of my reading of Winnicott's account of subjectivity might argue that in claiming that these two aspects of subjectivity are theoretically contradictory, I am either not accepting or else resolving (and thus reducing) a fertile Winnicottian paradox—namely, that they are *both* true. The term "paradox" is often invoked in Winnicott's work and commentaries. Anne Clancier and Jeannine Kalmanovitch (1987), for example, speak of the "many fruitful instances of paradox throughout Winnicott's work . . . [which] invariably attest to the originality of his thinking" (p. 92). Winnicott (1971) recommends that paradoxes be "accepted," "tolerated," and "respected" instead of being "resolved" and thereby reduced (p. xii). I can imagine certain cases in which an apparent contradiction—for example, that a transitional object is created *and* discovered by the infant—cannot be integrated into a more encompassing synthesis and should be allowed to exist as such. But I can also imagine other cases (and Winnicott's account of subjectivity is one) in which it might be fruitful to examine whether the invocation and valorization of paradox eclipses certain unresolved theoretical problems. The concept of paradox, in such a context, may hide unresolved theoretical tensions.

In order to clarify this theoretical difficulty with Winnicott's conception of subjectivity, I examine the second aspect of the paradox first, namely, that *"each individual is an isolate, permanently non-communicating, permanently unknown, in fact unfound"* (1963, p. 187). According to Winnicott, this "incommunicado" self is in tremendous danger.

This danger is only alluded to in his seminal paper on subjectivity, "Ego Distortion in Terms of True and False Self" (1960a), where he mentions the potential "exploitation" of the True Self that might result in its "annihilation" and, in extreme cases, even suicide (p. 143). In "Communicating and Not Communicating Leading to a Study of Certain Opposites" (1963) the terrifying dangers to the "incommunicado" self are presented more fully and starkly: "Rape, and being eaten alive by cannibals, these are mere bagatelles, as compared with the violation of the self's core, the alteration of the self's central elements by communication seeping through the defences. For me this would be the sin against the self. . . . The question is: how to be isolated without having to be insulated?" (p. 187).

Why did Winnicott conceptualize it this way? It is conceivable that one could be found and communicated with while retaining privacy. It is also possible to be found without being exploited and violated. Why did Winnicott stress *isolation* instead of relatedness-with-privacy or connectedness-without-self-violation?

I agree with Harry Guntrip's (1969) assessment of Winnicott's account of privacy and solitude. He calls Winnicott's problematic assertion about the necessary isolation of the "incommunicado" self a "dubious proposition" and suggests that the proper formulation is: "how to have *privacy* and *self-possession* without isolation or insulation" (p. 236). The sources of this "dubious proposition" are, in my view, *autobiographical*, not clinical.

Autobiographical elements of a theory are often signaled by theoretical reifications, universalistic concepts, extreme affect, striking imagery, repetition (or absence) of themes (Loewenberg, 1995, p. 150), and theoretical inconsistencies and lacunas. All of these are at work in the concept of the True Self and the "incommunicado" core. Let me give four examples. Other examples of autobiographical elements in Winnicott's theory will emerge as the chapter unfolds. The experience of being spontaneous, nonconforming, authentic, and nonreactive to the expectations of others is reified into a capitalized noun, the True Self.[2] Winnicott's specific insight about the potential danger to self-integrity posed by submission and unauthentic compliance—being-for-others—is generalized into the universalistic conception that human beings are permanently endangered by impingements from others. Impingements, in this view, are an inherent fabric of the human condition. The striking imagery and affect that Winnicott uses in equating the discovery of the "incommunicado" self with cannibalization and "rape" alerts the reader to the presence of a third and fourth possible autobiographical element in his theory.

There is scant biographical information about Winnicott (Grolnick, 1991). Available portraits tend to romanticize his family and his childhood. The accounts of F. R. Rodman (1987) and Winnicott's second wife, Clare (in Grolnick et al., 1978) are typical: the former claims that Winnicott "apparently had a happy childhood" (p. xiii), while the latter maintains that "there were no 'tragedies' in the Winnicott household" (p. 23), "he was a deeply happy person" (p. 25), and there "is no doubt that from his earliest years Donald did not doubt that he was loved, and he experienced a security in the Winnicott home which he could take for granted" (p. 21).

Brett Kahr's D. W. Winnicott (1996), the first book-length biographical study, does not present a romanticized account of his life. But it is, as the author acknowledges in the preface, "a mere sketch, and it does not in any way constitute a comprehensive biography" (p. xxix). The sketchiness emerges not so much in the details of his life, for it contains some realistic and disturbing facets of his family life and subsequent experiences, but in the insufficient exploration of their implications (e.g., Rubin, 1997b).

From Winnicott's unpublished autobiography, biographical information from two interviews with Clare Winnicott (1978; 1991), Winnicott's letters and a poem, and his theoretical writings viewed psychobiographically, a different and bleaker picture of his childhood emerges.

Winnicott was born on April 7, 1896, in Plymouth, England. He was the youngest child and only son of Frederick and Elizabeth Winnicott. His two sisters, Cathleen and Violet, were five and six years older, respectively. As a successful merchant and mayor of Plymouth, his father was involved with a variety of public responsibilities. From all available evidence, he had insufficient contact with his father. In his autobiographical notebooks, Winnicott indicated that he grew up "in a sense . . . an only child with multiple mothers and with father extremely preoccupied in my younger years with town as well as business matters . . . it is probably true that in the early years he left me too much to all my mother's. Things never quite righted themselves" (quoted in C. Winnicott, 1978, pp. 23–24).

In one of his final papers, "Fear of Breakdown" (1974), Winnicott asserts that the fear is actually fear from a breakdown that has already occurred but remains unremembered and "is not yet experienced" (p. 91).

The anticipated fear, in Winnicott's view, signals an unremembered and unexperienced trauma in the past. He likens fear of breakdown to fear of death:

Little alteration is needed to transfer the general thesis of fear of breakdown to a specific fear of death . . . the patient has a compulsion to look for death. Again, it is the death that happened but was not experienced that is sought. . . . Death, looked at in this way as something that happened to the patient but which the patient was not mature enough to experience, has the meaning of annihilation . . . a pattern developed in which the continuity of being was interrupted by the patient's infantile reactions to [parental] impingement, these being environmental factors that were allowed to impinge by failures of the facilitating environment. (Pp. 92–93)

Winnicott's autobiography, "Not Less Than Everything," begins with a description of his own death: "I died. It was not very nice . . . I was alive when I died" (quoted in C. Winnicott, 1978, p. 19). Winnicott emphasizes that he wishes to be alive at his own death. Is this wish a concretization of and an attempt to remember his own *psychic* death-in-life, which he experienced but could not remember or escape? A poem he wrote when he was sixty-seven called "The Tree" suggests an affirmative answer and provides a clue about the nature and genesis of this psychic death

> Mother below is weeping
> weeping
> weeping
> Thus I knew her
> Once, stretched out on her
> as now on dead tree
> learned to make her smile
> to stem her tears
> to undo her guilt
> to cure her inward death
> To enliven her was my living
>
> (Phillips, 1988, p. 29)

It is instructive to juxtapose this poetic remembrance of his mother with his theoretical remarks about early maternal caregiving:

Usually the mother of an infant has live internal objects and the infant fits into the mother's preconception of a *live* child. Normally the mother is not depressed or depressive. In certain cases, however, the mother's central internal object is dead at the critical time in her child's early infancy, and her mood is one of depression. Here the infant has to fit in with a role of *dead object*, or else has to be lively to counteract the mother's preconception with the idea of the child's deadness. Here the opposite to the liveliness of the infant is *an anti-life factor* derived from the mother's depression. The task of the infant in such a case is to be alive and to look alive and to communicate being alive; in fact this is the ultimate aim of such an individual, who is thus denied that which belongs to more fortunate infants, the enjoyment of what life and living may bring. To be alive is all. (1963, pp. 191–92)

When the poem and this passage are considered together, one gets the impression that his account of depressed maternal caregivers and their emotionally deprived, conforming, and self-subordinating progeny depicts, at least in part, his own experience of his mother's depression and her consequent inability to hold him. There is a sad irony in the fact that the poem depicts, as Adam Phillips (1988) aptly notes, the "absence of what became, in Winnicott's developmental theory, the formative experience in the child's life, the way the mother, in the fullest sense, 'holds' the child" (p. 30). In his brief medical duty as a surgeon-probationer during World War I, Winnicott, in his wife's words, had "much free time which he seems to have spent reading the novels of Henry James" (C. Winnicott, 1978, p. 27). Was Winnicott's interest in the novels of James, who was concerned with the "elusively absent" (Phillips, 1988), related to his own attempt to make sense of his mother's conspicuous and puzzling emotional absence from him?

A child who was not held, who had to "cure" his or her mother's "inward death" might, as the poem suggests, make a "living"—including being a psychoanalyst?—out of keeping mother(s) alive.[3] It is likely that such a child might have conflicts over authenticity and relatedness. The child might fear that the latter would lead to self-depletion, not self-enrichment. In the process of trying to "cure her inward death," Winnicott may have had to forsake his own spontaneous and authentic strivings and replace them with an inauthentic being-for-mother, a compliant, False Self mode of living that was deadly for his development.

Corroborating evidence for this assessment can be found in an interview with Clare Winnicott that appears in Peter Rudnytsky's *The Psychoanalytic Vocation: Rank, Winnicott and the Legacy of Freud* (1991): "there's one famous episode in his life, when he was nine, and he looked in the mirror and he said, 'I'm too nice.' And really, from this point he started coming bottom of the class. Blotting everything, blotting his copybook, shoving things around, torturing flies, pulling their wings off. You know, just doing naughty things. He wanted to find this other dimension [naughtiness] in himself. [Donald said] 'I'm too good! I'm coming top all the time! Everybody likes me too much! I must find the nastiness in myself!' " (p. 186).

But being authentic—including expressing nastiness—was greatly discouraged in Winnicott's family.[4] An excerpt from Winnicott's autobiography suggests that the father, who was a relatively absent figure in his developmental theory, was conspicuously present in inhibiting his own authentic development, including expressing aggression:

> When (at 12 years) I one day came home to midday dinner and said "drat" my father looked pained as only he could look, blamed my mother for not seeing to it that I had decent friends, and from that moment he prepared himself to send me away to boarding school, which he did when I was 13. (Quoted in C. Winnicott, 1978, p. 23).[5]

Winnicott's pathological self-blaming response suggests the extent to which the price of connecting with his father was to continue to bury his own spontaneity and authenticity. Compliance with his father's puritanical standards had replaced his own authentic emotional responses: "Drat sounds very small as a swear word, but he was right; the boy who was my new friend was no good, and he and I could have got into trouble if left to our own devices" (ibid.).

From this we can surmise that authenticity could be disastrous in the Winnicott household and that the last thing Winnicott was encouraged to be in his own home was himself. This may be why he would strikingly claim, as an adult psychoanalyst, that the "most aggressive and therefore the most dangerous words in the languages of the world are to be found in the assertion I AM" (1986b, p. 141).[6] It was safer to blame himself and take his parents off the hook than to recognize his parent's deficiencies and experience his own sense of deprivation or outrage. After being sent away to a day prep school at thirteen for his linguistic indiscretion, he wrote the following letter home:

> My dearest Mother,
> On September 2nd all true scouts think of their mothers, since that was the birthday of Baden Powell's mother when she was alive. . . . But to please me very much I must trouble you to do me a little favor. . . . I want you to go up into my bedroom and in the right-

hand cupboard find a small parcel. . . . Now have you opened it? Well I hope you like it. . . . My home is a beautiful home and I only wish I could live up to it. However I will do my best and work hard and that's all I can do at present. Give my love to the others: thank Dad for his game of billiards . . .

from your loving boy Donald.
(Quoted in C. Winnicott, 1978, p. 24)

By blaming himself and attempting to rid himself of his "badness," perhaps he kept alive the tenuous hope of garnering redemption and eventually reconnecting with his parents.

Winnicott had great difficulty separating from his family. Clare Winnicott (1978) indicated that he "did have a major problem, that of freeing himself from the family, and of establishing his own separate life and identity" (p. 25). This is painfully illustrated by a letter he wrote to a school friend, Stanley Ede, when he was sixteen. Ede had encouraged him to do what he wanted to do for a living instead of going into his father's business, which would have pleased his father.

> Father and I have been trying consciously and perhaps unconsciously to find out what the ambition of the other is in regard to my future. From what he had said I was *sure* that he wanted me more than anything else to go into his business. And so, again consciously and not, I have found every argument for the idea and have not thought much about anything else so that I should not be disappointed. And so I have learned to cherish the business life with all my heart, and had intended to enter it and please my father and myself. . . . I have for ever so wanted to be a doctor. But I have always been afraid that my father did not want it, and so I have never mentioned it and . . . even felt a repulsion at the thought. (Quoted in C. Winnicott, 1978, pp. 25–26).

Clare Winnicott (1991) adds that Donald "tried hard to make himself go into the business to please his father. But only his friend [Stanley Ede] said to him, 'What are you doing? You're absolutely mad. Do what you want to do.' And he [Donald] said, 'How wonderful. Do you think I really can?' " (p. 184).

There is some evidence that Winnicott's analysts—James Strachey and Joan Riviere—did not provide an environment conducive to working through his False Self proclivities. In fact, selections from Winnicott's theoretical writings, a letter from Winnicott to Melanie Klein describing each of his analysts, and his obituary of Strachey suggest that his analysts may have unconsciously recapitulated his conflicts.

In 1923 he began a ten-year analysis with Strachey, translator of the Standard Edition of Freud and author of a seminal paper, "The Nature of the Therapeutic Action of Psycho-Analysis" (1934), which stressed the centrality of mutative *interpretation* in the therapeutic action of psycho-analysis. Winnicott pointed to some positive facets of the analysis when he indicated that during treatment he experienced a long series of "healing dreams" that "marked my arrival at a new stage in development" (Winnicott, 1949b, p. 71). Some disturbing intimations about his first analytic experience can be inferred from letters between James Strachey and his wife, Alix. These letters indicate that Strachey would agree with the editors of his letters, who suggest that he viewed Winnicott as a "troublesome analysand" (Meisel & Kendrick, 1985, p. 313).

Letters from Strachey to his wife, for example, mention his irritation with Winnicott's leisurely style of paying (pp. 83–84, 106–7) and his wish to terminate in the midst of Winnicott's analysis (p. 125). A letter from Strachey's wife suggests that Strachey shared intimate details about Winnicott's sexual life with her. On December 29, 1924, Alix Strachey wrote back to her husband regarding his wish to terminate Winnicott's analysis. She was obviously privy to confidential sexual material: "Perhaps fresh data will turn up . . . Mr. W[innicott] will die or f–ck his wife all of a sudden" (p. 166).

Letters from an analyst to a spouse about an analysis do not offer conclusive evidence about the nature or results of a treatment, but one wonders how the "analytic attitude" (Schafer, 1983) could be present given Strachey's disparaging tone toward Winnicott in these letters. His hostility and devaluation of Winnicott suggest unexamined and unutilized countertransference manifestations, which undoubtedly compromised and cast doubt on the success of the treatment. Thus, with Simon Grolnick (1991), I believe that from these letters we "cannot help but be skeptical as to the success of Winnicott's analysis with Strachey" (p. 18).

Winnicott confided both to his wife Clare and to Dr. Margaret Little, a close colleague and patient, that his treatment with Strachey "did not help him as much as it should have done" (p. 54). In a letter to Ernest Jones on July 22, 1952, Winnicott wrote: "In 10 years' analysis Strachey made practically no mistakes and he adhered to a classical technique in a cold-blooded way for which I have always been grateful. He did, however, say two or three things that were not interpretations at a time when interpretation was needed. Each one of them has bothered me and at some time or other have come out in an unexpected way" (Rodman, 1987, p. 33). In his obituary of Strachey, Winnicott (1969) wrote: "It is my experience of analysis at the hand of Strachey that has made me suspicious of descriptions of interpretative work in analysis which seemed to give credit to the interpretations for all that happens, as if the process in the patient had got lost sight of" (p. 129).

Winnicott distrusted interpretations. "One of the purposes of interpreting," he suggested, "is to establish the limits of the analyst's understanding" (1989, p. 85). In a retrospective self-assessment of his work he says:

> I was getting away from the necessity of a verbal interpretation in its fullest form. I've been through the long process of interpreting everything I could possibly see that could be interpreted . . . feeling awful if I couldn't find anything, and pouncing on something because I found I could put it into words. I've been through all that and realised that in certain cases it was no good at all. (1989, p. 581)

Winnicott placed greater emphasis on the way the "facilitating environment," including the analytic setting and the relationship, could aid the unfolding of the inherent maturational processes in the person. "The individual," according to Winnicott (1974), "inherits a maturational process [that] carries the individual along in so far as there exists a facilitating environment" (p. 89). His belief in the maturational processes and the facilitating environment emerges in his remarks about children to a correspondent in Tanzania: "We cannot even teach them to walk, but their innate tendency to walk at a certain age needs us as supporting figures" (Rodman, 1987, p. 186). Psychoanalysis was better served, in his view, by stressing the developmental process and the natural growth tendencies of the patient as opposed to mutative interpretations.

Winnicott's remarks raise a series of questions: Did Winnicott highlight the importance of the patient's developmental process because this was absent or neglected in his analysis with Strachey? Was Winnicott's own conception of the mutative factors in treatment developed as a result of its absence in his analysis with Strachey? Did his experience of Strachey's interpretations *as well as* his interest in infancy and his belief in the patient's developmental process contribute to this skepticism of interpretation?

In 1935, a year after he finished his analysis with Strachey, Winnicott began supervision with Melanie Klein. Several years later, he began a roughly five-year analysis with Joan Riviere, a close colleague of Klein. Riviere summed up the Kleinian position by asserting that psychoanalysis was "not concerned with the real world, nor with the child's or adult's adaptation to the real world. . . . It is concerned simply and solely with the imaginings of the childish mind, the phantasied pleasures and dreaded retributions" (quoted in Grosskurth, 1987, p. 170). Given Winnicott's own denial of the pain of his childhood and Riviere's disinterest in both "the real world . . . [and] the child or adult's adaptation to the real world," one wonders how Winnicott's formative childhood traumas could even have been addressed let alone worked through in his analysis with Riviere.

His analysis with Riviere seems to have been a negative experience. Riviere, for example, made "caustic remarks about Winnicott's personality" during public, professional meetings. She announced to the audience at the medical section of the British Psychological Society that Winnicott "just makes theory of his own sickness" (quoted in Kahr, 1996, p. 62).

Winnicott's remarks about his second analyst suggest that his old conforming, placating ways were alive and well in adulthood:

> I said to Mrs. Riviere one day, "There's only just a line like that between me and the theory of delinquency and one day that's going to be something and then I'm going to be separate. And I feel it coming up you know." Only I couldn't do it while I was in analysis with her because—I don't say Mrs. Klein minded it, but—the psycho-analysts were the only ones for about ten or fifteen years who knew there was anything *but* environment. (1989, p. 577)

A letter to Klein on November 17, 1952, does nothing to discourage the impression that inauthenticity was being perpetuated rather than resolved in his second analysis:

> I think that some of the patients that go to "Kleinian enthusiasts" for analysis are not really allowed to grow or to create in the analysis and I am not basing this on loose fantasy but I am seriously bringing it forward as a matter for thought. I believe that the idea [the importance of the quality of actual infant care and the detrimental effects of not-good-enough caregiving] expressed in my paper ["Anxiety Associated with Insecurity"] however badly it is done, is in the direction of giving a new emphasis so that those who use your concepts and your ideas and your technique may not forget

something which it is disastrous to leave out. . . . This matter which I am discussing [intellectual rigidity which promotes not-good-enough relating and a non-facilitating environment] touches the root of my own personal difficulty so that what you see can always be dismissed as Winnicott's illness but if you dismiss it in this way you may miss something which is in the end a positive contribution. (Rodman, 1987, p. 37)

In the same letter, Winnicott revealingly refers to his two analysts:

What I was wanting on Friday undoubtedly was that there should be some move from your direction towards the gesture that I make in this paper. It is a creative gesture and I cannot make any relationship through the gesture except if someone came to meet it. I think that I was wanting something which I have no right to expect from your group, and it is really of the nature of a therapeutic act, something which I could not get in either of my two long analyses, although I got so much else. There is no doubt that my criticism of Mrs. Riviere was not only a straightforward criticism based on objective observation but also it was coloured by the fact that it was just exactly here that her analysis failed me. (P. 34)

Given Winnicott's own predilection for denying and rationalizing emotional injuries and deprivation, we do him a grave injustice if we too gloss over or in any way minimize his reservations or complaints. What was the "therapeutic act" that he did not get? How did his analysis with Riviere fail him? The "so much else" he got from his two analyses did not include something indispensable to the development of the self—namely, the meeting of the person's *spontaneous gestures*. It is instructive to quote at length Winnicott's (1960a) account of the importance of the meeting of the creative gesture in the development of self-authenticity and self-efficacy, for it is here that we gain an understanding of his view of the emotional cost of its neglect:

The *good-enough mother* meets the omnipotence of the infant and to some extent makes sense of it. She does this repeatedly. A True Self begins to have life, through the strength given to the infant's weak ego by the mother's implementation of the infant's omnipotent expressions. The mother who is not good-enough is not able to implement the infant's omnipotence, and so she repeatedly fails to meet the infant's gesture; instead she substitutes her own gesture which is to be given sense by the compliance of the infant. This compliance on the part of the infant is the earliest stage of the False Self, and belongs to the mother's inability to sense her infant's needs. It is an essential part of my theory that the True Self does not become a living reality except as a result of mother's repeated success in meeting the infant's spontaneous gesture or sensory hallucination. . . . There are now two possible lines of development in the scheme of events according to my formulation. *In the first case* the mother's adaptation is *good enough* and in consequence the infant begins to believe in external reality which appears and behaves as by magic (because of the mother's relatively successful adaptation to the infant's gestures & needs), and which acts in a way that does not clash with the infant's omnipotence. The True Self has a spontaneity, and this has been joined with the world's events. . . . *In the second case*, which belongs more particularly to the subject under discussion, the mother's adaptation to the infant's hallucinations and spontaneous impulses is deficient, *not good-enough* . . . the infant lives, but lives falsely . . . the infant gets seduced into a compliance, and a compliant False Self reacts to environmental demands and the infant seems to accept them. (Pp. 145–46)

From Winnicott's account, what seems to have occurred in his analyses was not the meeting of his spontaneous gestures—and the facilitation and emergence of his authenticity and aliveness—but the reenactment of the False Self mode of living characterizing his childhood, which inhibited the development of authentic and alive selfhood.

Winnicott (1960a) may have depicted his own experience of inauthenticity in analysis when he wrote:

A particular danger arises out of the not infrequent tie-up between the intellectual approach and the False Self. When a False Self becomes organized in an individual who has an intellectual potential there is a very strong tendency for the mind to become the location of the False Self. . . . [A] clinical picture results which is peculiar in that it very easily deceives. The world may observe academic success of a very high degree, and may find it hard to believe in the very real distress of the individual concerned, who feels "phoney" the more he or she is successful. . . . In psycho-analytic work it is possible to see analyses going on indefinitely because they are done on the basis of work with the False Self. (Pp. 44, 151)

Winnicott's unresolved conflict over authenticity—his simultaneous wish for and fear of it—emerges in his ambivalent relationship to psychoanalytic tradition and his unique and curious style of writing. On the one hand, he claims a spurious allegiance to and continuity with his theoretical predecessors (Freud) and colleagues (Klein), thus denying his theoretical originality. On the other hand, he consciously and defensively works in isolation, sequestering himself from the work of others and denying points of influence and intellectual convergence in order to preserve a precarious sense of autonomy. "From my point of view," he claims in a letter to Harry Guntrip, "any theories that I may have which are original are only valuable as a growth of ordinary Freudian psycho-analytic theory and practice" (Rodman, 1987, p. 75). A letter to Michael Fordham illustrates the opposite facet of the ambivalence: "I always admire people like yourself who really seem to read other people's papers; so very often I postpone reading something which is at all near my own subject because of the slight warp that it gives to the development of original ideas. When I have got something published, however, I then like to read around it. This is a rather weak policy but I must admit to it" (p. 74). In a retrospective evaluation of his work four years before his death, he indicated that he "realised more and more as time went on what a tremendous lot I've lost from not properly correlating my work with the work of others . . . it's a big fault" (Winnicott, 1989, p. 573).

His own innovative psychoanalytic contribution concerning the False Self is, not surprisingly, disavowed: "the idea of a False Self . . . can be discerned in the early formulations of Freud. In particular I link what I divide into a True and False Self with Freud's division of the self into a part that is central and powered by the instincts (or by what Freud called sexuality, pregenital and genital), and a part that is turned outwards and is related to the world" (1960a, p. 140). This is, as I argued earlier, a fallacious parallel. The True and False Self contrasts authentic, spontaneous aliveness and an inauthentic, compliant mode of being. Freud's ego and id contrasts functions geared to coping with the nature and demands of the external world and asocial, prewired drives. The issue of authenticity and aliveness that is crucial to Winnicott's formulations is absent in Freud's.

Winnicott's conflict over authenticity seems to have also been enacted stylistically. His writing is accessible and elusive, jargon-free and enigmatic, engaging and evasive, evocative and ambiguous. Novel ideas are shared but often underelaborated. Arnold Modell (1985b) aptly notes that Winnicott "does not pay sufficient attention to the intervening conceptual steps one must take to get from here to there" (p. 118) and there is sometimes an "absence of bridging concepts" (p. 120) in his work. The reader may feel welcomed in *and* left in the dark. Since Winnicott distrusted interpretations and recognized the dangers of impingements and the value of uncertainty and not-knowing, he may have wished for his reader, like his patients, to make their own interpretations and elaborations of his suggestive writings. In addition, perhaps his style of writing embodied a fertile paradox—namely, that he both wanted and did not want to be seen and found.

Winnicott's two theories of subjectivity depict his own conflicts about authenticity and relatedness arising from his experience with a depressed, emotionally unavailable mother, an absent and puritanical father, and two analysts who did not facilitate his authenticity and aliveness. Given the narrative I have been developing, Winnicott's claim that "it is a joy to be hidden but a disaster not be found" could be rewritten: "It is a joy to be hidden from my mother's depleting neediness and my father's rigid puritanicalness, and a disaster to not be found by the mother that I need to see and value me."

From a psychobiographical perspective, Winnicott's emphasis on unburying the True Self *and* not finding the "incommunicado" self is not a heuristic paradox of a universal truth of human experience. Rather, it is a symbolic encapsulation of two frightening dangers in his life: (1) conforming, being inauthentic, feeling unknown and constricted, and (2) being found and swallowed up in the demands of others.

His contradictory theory of subjectivity exemplifies his efforts both to regain a sense of authenticity and aliveness that was threatened by his being-for-others and to protect his own precarious sense of selfhood from being cannibalized by creating an illusion of an autonomous self existing in isolation. It is likely that Winnicott stressed unfreezing the authentic self as a protection against remaining compliant, inauthentic, isolated, undiscovered, and virtual. And he may have emphasized that the self remain isolated as a protection against the dreaded danger of being found, absorbed, and swallowed up in the demands of others.[7]

The roots of Winnicott's concept of subjectivity are autobiographical. This does not invalidate his formulations, but it does suggest caution in positing their universality. Not everyone, for example, feels that intimacy inevitably leads to usurpation and self-loss and that one must remain essentially hidden and unrelated in order to avoid being exploited. In fact, for many of the people contemporary analysts work with, being seen and heard in all their depth, vulnerability, and uniqueness seems essential to the self-healing and self-enrichment that they seek.[8] Winnicott does not imagine that there could be human connectedness that fosters the enrichment rather than the depletion of the self. He thus posits an excessively isolated and isolating conception of self and relationships in which insularity-with-authenticity is the highest virtue.

When subsequent psychoanalysts also emphasize an essentially isolationist and self-centered view of self and relationships—treating the other as merely an object of the self's needs rather than a *subject* with its own interests and values—then Winnicott is being treated as an idol of worship instead of a facilitator of their own independent thinking. Psychoanalysts are then ironically enacting the same restrictive relational pattern in their relationship to Winnicott that he assumes about the self: exemplifying the way connectedness can lead to usurpation. For psychoanalysts to be related to Winnicott without being usurped by him, they need less schizoid views of self and relating. They need to see the other as a *subject*, not as an object for the self's use.

Like Winnicott, we need to strive to be connected and related even as we attempt to be personally authentic and alive. Winnicott's life and work suggest both pitfalls and possibilities on this journey to greater humanness. We are infinitely more attuned to the vicissitudes of that process because of the human journeys Winnicott made us privy to, including his own life.

# 6

# Does the True Self Really Exist?
## A Critique of Winnicott's True Self Concept

This above all: to thine own self be true,
And it must follow, as the night the day
Thou canst not then be false to any man.
—William Shakespeare, *Hamlet*

A *picture* held us captive. And we could not get
outside it, for it lay in language and language
seemed to repeat it to us inexorably.
—Ludwig Wittgenstein, *Philosophical Investigations*

It may be that in some ways the concept
[of the True Self] itself will be modified.
—D. W. Winnicott, *Ego Distortion in Terms of True
and False Self*

The search for the authentic core of the self plays a prominent role in both psychoanalysis and popular culture. Finding what Winnicott termed the "buried True Self," by which he meant who we really are, is a central preoccupation of many people inside and outside of psychoanalysis. The concept of the True Self was central to Winnicott's work because it exemplified the healthy self, that is, what would happen when parenting or psychoanalytic treatment optimally facilitated self-development. The importance of Winnicott's notion for my argument in this book is twofold: (1) the notion of the True Self enjoys a central importance in postclassical perspectives on selfhood; and (2) it illustrates the dangers of even an analytic innovator being idealized and relatively immunized from analytic scrutiny.

The ability to play with ideas, in Winnicott's view, is essential to the evolution of both psychoanalysis and people: "Psychotherapy takes place in the overlap of two areas of playing, that of the patient and that of the therapist. Psychotherapy has to do with two people playing together" (1971, p. 38). In this spirit I will play with Winnicott's concept of the True Self, a central notion of his enlightening work on individual development.

This chapter critiques the notion of the True Self and argues that the quest for it is misguided as well as limiting. Challenging a vision of self-experience that holds patients and analysts captive can broaden the way analysts think about the nature of self and the process of constructing an identity. Psychoanalysts would then be encouraged to conduct treatment in new and vital ways.

The belief in the notion of a True Self enjoys great popularity in our culture and seems, prima facie, to be intuitively correct. It resonates with personal and clinical experience. Consider what is reflected in the statements "I don't feel like myself," "That's not me," and "That's who I really am." From the sneaker commercial that admonishes "You Be You" to the voices of popular psychology that encourage us to follow our own drummer, the language of everyday life—conversations, movies, books, television commercials, and analytic sessions—is filled with such expressions.

Winnicott was very wary of rigid theory and the idolatry of concepts. In a letter to Roger Money-Kyrle, he writes: "I think what irritated me was that I faintly detected in your attitude this matter of the party line, a matter to which I am allergic" (Rodman, 1987, p. 79). Orthodoxy leads to theoretical ossification, which is, in Winnicott's view, deadly. In a letter to Melanie Klein, he says:

> I personally think that it is very important that your work should be re-stated by people discovering in their own way and presenting what they discover in their own language. It is only in this way that the language will be kept alive. If you make the stipulation that in the future only your language shall be used for the statement of other people's discoveries then the language becomes a dead language, as it has already become in the Society [British Psycho-Analytical Society]. . . . Your ideas will only live in so far as they are rediscovered and reformulated by original people in the psychoanalytic movement and outside it. (Rodman, 1987, pp. 34–35)

Winnicott believed that even his own concepts should not become too rigidly formalized. In a letter to L. Joseph Stone, he writes: "how reluctant

I am to start up a 'squiggle technique' as a rival to other projective techniques. It would defeat the main object of the exercise if something stereotyped were to emerge like the Rorschach test. Essential is the absolute freedom so that any modification may be accepted if appropriate" (Rodman, 1987, p. 178). Yet Winnicott's concept of the True Self has not been given sufficient critical examination. Ironically, this has made it into a sacred doctrine that has stifled creative thought about the nature of self-experience.

Winnicott's writing demonstrates a deep respect for human individuality and complexity and an exemplary capacity to facilitate human aliveness, authenticity, and creativity. In an interview, the French analyst Daniel Widlöcher stresses the "freedom of thought" that Winnicott "helps one to acquire" (Widlöcher, 1993, p. 182). Winnicott was, in the experience of Evelyne Kestemberg (1993), a "yeast" for others' thoughts (p. 168).

Margaret Little's (1993) treatment experience with Winnicott illustrates the way he ardently defended and facilitated individuality in his patients: "I was allowed to work at my own pace, and he adapted himself to it. . . . It allowed me to be myself, to have a pace that was my own" (p. 127). Feeling exhausted and deeply depressed after a severe attack of gastroenteritis, Little was unable to go to her sessions. "D. W. came to my home—five, six, and sometimes seven days a week for ninety minutes each day for about three months" (p. 129).

Conventional analytic wisdom about Winnicott aptly highlights this dimension of his theories and practice. The difficulty with this viewpoint is that it does not account for a subtle countertendency in his writing on the True Self. Taking this tension seriously, rather than immunizing Winnicott from theoretical critique and revision because we idealize him, may deepen our understanding of his work and enrich our sense of the process of constructing an identity.

Authentic living, in Winnicott's view, is not a given of human experience. Reactiveness to the expectations of others may dominate one's life and replace one's own somatic and psychological experience. Winnicott (1960a) terms this mode of nonliving the "False Self." The False Self serves as a *caretaker* for the True Self, which is frozen and goes into hiding. The False Self attempts to "hide the true self, which it does by compliance with environmental demands" (p. 147). The False Self mode of living is impoverished, characterized by compliance, imitation, inauthenticity, unaliveness, neglect of "psychosomatic existence" (p. 144), and an inability to use symbols or play.

Winnicott spends more time defining the False Self than the True Self. He admitted that the latter was an imprecise concept: there was "but little point," he said, "in formulating a True Self idea except for the purpose of trying to understand the False Self," because the former did "no more than collect together the details of the experience of aliveness" (1960a, p. 148).

Winnicott described the "True Self" as "the inherited potential which is experiencing a continuity of being, and acquiring in its own way and at its own speed a personal psychic reality and a personal body scheme" (1960b, p. 46). It "comes from the aliveness of the body tissues and the working of the body-functions . . . and is, at the beginning, essentially not reactive to external stimuli but primary" (1960a, p. 148).[1] It arises as a *result* of "good-enough" caregiving in which the mother is especially devoted and attuned to the infant's needs. The mother provides a *"live adaptation to the infant's needs"* (1960b, p. 54). Thus, the infant can exist and does not have to react to or comply with external demands. When there is "good-enough parental adaptation to the infant's living needs" the True Self becomes a "living reality" (1960a, p. 149). The True Self mode of being is characterized by spontaneity, aliveness, and "creative originality" (p. 152), including the use of symbols and play. It is expressed in the person's spontaneous gesture, which needs to be met by the caregivers. Meeting the creative gesture promotes one's confidence in his or her efficacy and in the world's responsiveness and availability as a canvas on which one can create.

Christopher Bollas's (1989) discussion of the True Self makes explicit what is sometimes apparent in Winnicott's account of this concept understood as inherited potential, namely, that the doctrine can be used in a way that gives priority to something fixed in the past rather than something continually created, transcended, and re-created in the present: "A genetically based set of dispositions, the true self exists before object relating. . . . [I]nfants, at birth, are in possession of a personality potential that is in part genetically sponsored and . . . this true self, over the course of a lifetime, seeks to express and elaborate [itself] . . . through formations in being and relating" (pp. 9–11).

The clinical data Winnicott offers about the True Self is sparse and unspecific: "The best example I can give [of the True Self] is that of a middle-aged woman who had a very successful False Self but who had the feeling all her life that she had not started to exist, and that she had always been looking for a means of getting to her True Self" (1960a, p. 142). This vignette raises more questions than it answers. How does Winnicott's patient know about her True Self if her whole life has been inauthentic? Is her False Self organization *completely* inauthentic? Does she have any moments of authenticity or aliveness? If she is completely inauthentic and unalive, how did she manage to enter treatment with Winnicott? Does shedding her False Self lead directly to embodying her True Self? Does getting to her True Self involve only shedding her False Self? Is there *one* True Self?

Successful treatment of the False Self, according to Winnicott's theory, involves finding the lost or frozen True Self. This is illustrated by Winnicott's (1954) remark about a patient with "a very early development of a false self": for treatment "to be effectual, there had to be a regression in search of the true self" (p. 280). Bollas's (1989) comment on "moods" provides a contemporary reiteration: "It will become necessary at some time to reach the person while he is 'inside' the mood. . . . This often means contacting part of the individual's true self, but a true self that may be frozen at a time when the self experience was traumatically frozen" (p. 112). It is implicitly assumed, without actually being clinically demonstrated, that putting the patient in touch with this nascent core will provide a direction for the conduct of life and make possible the completion of the construction of the self.

Winnicott never presented definitive or systematic guidelines for doing this. In "Ego Distortion in Terms of True and False Self" (1960a), his central text on these issues, he is vague about the treatment process and the analyst's role in facilitating the emergence of the True Self. He stresses some of the difficulties and the dangers of working with the False Self, including failing to diagnose cases of False Self personality and inadvertently working with the compliant, False Self proclivities of the analysand. He also emphasizes the importance of the analyst's meeting the analysand's excessive vulnerability and dependence during the "period of extreme dependence" (p. 151)—which is crucial, in his schema, for facilitating authenticity. He also alludes to the importance of the emergence of the patient's creative originality (p. 152).

Hints for how the analyst can facilitate the patient's movement from inauthenticity to authenticity are sprinkled throughout Winnicott's corpus and center around two interrelated themes: (1) a particular analytic ambience—the "facilitating environment" created and maintained by (2) specific qualities and attitudes on the part of the "good-enough" analyst.

What the analysand struggling with inauthenticity needs, in Winnicott's (1971) view, is "a new experience in a specialized setting" (p. 55); an experience in which the analyst profoundly adapts to the analysand's needs so that the analysand is in a state of "not having to react [to the analyst] which is the only state in which the self can begin to be" (1949a, p. 183). This may in certain cases include a "period of extreme dependence" (1960a, p. 151) on the analyst, in which the good-enough analyst is flexibly responsive to the unfolding needs of the patient. Having to react to the analyst—for example, by conforming to the analyst's theoretical or clinical expectations—impinges on the analysand and generates a "false and unhealthy forward movement in emotional development" (1949a, p. 183), especially a "phase of reaction and therefore of loss of identity" (ibid.).

The good-enough analyst facilitates the birth of the self by being "alive, awake, and ready to make active adaptation through the quality of being devoted" (1949a, p. 183). She or he needs to be a tolerant, nonintrusive presence who understands and reflects the patient's reality: "the sense of self comes on the basis of an unintegrated state which, however, by definition, is not observed and remembered by the individual, and which is lost unless observed and mirrored back by someone who is trusted and who justifies the trust and meets the dependence" (p. 61 n. 1).

In an analytic environment and ambience in which the analysand can exist and be, the self-protecting and constricting shield that formerly safeguarded the analysand from anticipated psychic danger recedes. This is often expressed in the emergence of a creative or spontaneous gesture— "the True Self in action" (1960a, p. 148)—on the analysand's part.

The True Self only becomes a living reality when the analyst meets the spontaneous gesture. This experience "allows for the patient's capacity to play, that is, to be creative in the analytic work" (1971, p. 57). Then the patient "believes in external reality" (1960a, p. 146) and his or her own efficacy and agency, including the capacity to create and play. The patient then can "come together and exist as a unit, not a defence against anxiety but as an expression of I am, I am alive, I am myself. From this position everything is creative" (1971, p. 56).

There is something profoundly alluring about unmediated contact with our essential nature. Connecting with one's True Self has an appeal for most people, regardless of their familiarity with Winnicott's work. It is beyond the scope of this chapter to discuss all of the numerous meanings and functions such a wish serves. Let me mention six appeals his notion has:

1. It keeps alive the hope of a link to one's past so as to ward off the mourning that may arise when one recognizes the irremediable loss in one's life—especially possibilities that will never be.

2. It decreases one's painful sense of the profound unsettlement pervading postmodern life by offering an essence to one's life and the promise of a guiding direction for living it, which provides a reassuring illusion of self-substantiality and stability.

3. It lessens the fear of usurpation. Arnold Modell (1985a; 1986) describes patients for whom trusting the analytic process and the analyst is intensely conflictual as a result of developmental trauma or developmental impingement. These patients have a "fear of being controlled" by others and a compensatory, self-protective "need to control the object" (1986, p. 371). One manifestation of this vulnerability is a need to "maintain a system of thought that is entirely within their own omnipotent control" (p. 97). Positing the existence of a core self simultaneously provides the missing guiding ideals caused by the unidealizability of one's parents and their inability to provide a familial milieu in which one can fashion one's own ideals. It can also create an illusion of self-sufficiency that protects one against anticipated parental (or analytic) dependence and control. One could find the guiding direction for one's life not by interaction with "dangerous" others who might usurp one's autonomy, such as one's parents or analyst, but by consulting one's buried core self. One's freedom can thus be preserved.

4. The concept of a True Self also lessens the anxiety of *self-authorship*, one facet of freedom. Freedom can generate tremendous anxiety. Reified concepts can seemingly decrease such anxiety. Winnicott was aware of the dangers of such essentializing concepts. In saying that the notion of the True Self did "no more than collect together the details of the experience of aliveness" (1960a, p. 148), he was expressing his reluctance to essentialize this or any other concept. Nevertheless, the concept has sometimes come to be understood, and even used, by Winnicott and others in an essentializing way—as if it is an antecedent reality that one might discover—which courts potential difficulties. Such an understanding of the notion of the True Self might lessen the anxiety of self-authorship. Maintaining that the True Self is responsible for who one is and

how one behaves removes one from the terrible burden and danger of taking responsibility for one's actions. In this light, the concept of the True Self could be viewed as "disclaimed responsibility" (Schafer, 1976) for fashioning one's own identity.

5. In the opposite vein, finding a core self may offer one the chance to have an unconstricted and uncontaminated realm of noncompliance with and freedom from parental expectations and impingements. Living in accordance with one's core self provides the possibility of being free from a self-denying attachment to and absorption in the needs of narcissistic parents or an exploitative world. It would have offered Winnicott a region in which he was free to say the word "drat" or express whatever emotions he felt, regardless of whether it disturbed a parent or parental surrogate.

6. One feature of adulthood is the dawning awareness of the tragic dimension of human experience: the inevitability of ambivalence, conflict, inauthenticity, death, and loss. The True Self expresses the longing for an uncorrupted time, unconstrained by external demands and devoid of inauthenticity; a time animated by spontaneity, playfulness, and freedom. This offers the promise of decreasing one's sense of human mortality and privation.

My own clinical experiences with people struggling with inauthenticity and compliance indicate that the concept of the True Self is alluring but clinically problematic and thus in need of critique and revision. I do not wish to deny the clinical importance of "False Self" experiences. Inauthenticity and compliance certainly exist and require therapeutic investigation and working through. Furthermore, skills, talents, and self-potentials can be arrested, hidden, compromised, and unrealized. Patients act, at times, in ways that are self-compromising and incongruent with their interests, values, and ideals. It can be clinically useful to identify and work through these experiences.

But when analysts or patients focus on discovering a True Self, the theoretical trouble begins. This concept is based on at least five problematic assumptions:

1. The concepts of the True and False Self are more conceptually imprecise and interrelated than Winnicott and most subsequent commentators recognize. Winnicott does not maintain that these concepts are conceptually precise or segregated—he acknowledges, for example, that there are degrees of False Self behavior—but he does not offer a nuanced discussion of the subtle interplay of authenticity and inauthenticity, although a sensitivity to such an interplay between self and other, illusion

and reality, and so forth pervades his work. Since concepts all too frequently get reified in a way that the originator did not intend, the lack of elaboration about the complexity and interpenetration of authenticity and inauthenticity may open the door to misuse and thus detract from Winnicott's overall contribution.

The work of the French philosopher Jacques Derrida (1981) has highlighted the fallaciousness of binary oppositions, and the way apparent theoretical dichotomies and polarities such as nature/culture, good/evil, and truth/fiction are conceptually interrelated. Deconstructionist readings of humanistic and social science texts repeatedly demonstrate that there is always an interplay and mutual influence between concepts that thinkers ordinarily polarize. Culture partakes of nature, what is absent may shape what is present, death is a part of life, and authenticity and inauthenticity inhere in the same person.

Given the multiple meanings and purposes of psychic events, demarcations of authentic and inauthentic experience are, as Stephen Mitchell (1993c) notes, complex and problematic. Self-accommodation to the needs of another—which appears to embody inauthenticity—does not necessarily signal a self-betraying False Self mode of being if altruism and connectedness are part of one's cherished ideals and motivationally salient at that time (Dorthy Levinson, personal communication). Apparent spontaneity and vitality, which seem to represent self-chosen initiative and authentic existence, may also serve to express a self-alienating manic defensiveness or an unconscious need to *justify* one's existence. The True Self, for Bollas (1992), designates "the sign of life." Yesterday's "sign of life" may be tomorrow's *obstacle* to living. An authentic action in the past may subsequently be experienced as an inauthentic choice.

A person a clinician might describe as dominated by a True Self organization may display inauthenticity and compliance. Assuming otherwise is tantamount to claiming that such a person has no moments of unconsciousness or self-blindness and is completely authentic, spontaneous, and alive at every moment of his or her life. And a person one might describe as being dominated by a False Self organization may also exhibit authenticity. The False Self is not all false: Winnicott's paradigmatic clinical illustration, his patient with a lifelong False Self personality, managed—presumably without being coerced—to pursue and participate in treatment with Winnicott.

2. There is a tension in Winnicott's discussion of the True Self between two conceptions of self—a nonreified self, and a reified, singular sense of

self—which may undermine his enormous contribution to a psychoanalytic understanding of human subjectivity. When Winnicott asserts that there was "but little point in formulating a True Self idea except for the purpose of trying to understand the False Self" because the former did "no more than collect together the details of the experience of aliveness" (1960a, p. 148), he acknowledges the danger of fashioning a stultifying definition of authentic selfhood. He resists defining it because he does not wish to constrain the *experience* of aliveness.

Winnicott also gives the experience of authenticity and aliveness—which is, as he acknowledged, fluid, multidimensional, and ever-changing—a *capitalized* name, the True Self, which reifies it. In addition, he locates and localizes it in the past: "For treatment to be effectual, there had to be a regression in search of the true self" (1954, p. 280). This rhetorically establishes the expectation in the mind of the reader of a singular essence in the past that one must discover.[2] An emphasis on process permeates Winnicott's writings. In *Playing and Reality*, for example, he uses the verb "playing" to talk about intersubjectively shared realities (Modell, 1985a, pp. 126–27). Treating the experience of authenticity and aliveness as a noun, the True Self, may eclipse the attunement to process that Winnicott emphasizes elsewhere.

Theoretical reifications, as I suggested in the previous chapter, signal blind spots in a theorist's vision. The reification of the True Self illustrates Winnicott's unconsciousness of himself. Given the conformity and inauthenticity in his life, he may have needed to symbolize concretely personal integrity (making it a reified thing) instead of seeing it—as he did elsewhere (e.g., Winnicott, 1971)—as a moment-to-moment process. Reifying what he does not understand about himself, he turns the experience of authenticity into an absolute, universalistic, thing-like entity.

Such a perspective has the potential to limit rather than enrich the way we conceive of the self. There is no *one* True Self that can be defined or isolated from the relational context in which it is manifested. Winnicott does not actually say that there is a single self, but referring to authenticity as a thing to be found implies that it is a preexisting essence that is uncovered, rather than ever-shifting perspectives on oneself that are collaboratively constructed through the analytic dialogue and relationship. Winnicott, of course, also offers tremendous resources to "free" the self even as he fixes it. In his suggestive essay "Mind and Its Relation to the Psyche-Soma" (1949b), for example, he illuminates the dangers of treating the mind fetishistically and points toward a liberating state of un-self-conscious self-forgetfulness (which I discuss in greater detail in the next chapter) that fosters mind/body integration and creative living.

3. The process of searching for one's True Self, regarded as a singular entity waiting to be found, is a quixotic enterprise that may promote self-restriction and self-alienation. "I am large," Walt Whitman wrote, "I contain multitudes." Since selfhood is not a singularly definable entity developing or arising outside a human context, but rather a heterogeneous and complex phenomenon that is context-dependent, singular notions like the True Self subjugate selfhood's possibilities by obscuring and limiting its multidimensionality. Facets of self-experience that do not fit into preexisting images of who one *really* is are neglected or not assimilated into one's sense of identity. Opportunities for complicating and transforming one's sense of self—what Thomas Ogden (1994) has termed "destabilizing the static" (p. 41)—are thus severely restricted (Sennett, 1970). The doctrine of the True Self, from my perspective, could be used in a way that might not constitute the solution to Winnicott's patients' False Self mode of being. Rather, it might function as what Erich Fromm (1941) termed an "escape from freedom"—the never-ending possibility and responsibility for creating who we are. Not only is a monolithic sense of self limiting, but psychological health may involve access to, and comfort with, our multidimensionality. From this perspective, a sense of the complexity, multidimensionality, and polyvalency of the self is a developmental milestone and achievement.

4. Viewing the doctrine of the True Self as an essence to be discovered in the patient's past, which is one way Winnicott and subsequent commentators sometimes speak of it, can result in a neglect of an essential feature of subjectivity—the role of agency or will: the way we actively create and shape our lives by our choices and commitments in the present. This includes but is not limited to the crucial task of what Richard Rorty (1989) terms "self-creation"—giving form and substance to the self in the present. Self-creation involves creatively reworking and transforming the past as it has shaped us through ongoing self-analysis, relational affiliations, choices, and commitments based on one's values, goals, and interests. In this perspective, both the past *and* the appropriation of the past in the *present* shape who we are.[3]

Living a human life is more like extemporaneously constructing a building out of materials from the past and present in the present—including the enduring images of self and others and the associated affects that organize and thematize personal, subjective worlds—rather than discovering a frozen, nascent self-state from the past. Such discovery, however, may add a crucial element to the person's ongoing self-creative efforts. Self-creation in the present plays a more significant role in self-experience than is accounted for in the notion of the True Self.

5. The therapeutic process of facilitating authenticity is more complex than Winnicott and theorists inspired by his work have suggested. Bollas (1987), for example, stresses the need of certain patients "to use the analytic setting and process to be unburdened of the false self and collapse into true Self" (p. 256). There is no True Self waiting to be discovered underneath the analysand's inauthenticity and compliance, but rather an inchoate sense of self. Psychoanalytic treatment with False Self issues thus involves *building* rather than simply or only finding a self.

Winnicott's work collapses and conflates two different processes: (1) detecting and working through inauthenticity, and (2) self-construction leading to living authentically and vitally in the present. Discovering a nascent, buried aspect of oneself does not automatically provide direction for the conduct of one's life and complete the aborted task of constructing the self. That the discovery of a valued, buried part of oneself is insufficient for leading an authentic life in the present is implicit in Winnicott's description of the case of a man in treatment who "had a considerable amount of analysis before coming to me. . . . *My work really started . . .* when I made it clear to him that I recognized his non-existence [being a false self]" (1960a, p. 151; italics added). Since Winnicott does not offer an account of the subsequent stages of that work he had "started," we are left without a sense of how he approached the task of facilitating the patient's True Self. Because he omits the crucial task of self-construction *after* inauthenticity, Winnicott's formulations on clinically addressing inauthenticity are incomplete. Working through inauthenticity is a necessary but insufficient aspect of the treatment of people struggling with such issues. Self-construction necessitates a somewhat different and more active role for both the analyst and the analysand than Winnicott's formulations imply.

Some, if not all, patients struggling with inauthenticity have a tenuously held sense of self. They have scant belief in the validity of their perceptions or judgments about themselves or others. They may doubt or dismiss their own emotional reality. Their experience of emotional compliance or deprivation, for example, may be denied or minimized. A person's sense of and confidence in the reality and substantiality of subjective

experience develops as a result of parental attunement to his or her subjective world, including positive and negative affect states. Central to this
is what Robert Stolorow, George Atwood, and Bernard Brandchaft
(1992) and Stolorow and Atwood (1992) term a *"self-delineating selfobject function,"* namely, aiding "the articulation and validation of a child's
unfolding world of personal experience" (p. 27). Knowledge of and belief
in one's own subjective reality is deeply compromised when such parental
attunement is absent. Stolorow and Atwood (1992) pinpoint some of the
devastating consequences: "Perceptions remain ill-defined and precari-
ously held, easily usurped by the judgments of others, and . . . affects tend
to be felt as diffuse bodily states rather than as symbolically elaborated
feelings" (pp. 34–35). In such cases the child may subordinate—to the
extent of negating—his or her own sense of self and the world to caregivers in order to maintain a sense of connectedness to them. The analysand is likely to reenact this subordination with his or her analyst, which
creates a breeding ground for compliance and inauthenticity. For this
reason, it is more difficult to avoid analytic impingement than Winnicott
implied.

Unless an analyst possessed total self-consciousness and no countertransference—which is impossible—therapeutic influence and impingement are inevitable. The specialized nonimpinging setting Winnicott recommends thus provides necessary but insufficient conditions for facilitating authenticity. Since impingements are inevitable, analyzing their
impact is essential.[4] Otherwise, the perpetuation of compliance and inauthenticity goes underground. The interesting therapeutic question is not
how to eliminate misattunement and impingements—which are
unavoidable—but how to understand the analysand's participation in
them and *experience* of their impact.

The analyst's attunement to the analysand's experience from within
the latter's own vantage point—which Heinz Kohut termed "empathy"—
is crucial to the process of clarifying and further consolidating the analysand's inchoate subjective reality. This may include such things as the
analysand's experience of the analyst's impingement, affective discontent
about the analyst or the analysis, and vulnerability and ambivalence
about experiencing and articulating his or her tenuously held affective
reality because of fear of the repetition in the therapeutic relationship of
traumatic affective misattunement. Once this sort of analytic environment
is established and, when necessary, reestablished, it is somewhat less dan-

gerous for the analysand to experience and articulate a range of affect. This may then lead to the emergence of formerly disavowed states that are inconsistent with or threaten the reign of compliance.

The analysand's subtle affective discontent—for example, his or her irritation, boredom, or muted disappointment—can represent the first faint manifestation of authenticity, which will probably be experienced by the analysand as unfamiliar, trivial, strange, or silly. The analysand may disbelieve, dismiss, or devalue moments of authenticity, just as important caregivers failed to value and encourage the belief in and expression of those aspects of the analysand's subjective world at earlier stages of his or her development. The analyst's attunement to these intimations of authenticity will aid in their further expression and clarification. This, in turn, will eventually lead to the analysand's strengthened recognition of and belief in his or her existence and validity.

But before this happens, a terrifying process may occur. Intimations of authenticity constitute a profound threat to self-organization in two fundamental ways: (1) they undermine established ways of organizing experience, and (2) they erode archaic emotional allegiances with caregivers based on accommodation and self-disavowal. The tremendous psychological dislocation this generates may be symbolized by the analysand's pervasive hypochondriacal concerns (Kohut, 1979, p. 19), concrete symbols of disaster such as "earthquakes, thunder, lightning" (Brandchaft, 1993, p. 226), and nihilistic images of doom and barrenness. One patient who was just beginning to "feel his oats" and challenge and venture out from the pervasive tendency that characterized his life with his parents, namely, to subordinate himself to the needs of others and neglect his own feelings, informed me that being authentic felt like entering a postapocalyptic universe of desolation, aloneness, and sterility.

Attunement to the *analyst's* experience can also aid in facilitating the emergence of the analysand's authenticity. For example, I was able to detect the aforementioned patient's subtle compliance with me by attending to my own experience of excessive efficacy and ease in the treatment, which signified, not that the analysis was proceeding in an unequivocally successful manner, but that it was permeated by the analysand's unconscious conformity to what he assumed I wanted. The sense of therapeutic ease was as much an artifact of the analysand's conformity as it was an indication of the correctness of my interpretations. Attention to this dimension of the analyst's experience can aid in reexamining subtle aspects of compliance in the therapeutic interaction, which can encourage transference analysis of this formerly neglected area.[5]

The answer to the question posed in the title of this chapter is, "No, the True Self does not exist." The concept of the False Self can be clinically valuable in helping facilitate greater authenticity and aliveness in the analysand. The concept of the True Self demonstrates that any concept is prone to reification, even when it is used by someone as flexible and creative as Winnicott. Winnicott would have been more consistent with his own most innovative thinking if he had spoken of moments of authenticity, preferred selves, and multiple selves rather than the True Self. His theoretical account of authentic selfhood would then have embodied the openness and fluidity that he valued and fostered in his clinical work.

Winnicott's work illustrates the difficulty we all have in experiencing our self in all its polymorphous and untidy complexity. To survive in our heterogeneous world, we need to appreciate and experience the multidimensionality of the self even as we inevitably strive for self-unity.

# 7

## Kohut's Bipolar Self Revisited

A worshipful attitude toward established explanatory systems—
toward the polished accuracy of their definitions and the flawless
consistency of their theories—becomes confining in the history of
science—as do, indeed, man's analogous commitments in all of
human history. Ideals are guides, not gods. If they become gods,
they stifle man's playful creativeness; they impede the activities of
the sector of the human spirit that points most meaningfully into
the future.              —Heinz Kohut, *The Restoration of the Self*

Heinz Kohut, like D. W. Winnicott, richly contributed to
opening up the territory of self-experience eclipsed by Freud and his successors. Human subjectivity is central to the work of Kohut, whose pioneering investigations of narcissism and selfobject transferences, those
archaic forms of interpersonal relatedness in which the subject attempts
to utilize the other to compensate for his or her sense of defectiveness or
incompleteness, have deepened and enriched psychoanalytic understanding of what helps or hinders the optimal development of the self. Kohut's
innovative theoretical and clinical investigations have widened the scope
of psychoanalytic treatment and enabled analysts to treat successfully
forms of human suffering that were formerly thought to be outside the
scope of psychoanalytic intervention.

In this chapter I explore the way Kohut's map of the self partakes of
the conflict between the wish-to-know and the wish-*not*-to-know, thus
impeding movement into the "new territory" Kohut (1984) himself valued.[1] If the tension between knowing and not-knowing also exists in self
psychology, then detecting it and working through it may increase self
psychology's capacity to experience what Paul Ornstein (1993) has
termed its "multiple trajectories" (p. 3).

In the preface to Kohut's posthumously published *How Does Analysis
Cure?*, his widow, Elizabeth Kohut, indicated that her late husband

expressed the hope that his colleagues, particularly those of the younger generation, would do further research on the many questions he has raised during the course of his work. He also expressed the hope that his thoughts would stimulate them to raise questions of their own . . . in order to contribute to the advance of the science of psychoanalysis. (1984, p. xi)

Kohut's work has been enormously enlightening to my own theoretical understanding and clinical practice and has also raised fertile questions about the nature of human subjectivity. In this chapter I heed Kohut's invitation and examine the concept of the bipolar self with a spirit of "playful creativeness" rather than worshipfulness. First, I briefly outline Kohut's well-known views of the self. Then I reflect on several questions his work has raised for me regarding the role of gender and culture in identity, the value of unintegration, and the patient's role in constructing an identity. Because I deeply value Kohut's contributions to illuminating human subjectivity, my reflections are meant in the spirit of constructive critique aimed at emending and extending his contributions.

The central motivation in human experience, according to Kohut (1984), is "the self and the survival of its nuclear program" (p. 147). The nuclear program is "the basic program of the personality that was outlined in early life" (p. 100). The "ultimate achievement of Tragic Man," Kohut's alternative to Freud's Guilty Man, is the "realization through his actions of the *blueprint* for his life that had been laid down in his nuclear self" (Kohut, 1977, p. 133 n. 15).

During early psychic development a nuclear self is formed, which Kohut (1977) conceives of as being bipolar—composed of (1) basic ambitions and ideals that thrive or are thwarted by the presence or absence of mirroring, and (2) idealizing selfobject functions. *Mirroring*, in Kohut's schema, refers to the caregiver's appreciative and affirming responses to the child's actions. It is the gleam in the parent's eye when the child takes a new developmental step or the caregiver's enthusiastic reaction to the child's successes. By *idealizing* Kohut means the caregiver's availability to serve as an idealized source of strength, calmness, and wisdom for the child to identify with and draw sustenance from. A "tension arc" is said to lie between these two poles of the self and serves as the basic source of human motivation. *Tension arc* refers to the "abiding flow of actual psychological activity that establishes itself between the two poles of the self, i.e., a person's basic pursuits toward which he is 'driven' by his ambitions and 'led' by his ideals" (p. 180). The nuclear self comprises the "patterns of the basic ambitions and ideals that were laid down in the two polar areas" (p. 49). It is an innate "blueprint" of the self, revealing its structure, nature and destiny.

A "blueprint" gives us a plan for how something should be built, while "destiny" suggests psychological predetermination. The nuclear program serves as a kind of innate, buried psychic design of the self that suggests what we should value and aspire to. The job of the analyst and the analysand is to be responsive to this blueprint so as to enable it to emerge. Analysis can then help provide a direction for conducting our lives and completing the aborted task of constructing the self.

The concept of the bipolar self enjoys a relatively unquestioned role in self psychology.[2] It also resonates with both personal experience and prevalent trends in our culture involving the search for the buried, authentic self in the past or one's "destiny," which is assumed to provide direction for our lives in the present. In a world with a scarcity of viable ideals, it can be reassuring to believe that one can discover ideals within oneself.

With its "new definition of the essence of the self" (Kohut, 1984, p. 8), the nuclear program, the concept of the bipolar self is, in my clinical experience, theoretically alluring but clinically problematic. It provides a *necessary* but insufficient account of self-experience in general and in women[3] in particular. Although I believe, with Jill Gardiner (1987), that self psychology "holds great promise for feminist theory" (p. 762), in positing ambitions and ideals as the essential components of selfhood, the concept of the bipolar self eclipses the complexity of self and the experience of women (and some men) and is thus in need of further examination and perhaps revision.

At first glance, such goals and values appear to be self-evident and natural. How can one challenge them? But further reflection raises important problems. I do not wish to deny that ambitions and ideals are central to the self-experience of many, if not most, people. Not living in accordance with one's ambitions and ideals can be self-impoverishing and self-alienating. And it seems true that patients, as well as analysts, experience themselves as either (1) having gotten in touch with ambitions and ideals that guide the conduct of their lives or (2) feeling they have (or have not) lived out their destiny. And patients and analysts do act, at times, in ways that seem self-compromising and incongruent with their interests, values, and ideals. It can be clinically useful to identify and investigate these kinds of self-experiences, as well as to transform analytically this facet of an analysand's life. But when analysts or patients think of ambitions and ideals from the past as the *essence* of the self, the theoretical trouble begins.

Kohut's emphasis on ambitions and ideals as the heart of the self may express an unconscious cultural and androcentric bias in his theory. The impact of the culture we live in—like the air we breathe—is not always easily detectable because it is too familiar and close-at-hand. One central influence of American culture is the ideology of individualism, with its emphasis on the instrumentally oriented, autonomous, self-contained, self-interested individual. In the culture of individualism, the *doing* that is often central to pursuing ambitions and ideals—evident, for example, in a concern with autonomy, achievement, productivity, and consumption—is consciously and unconsciously valorized and encouraged more than a non-goal-oriented way of living.[4] But many women and some men resonate to the beat of a different, less instrumental drummer. Worshiping ambitions and goals as the acme of psychological sanity or health affirms and treats as self-evidently normal and valid "free-market" values that often have harmful psychological and social consequences. It is perhaps insufficiently recognized that such an accomplishment orientation can be a form of pathology—an unconscious attempt, for example, to prove one's sense of worthiness and thus justify one's existence.[5] There are patients, notes Joyce McDougall (1995), who "need to learn how to *stop* working, or to discover that their pleasure in their work conceals a compulsive, perhaps even a perverse, dimension—those, for example, who use their work as others use drugs: to escape mental pain and avoid reflecting on the factors that have caused it" (p. 223). Individuals who are "preoccupied with 'doing' rather than 'being,' " she continues, "leave no space in their lives for imagination and dreaming" (ibid.).

Just as there may be a hidden cost to overweaning ambition and an instrumentally oriented state of being, a noninstrumental orientation may hold unsuspected possibilities. Such an orientation toward life can, for example, be a facet of health—provided it is not defensive nonambitiousness—as well as a challenge to the individualist ethos. Nonpurposive states are implicated in and contribute to creativity, intimacy, spiritual experiences, and psychological well-being (e.g., Rubin, 1996b).

One of Kohut's seminal contributions to psychoanalysis is his critique of the self-contained individual of the culture of individualism. One could even argue that self psychology pinpoints psychopathology resulting from problematic selfobject relationships that American individualism promotes with its focus on achievement and social mobility (e.g., Roland, 1996, pp. 12–13). The problem is that this view does not account for an important countervailing tendency in his work. There is a tension in Kohut's writings between an emphasis on relatedness and a stress on individuality. On the one hand, he unequivocally challenges and offers a convincing alternative to traditional, individualistically oriented conceptions of human development with his assertion that *interconnectedness* rather than individuation is the apex of development. On the other hand, the claim that the nuclear program—with its emphasis on an individual following the ambitions and ideals residing within and thereby fulfilling his or her destiny—is the "basic force in everyone's personality" (1984, p. 147) is underwritten by assumptions that are central to the ethos of individualism.

As studies of non-Western cultures teach us, other meaningful ways of being exist. For example, certain nonpathological, non-achievement-oriented, non-self-centered states of being may be more important for many people than pursuing ambitions and ideals.[6] These alternative ways of being are either missed or pathologized when one assumes that the individualistic ethos of the northern European and North American individualized self is a universally valid and superior mode of being.[7]

Non-self-centered subjectivity, as I suggest in chapter 10, is a psychological/spiritual phenomena implicated in a wide range of adaptive behaviors ranging from art to psychoanalytic listening to intimacy. It is an unconstricted state of being, a non-self-preoccupied, non-self-annulling immersion in whatever one is presently doing in which there is heightened attentiveness, focus, and clarity. Action and response are unconstrained by self-concern, thought, or conscious effort, and restrictive self-identifications and boundaries are eroded. This facilitates a greater sense of freedom and an inclusiveness of self-structure. When excessive self-preoccupation wanes—as may occur, for example, while one is deeply immersed in playing a musical instrument, watching an engrossing cultural event, playing with a child, or making love—one may experience a heightened sense of living.[8]

Empiricism is for Kohut, as for Freud, a touchstone of a theory's validity. Kohut (1984) admits that his theory is tautological: "all value judgments are to a certain extent self-fulfilling prophesies and the procedure employed by the psychology of the self is no exception" (p. 210 n. 1). But this is not a cause for despair. The validity of a theory, according to

Kohut, is "based on a claim that rests on empirical data and can therefore be either proved or disproved by observation" (ibid.).

The fact that fifteen of the seventeen cases in *The Analysis of the Self*, where the theory of the nuclear program is first formulated, are *men*, strongly suggests that Kohut's theory is not based on the experience of women (Layton, 1990), for whom non-self-centered states of being may be more central than for men. Kohut's claim about the importance of ambition and ideals seems more applicable to men than to women. The experience of women may be eclipsed in formulations that unconsciously treat experiences related to doing, rather than being, as the norm.

The neglect of gender and the generic use of "Man" in Kohut's theory suggests, as Gardiner (1987) points out, that he "does not consider gender as a significant variable when meditating about individual psychology and our cultural condition" (ibid.). This is not to deny that his theories and clinical practices can be and have been clarifying and empowering for many women. They undoubtedly have been deeply important for women as well as men. But in valorizing facets of self-experience that seem more central to men than to women, the concept of the bipolar self may neglect the experience of women and some men.

The second question I have regarding Kohut's concept of the self involves the notion of *self-cohesion*. Self-cohesion, an integration of mind and body and the thoughts, feelings, and fantasies that comprise a life, is ordinarily assumed to be unequivocally positive, a developmental achievement. From multiple personality disorders to schizophrenia, psychoanalysis has illuminated the psychological catastrophes and suffering that disintegration, the pathological counterpart to self-integration, spawns. Self-cohesion is thus obviously crucial to a healthy experience of self and others.

And yet, despite the indispensable role that self-cohesion plays in living a fulfilling human life, many people inside and outside of analysis suffer from being *too* cohesive, too integrated, too tightly wound, incapable of relinquishing rigid control of mind and body and letting go and letting be. Too much cohesion and integration can be restrictive and limiting. It can keep us too controlled, unreceptive to the unknown, inflexible, incapable of surprise. Sleeplessness, hyperigidity, a paucity of playfulness and imagination, and sexual inhibitions are some of the clinical manifestations of too much integration.

The problem with the notion of self-cohesion is that there are both *pathological* states of integration and nonpathological, *healthy* states of unintegration. Unintegration has a more positive role in self-experience than Kohut's formulations may recognize. It is not always pathological disintegration; rather, it may be necessary for health (Winnicott, 1986b). Winnicott (1986b) recognized, for example, that "it is out of the unintegrated state that the creative impulse appears and reappears. Organized defence against disintegration robs the individual of the precondition for the creative impulse and therefore prevents creative living" (p. 29). Uncohesive states are involved in such things as dream mentation, aesthetic creation, intimacy, and spiritual experiences. In a world without unintegrated states—without the ability to live in uncertainty, to wander, flounder, muddle, to be without orientation, to lie fallow, to exist without needing to either act or react (e.g., Winnicott, 1958)—human beings would, I suspect, be impoverished.

The very urge for self-cohesion may not be an inevitable, "normal" state of self-experience, but a reaction to an already existing sense of self-division. It may only be when we feel not integrated that we worry about being cohesive. Self psychology may thus make the core of self-experience something that only arises when there is an anomaly in development.

The clinical implications of conceiving of both self-cohesion *and* unintegration as essential to the health of the self are at least twofold. First, it would aid analysts in pinpointing kinds of psychopathology that Western culture may reward—and psychoanalysis may too often neglect—such as an unconscious addiction to productivity and success. These and other kinds of cultural pathologies may be part of what could be termed the social/cultural unconscious and are thus ordinarily difficult for psychoanalysis to detect. Elucidating these and related aspects of self-experience and working through fears of and resistances to constructive states of disintegration might deepen the possibilities for self-enrichment in treatment. Second, a psychoanalysis that appreciated more of the value of states of unintegration might foster a greater capacity for dreaming, playfulness, creativity, intimacy, and spiritual experiences in those we work with.

Let me now briefly consider a third question I have about Kohut's conception of the self. In viewing the blueprint for one's life residing within the nuclear program as a "preexisting potential" in the "prenatal or genetic prehistory of the individual" requiring only the opportunity to become actualized" (Stolorow & Atwood, 1992, p. 17) by a responsive milieu, Kohut's theory may unwittingly create a teleological conception of subjectivity that places too much explanatory weight on the past and perhaps neglects—at least in *theory*—how self-experience is deeply shaped by later intersubjective contexts in which it is embedded, as well as subsequent developmental experiences. No self psychologist would recognize his or her own therapeutic work in my description, since fostering the spontaneous emergence of selfobject transferences and working through them in the *present* is an indispensable facet of self-psychologically informed clinical practice. But if Kohut's theoretical remarks about the nuclear program are taken literally, there is an agenda predisposing a return to the patient's *past*.

Kohut (1977) himself warned of the dangers of an excessive preoccupation on the analyst's part with one facet of the patient's experience, such as the past:

> The analyst's conception of the conditions that exist in infancy often decisively influences his outlook on the conditions he encounters in adults, particularly in the therapeutic situation . . . the shift in outlook concerning the conditions in early life impoverishes the analyst's perception of the varieties of significant human experiences and brings about a narrowing of the focus of his attention upon a single thread in the complex weave of the patient's psychopathology. (P. 101)

Kohut's overemphasis on the past and consequent neglect of the shaping role of the present are suggested by his comment that the process that "lays down a person's self"—namely, the selfobject's empathetic responces to "certain potentialities of the child"—"continues throughout childhood and to a *lesser* extent later in life" (1977, p. 100), as well as his claim that "psychoanalysis does not lay down new structure . . . the analytic process, so far as we know, cannot establish a nuclear self de novo" (1984, p. 99).[9]

Underlying the concept of the nuclear program is the problematic assumption that there is a definite program of action to be found in one's past that can be a reliable guide for conduct in one's present life. Though there are genetic influences and predispositions and differences in temperament, there is no antecedently given identity. It is an idealization and romanticization of the past and a denigration of the present to claim that the best of an adult is embryonically in the infant and that a nascent version of oneself is the best guide for the conduct of an adult's life. Understanding one's past is crucial for self-vitality, personal freedom, and a depth of interpersonal relatedness, but reconnecting with an earlier version of oneself is insufficient for conducting one's present life. A buried blueprint would offer, not a clear direction for one's present life, but a snapshot of an earlier, less maturely constructed self-system. It is far from self-evident how the less highly developed experience of self in infancy or childhood would illuminate the questions and conflicts one has about oneself, one's relationships, or one's life in adulthood.

The clue as to why Kohut might adopt the problematic metaphor of a blueprint may lie in the personal realm. Only scant biographical information is available on Kohut. The available information hints at a geographically and characterologically absent father (Strozier, 1985) who may have been unavailable as a source of guiding ideals, and a highly critical and intrusive mother who, for example, apparently used to pick his pimples when he was an adolescent. Is it possible that the "distant-understimulating parental selfobjects" and the "excessively close, over-stimulating selfobjects" (Kohut, 1984, p. 11) Kohut implicates in the aetiology of narcissistic personality disorders and classical neuroses, respectively, also describe his father and mother? Although I cannot prove it because of the dearth of biographical material, my speculation is that the concept of a buried blueprint in one's past that serves a guiding direction in one's present solved in one stroke a nuclear dilemma of Kohut's childhood. That is, the buried blueprint provided missing ideals and direction from his absent father, while protecting them from usurpation from his intrusive mother. Is it possible that by positing ideals existing *within*, Kohut could rectify his father's depriving absence while averting his mother's problematic presence?

Privileging the past in one's conception of the self in the present may have other problems. One can conceive of one's values and ideals in at least several ways, which would change in emphasis depending on the nature of the various relational contexts in which one was embedded. What seems like a nuclear ideal or goal may, for example, represent unconscious accommodations to one's parents (or one's analyst) designed to maintain a sense of connectedness or to be valued. An ideal from the past may be self-compromising and self-alienating in the present. Conversely, vital ambitions and ideals that have never been mirrored or delineated by caregivers (or one's analyst) may remain inchoate and thus never become integrated into one's essential goals and values.

Kohut's conception, like Winnicott's, seems to neglect an essential feature of subjectivity: the role of agency or will. The patient's contributory role in continually re-creating and perpetuating his or her difficulties in living in the present is likely to be slighted when attention is placed on the centrality of buried ambitions and ideals from the past. This may eclipse the *patient's* unconscious contribution to his or her self-enslavement, that is, the recurrent unconscious ways a particular analysand often perpetuates the feared and troubling past by assimilating new experiences and relational possibilities into old, familiar, and constricting modes (Wachtel, 1977).

By selectively attending to new positive experiences and relationships that might challenge old, excessively narrow, and self-denigrating ways of thinking of herself, a female analysand who had been sexually abused as a child by a sibling continually reconfirmed her sense of self-contempt originating in childhood. Only when we worked through her pervasive tendency in the *present* to treat herself as her brother and father did in the past—that is, to exploit her as her brother did, and prosecute herself for imagined errors, ignore her accomplishments, and fail to protect her as her father did—did she begin to experience a sense of personal value, purpose, and direction in the present.

It is assumed, in what might be termed Kohut's "derailment-rerailment" theory, that one's life will proceed smoothly once derailments in development are detected and analytically worked through (once one gets back on the "right track"). Just as the life of a slave *begins* once she or he is released from bondage, detecting one's earlier ambitions and ideals provides a necessary but insufficient perspective for living a life.

Because there is no fully developed self waiting to be discovered, but rather an inchoate sense of self, the therapeutic process involves *building* an identity rather than finding a blueprint. An important implication is that ambitions and ideals are seen as constructions arising in specific intersubjective contexts, rather than irreducible foundations of one's psychic life. The particular ambitions and ideals that emerge in treatment are viewed as one of a multitude of possible ambitions and ideals shaped by the relational matrix in which they emerge and are articulated. In a different relational matrix, other values might take on heightened importance.

The history of psychoanalysis is a testament to the way the past deeply influences the present. That the *present* as well as the past plays a formative role in self-development is suggested by research on traumatized children, who do not always subsequently show the expected effects of early trauma (e.g., Anthony & Cohler, 1987); by the way neurotic structures that may not have an infantile source develop later in life than analysts commonly assert (Emde, 1985); and by the mutative impact of successful psychoanalytic treatments.

It is thus not a question of *whether* the past influences the present, but *how* it does so. In what might be termed my historical-existential,[10] developmental-structural view of development, a focus on both the developmental origins and vicissitudes of psychological phenomena *and* the organizing principles or patterns that are currently operative are essential (Atwood & Stolorow, 1984, p. 38).[11] The present is often assimilated into the past even as the past is sometimes transformed by/in the present. What Jean Piaget termed "accommodation" and "assimilation" are both central to selfhood.

The process of constructing the self involves understanding the shaping power of the past and creatively reworking and transforming its legacy in the *present* through ongoing self-investigation, emotional commitments, and involvements based on our values, goals, and interests. In this perspective, both the past *and* the present shape who we are. Living a human life is more like extemporaneously creating a work of art utilizing materials at hand from the past and present, rather than discovering and following a buried blueprint from the past.

## Back to the Future: Self Psychology and the "Blindness of the Seeing I"

The concept of the bipolar self has both highlighted the centrality of ambitions and ideals in self-development and our patients' lives and offered a powerful and heuristic alternative explanatory framework to the motivational priority of drives in self-experience, even as it may have eclipsed the experience of some women and men and the importance of unintegration, the present, and the patient's will in constructing an identity. Obviously, it is therapeutically meaningful to help analysands clarify and attempt to embody their values and goals. This can best be accomplished by the ongoing process of exploring and transforming the past as it lives in the present, rather than searching for a buried, innate nuclear program in the past. We need to look forward as well as backward—to the patient's present as well as her past—if the self of the patient's future is to reach its full potential.

Self psychology will more readily fulfill its own enormous potential when the impact of gender and culture on theorizing and clinical practice in general and human subjectivity in particular are more fully elaborated. By drawing on the experience of women as well as men in formulating hypotheses and theories about self experience, self psychological conceptualizations of human subjectivity can be both complicated and greatly enriched.

# 8

# Psychoanalysis Is Self-Centered

Psychoanalysis is arguably the preeminent discourse in the twentieth century for investigating the nature and vicissitudes of self-experience. From Freud's account of self-unconsciousness, to Jung's description of self-division and self-integration, to Winnicott's depiction of compliance and authenticity, to Kohut's discussion of self-depletion and self-restoration, psychoanalysis has explored various facets of self-experience with lapidary precision. In this chapter I suggest that there is more in the nature of selfhood than is dreamt of in psychoanalytic psychologies. More specifically, the fertile, authentic subjectivity that contemporary psychoanalysts of every stripe have so ably illuminated and facilitated fosters a normative egocentricity that may contribute to self-constriction and alienation from self and other. Psychoanalytic treatment can reduce narcissism and provide a valuable alternative to the painful isolation and excessive privatism of our culture. But, the excessive narcissism in psychoanalysis—the overinvestment many analysts have in their own theories and practices, the intolerance of unorthodox and revisionist thinking, and so forth—suggests that successful treatment does not inevitably lead to reduced egocentricity.

In promoting an egocentric vision of self, psychoanalysis may also eclipse a vital facet of self-experience, namely, *non-self-centered subjectivity*, by which I mean a non-self-preoccupied state of being in which one is open to the moment without a sense of time, un-self-conscious but acutely aware, self-"forgetful" yet not self-neglectful, highly focused and engaged although relaxed and without fear. In non-self-centered subjectivity we experience a sense of self-vivification, self-renewal, and self-transformation and we live, relate, and play with greater creativity, joy, and efficacy than we normally experience. The neglect of non-self-centered subjectivity and the spirituality of which it may be a part leads to an impoverished view of self, a narcissistic conception of relationships, and an incomplete account of morality. Psychoanalysis offers a necessary, albeit insufficient, perspective for thinking about morality. The greater self-acceptance and lessened narcissism that analytic treatment fosters exists without the larger perspective of non-self-centered subjectivity, wherein one's own experience is viewed as a *part* of a more encompassing reality. Freed from a picture of the self that has often held analysts captive, we might be encouraged to conceive of subjectivity in more expansive and less self-alienating ways. We might then have a psychoanalysis of greater tolerance and civility that could contribute to contemporary debates over the revitalization of civic culture.

The vast majority of psychoanalysts agree that a fundamental aspect of analysis is an expanded and nuanced experience and understanding of "I-ness," that is, the sense of ourselves as physically bounded subjects who reason, fantasize, desire, fear, hope, choose, and act. In his synthetic overview of postclassical psychoanalytic views of the self, Stephen Mitchell (1991) suggests that each school of psychoanalysis illuminates a different aspect of selfhood. Mitchell distinguishes three views of the self: the Freudian view of the self as separate and integrated, the object relations and interpersonal view of it as multiple and discontinuous, and the self psychological view of it as integral and continuous.

The dialogue between Sigmund Freud and his friend Romain Rolland concerning religion implicitly suggests that there is more in the nature of selfhood or "I-ness" than these accounts of subjectivity imply. Responding to Freud's critique of religion in *The Future of an Illusion*, Rolland, a poet and student of the Indian saint Ramakrishna, indicated that Freud's negative assessment had much merit but neglected the most important source of the religious sentiment, a "sensation of 'eternity,' a feeling of as something limitless, unbounded." In *Civilization and Its Discontents*, Freud (1930) admitted that he could not discover this "oceanic" feeling in himself and voiced discomfort in coping with these "obscure modifications in mental life" (p. 73). Subsequent psychoanalysts, with rare exceptions (e.g., Loewald, 1978; Kovel, 1991), followed Freud's lead and also neglected and pathologized this facet of self-experience.

Psychoanalysis has elucidated pathological facets of such oneness experiences, by which I mean experiences in which one feels a sense of interconnection with the world, in its accounts of the characteristic boundary problems of schizophrenics or the way fusion experiences may ward off feelings of disappointment, loss, or Oedipal conflicts (e.g. Silverman et al., 1982). But it has neglected the adaptive possibilities of such experiences,[1] particularly non-self-centered subjectivity, which is characterized by heightened attentiveness, focus and clarity, attunement to the other as well as the self, non-self-preoccupied exercise of agency, and non-self-annulling immersion in whatever one is doing in the present. It is something many people have experienced—whether absorbed in nature, a play, or making love. Non-self-centered subjectivity is implicated in a range of adaptive contexts ranging from psychoanalytic listening to creating or appreciating art to emotional intimacy. The adaptive dimensions of non-self-centered subjectivity raise important questions for psychoanalysis: Do self-transformations that may occur in this state of being ever enrich self-experience? Might such experiences aid analysts and analysands in envisioning selfhood in new and more expansive ways?

## Psychoanalysis and Individualism

Sociologist Philip Rieff (1963) maintains that four character ideals have vied for center stage in the history of Western life: the "political" subject of classical antiquity, who participates in public life; the "economic" subject, who retreats into a search for private fulfillment while enjoying the fruits of citizenship; the Hebraic and Christian "religious" person, who substitutes faith for reason; and the "psychological" subject of the late nineteenth and twentieth centuries, who eschews any redemptive external doctrine or creed—whether political or religious—and attends to the workings of his or her own private universe of thoughts, feelings, dreams, and symptoms.

Psychoanalysis arose from the soil of the modern period, in which there was a "despiritualization" of subjective reality (e.g., Kovel, 1991), by which I mean a devaluation, marginalization, and pathologization of the spiritual. Spirituality does not flourish in a world in which mechanistic science is the arbiter of reality. The "psychological" subject monopolized the stage of intellectual life in the West during the formation and development of psychoanalysis. "In the age of psychological man, the self," notes Rieff (1963) "is the only god-term" (p. 23). Selfhood, according to Roy Baumeister (1987), became a problem in the modern period.

> During the Victorian era (roughly 1830–1900), there were crises with regard to . . . four problems of selfhood . . . how identity is actively or crea-

tively defined by the person, what is the nature of the relationship between the individual and society, how does the person understand his or her potential and then fulfill it, and how and how well do persons know themselves. . . . Early in the 20th century, themes of alienation and devaluation of selfhood indicated concern over the individual's helpless dependency on society. (P. 163)

For psychological man, self-maximization, not participation in the polis, is the chief vocation. Interest in the workings of one's psyche replaces commitment to the life of the commons. Psychotherapeutic concern for the meaning of symptoms replaces questions about meaning or "ultimate concern." Better living, not the Good Life, becomes the main psychoanalytic preoccupation (Rieff, 1963).

Contemporary psychoanalytic assumptions about the self—even within relational schools—are underwritten by Western values, particularly the Northern European/North American cultural values and philosophical assumptions of individualism (Roland, 1996).[2] The individual in individualism is sacred: "the supreme value in and of himself or herself, having his or her own rights and obligations. . . . Society is considered to be essentially subordinate to the needs of individuals, who are all governed by their own self-interest" (Roland, 1996, p. 6).[3]

According to Robert Bellah, four types of individualism have dominated Western culture: biblical, republican, utilitarian, and expressive. In biblical individualism, "creation of a community in which a genuinely ethical and spiritual life could be lived" was crucial (Bellah et al., 1985, p. 29). The republican individualist tradition originated in classical Greece and Rome and flourished in the civic humanism of late medieval and early modern Europe. It presupposes that "the citizens of a republic are motivated by civic virtue as well as self-interest." "Public participation," in the tradition of republican individualism, is viewed as a form of "moral education" aiming toward "*justice and the public good*" (Bellah et al., 1985, p. 335). Utilitarian individualism is focused on the maximizing of self-interest. Expressive individualism "arose in opposition to *utilitarian individualism*" (Bellah et al., 1985, p. 333). It asserts that "each person has a unique core of feeling" that should "unfold or be expressed" (Bellah et al., 1985, p. 334). Psychoanalysis is an exemplary psychological version of Western expressive individualism. In the next section I reflect on some problems with psychoanalytic individualism.

## Beyond Psychoanalytic Individualism

Individuality and the "uniqueness of personality" are arguably the hallmark and greatest achievement of modern culture. Individualism has promoted such things as the importance of human dignity and rights, even as the "limits of individualism" (Gaylin, 1988, p. 59)—the materialism, greed, and xenophobia it also bequeaths us—cry out to us on a daily basis. Gregory Bateson (1972) claims that the concept of a separate "I" is *the* epistemological fallacy of Western civilization. It could be argued that narcissism is at the root of the pervasive intolerance, oppression, inequality, and injustice in the world. Narrow and narcissistic conceptions of self seem to be implicated in many contemporary crises—ranging from a resistance to utilize available resources to remedy world hunger to the scapegoating of the oppressed.

The rampant fundamentalism, racial and religious scapegoating and bigotry, and ecological insensitivity in our world suggest that the narcissistic and disconnected sense of self is dysfunctional, both cause and result of much of the suffering and disharmony in late twentieth-century life. Psychoanalysis has not caused the narcissistic or disconnected sense of self, or the mayhem in our world. In fact, it can do the opposite: it can bring more reason to bear on our asocial, self-centeredness, lessen irrational conscience, and improve our standard of conduct (e.g., Gedo, 1986, p. 207). But its self-centered conceptions of self might foster a normative narcissism that contributes to viewpoints that fuel suffering and alienation from self and others.

Ernest Wallwork and Roy Schafer claim that psychoanalysis could actually lessen narcissism. Wallwork (1988), for example, argues that psychoanalysis offers a "way out of the isolated individualism and exclusive privatism of contemporary American culture" (p. 204). Schafer (1992) claims that at the termination of a successful treatment, "benevolent self-interest" (p. 8) and benevolent interest in the selves of others replaces "malevolent self-interest" (p. 9), leading to an interest in others.

While the two seem linked, the historical record within psychoanalysis raises questions about the "inseparability" (p. 20) of benevolent self-interest and interest in others. If they were indissolubly connected, I suspect that we might have a psychoanalysis of greater tolerance and civility. Analysts would be less narcissistically overinvested in the ultimate validity of their own formulations, and dissident thinkers would confront less pathologization and marginalization. The narcissism permeating psychoanalysis seems to suggest that either (1) the analysis of many analysts was unsuccessful or (2) Schafer's claim about the mitigation of narcissism is partially true but incomplete. If "infantilism" was the malady afflicting the unreflective, pre-self-conscious protoindividual symbiotically immersed in the tribal mind (e.g., Houston, 1980, p. 27), then narcissism, disconnection, nihilism, and anomie may be the pathology characterizing the autonomous, self-sufficient, atomized, Promethean man of our hyper-self-conscious individualistic society. Thus, the path to social order may lie, not, as Freud (1933d) claimed, in conquering instinctual aggression through rationality and renunciation, but in mollifying narcissism and increasing understanding and tolerance of the other.[4]

Psychoanalysis's egocentric conception of "I-ness" fosters a type of self-blindness and self-impoverishment. Thinking of the self as the center of the psychological and moral universe can foster a narrow and problematic way of seeing and relating to ourselves and others. For example, it encourages an inflated sense of self-importance and may thus promote ethnocentrism and xenophobia. "Every spirit," says Ralph Waldo Emerson (1968) at the end of *Nature*, "builds itself a house and beyond its house a world, and beyond its world a heaven." "Know then," he continues, "that the world exists for you. For you is the phenomenon perfect. What we are, that only can we see." While every person may be at the center of his or her own world, no one is the center of the whole world. Thinking that we are—which individualism encourages—may compromise empathy and tolerance, foster disconnection from others, and engender self-alienation.

The psychoanalytic conception of subjectivity that arose in nineteenth-century Victorian Europe was particular and partial. Psychoanalysis's emphasis on the development of the psyche of the "psychological" subject offered psychological grounding and comfort for the dehumanized and alienated early twentieth-century citizen. It also seems to jibe with (and perpetuate) the post–World War II consumer economy with its empty individual who needs to acquire and consume constantly (Cushman, 1995, p. 160).[5] But in overemphasizing a reified, egoistic individualism, psychoanalysis necessarily promotes excessive self-centeredness and eclipses certain possibilities and features of subjectivity, including non-self-centric modes of being.

Because autonomous, differentiated identity—which is a more self-centered aspect of subjectivity—has traditionally been viewed as the apex of human development by most psychoanalysts (except Kohutians), non-self-centric modes of being have been interpreted by most psychoanalysts as symptoms of psychopathology. From traditional analytic perspectives, such experiences are most often viewed as a regressive attempt to merge with the pre-Oedipal mother. In the self psychology tradition, permeability of self-boundaries and alternations in self-cohesion—such as might occur in self-transformative moments of non-self-centered subjectivity— appear to be viewed as symptoms of a vulnerable, besieged, or under-structuralized self.[6]

But experiences of self-transcendence, in which there is non-self-centricity and at least a transient loss of self-differentiation, may embody a nonpathological, expanded sense of self[7] that is quite different from archaic states of nondifferentiation. The non-self-centric is usually conflated in psychoanalysis with pathological self-loss. Non-self-centered subjectivity does not have to be a reflection of the failure to have achieved psychological separation during infancy. There can be an expansion of self-structure that is not necessarily indicative of an ego defect or a boundary problem and that is self-enriching and not self-annihilating.[8]

It is difficult to paint a picture of these experiences because in authorizing us to "think and speak in terms of single, stable self-entities" (Schafer, 1989, p. 159), the English language offers an impoverished vocabulary for evoking non-self-centric states of being. In non-self-centered subjectivity we are un-self-preoccupied yet highly attentive, receptive to the moment but without a sense of time, attuned to the other but not neglectful of the self. We live and relate with greater awareness, receptivity, creativity, and efficacy than we normally experience. Hans Loewald (1978) depicts some manifestations of these self-enriching facets of non-self-centered subjectivity that many people have probably experienced:

> We get lost in the contemplation of a beautiful scene, or face, or painting, in listening to music, or poetry, or the music of a human voice. We are carried away in the vortex of sexual passion. We become absorbed in . . . a deeply stirring play or film, in the beauty of a scientific theory or experiment or of an animal, in the intimate closeness of a personal encounter. (P. 67)

In these non-self-preoccupied states of being there is a nonpathological reduction of boundaries between self and world, a self-empowering sense of connection that results in a lack of self-preoccupation, a sense of timelessness, efficacy, and peace. Such moments of non-self-centricity—

whether surrendering, merging, yielding, or letting go—are part of most spiritual traditions.

There are at least four reasons why spirituality has been neglected or pathologized in psychoanalysis. First, as Freud (1927) emphasized, religion has been guilty of many "crimes" and "misdemeanors" (p. 27), ranging from rationalizing authoritarian behavior and intolerance to physically and psychologically persecuting dissenting thinkers, in its attempts to ward off and make tolerable human existential feelings of helplessness. Second, oneness experiences may stir up various internal and interpersonal anxieties and dangers, including fears of engulfment and self-loss. Freud may have unconsciously connected and conflated religion and the feminine. His dismissal of the former may have been profoundly shaped by the negative and mystifying experiences with the latter (his mother) explored in the first chapter. The third reason for spirituality's dismissal in psychoanalysis was that James Strachey's English translation of Freud's German was shaped and delimited by positivistic assumptions, which lent a scientized cast to Freud's humanistic insights and made the spirit seem even less relevant to psychoanalysis (e.g., Bettelheim, 1982). It is inevitable that a soulless version of Freud would neglect spirituality. And finally, exploring the realm of spirituality opens up the question D. W. Winnicott recognized psychoanalysis—with its essentially "tragic" worldview (Schafer, 1976), its recognition of the inescapable mysteries, afflictions, and losses pervading human existence—has rarely addressed: "What is life about, apart from illness?"[9]

The plethora of analysands and analysts who are pursuing various forms of spiritual practice, the increasing number of conferences and articles on spirituality and psychotherapy, and perhaps the burgeoning attention to subjectivity and relationship issues in treatment suggest we may be witnessing a hunger for and a return of the (spiritual) repressed in contemporary psychoanalysis. In the spring of 1994, for example, more than five hundred therapists and Buddhists participated in a conference on Healing the Suffering Self at the Harvard Club in New York City. Might many analysands and analysts turn to the meditation cushion (or yoga ashram) in addition to the psychoanalytic couch, because psychoanalysis may not fully nourish their spiritual needs or hunger?

Psychoanalysis's impoverished view of relationships may be related to its narcissistic view of the self. It may not be accidental that psychoanalysis calls the other an "object" and relations with others "object relations." The word *object* connotes a thing and predisposes one to adopt a depersonalized view of (Buccino, 1993, p. 130) and narcissistic relation to others. The narcissistic view of relationships emerges in the psychoanalytic vocabulary of "bad objects," "part-objects," "need-satisfying objects," and "selfobjects." The other tends to be viewed, in psychoanalysis, as an object rather than a *subject*. From such a perspective, one focuses on what the other needs to do for the self rather than what the self might do for the other. This fuels an absence of recognition of the other as a separate, individual center of initiative, experience, need, and desire. The complexity of relatedness and the subjectivity of the other is eclipsed by such egocentric conceptions of other people.

That psychoanalysis—even in its relational versions—treats the other reductively is suggested by its notion of the other as an object, its failure to articulate a workable theory of intimacy, and its egocentric conception of moral responsibility. The word *responsibility* hardly appears in the *Standard Edition* of Freud and is usually absent from psychoanalytic discourse. The notion of responsibility emerges in relation to the "evil" content of one's dreams rather than questions of morality between people (Freud, 1925a, p. 133). Despite the relational turn in psychoanalysis in the last fifteen to twenty years, the morality underpinning psychoanalysis is based on a one-person, nonrelational model of human beings. Although contemporary psychoanalysis charts relational influences on development and treatment, it does not yet offer a relational perspective on moral responsibilities. In contemplating action and moral decisions, we unconsciously import a one-person perspective on morality. When patients struggle with ambivalence about a relationship or moral dilemma—should one, for example, allow his or her aging parent to move in?—we psychoanalysts usually ask the person not "what do you think is right or just?" but "what do *you* feel, want or need?" Our very question about what the lone individual wants or needs predisposes us to think in terms of the discrete desires of isolated, disconnected individuals, not of people inextricably involved in a network of relations (Marilyn Saur, August 1995, personal communication). Identifying the locus of value in the desires or authenticity of the separate, isolated individual ("if it feels good [or true] to you, then do it") encourages expressive individualism, which erodes republican individualism and civic engagement. It is possible that some of the disconnection and alienation that analysands experience is related to the ascendency of expressive individualism and the decline of civic engagement. In dissolving the separation between self and other, moments of spirituality usher in a different kind of consciousness of self in relation to other. One can then sometimes ask not "what did the other do for the self?"—the question psychoanalysis usually focuses on—but rather, "what might the self do for the other?" A spiritual perspective might offer an alternative vision to the solipsistic psychoanalytic sense of self. Concern with the other as well as the self allows us to view morality in a more complex and nuanced way. One of the tasks confronting contemporary psychoanalysis might be to develop a relational view of morality that retains both what Paul Ricoeur (1970) terms a "hermeneutics of suspicion"—a challenging of motives and meaning arising out of the recognition of the shaping role of unconsciousness and the pervasiveness of psychological complexity and conflict—*and* a spiritual perspective of a larger reality in which all individuals are embedded (e.g., Rubin, 1997a).

It is not surprising that psychoanalysis lacks a nuanced and compelling account of emotional intimacy among egalitarian subjects. How could there be an adequate account of intimacy when the other is seen mostly in terms of what it does (or does not do) for the self? In a theoretical world in which "relationships are secondary phenomena and emotions are derivative, love will never be discovered" (Gaylin, 1988, p. 44). The complexity of intimacy and love cannot be adequately explained when human beings are valorized as self-centered and hedonic monads accountable only to the dictates of their own personal tastes and dispositions.[10]

The psychoanalytic neglect of otherness effects its view of morality, or how we treat each other, as well as interpersonal relationships. It is beyond the scope of this chapter to attempt the complex task of delineating a psychoanalytic morality. Let me, however, briefly reflect on psychoanalytic perspectives on morality.

Psychoanalysis may now be very far from Heinz Hartmann's (1960) assertion in *Psychoanalysis and Moral Values* that it is a clinical procedure without moral considerations. Hartmann's position seemed to echo Freud's (1933d) claim that psychoanalysis does not posit any values beyond those within science as a whole. However, there still seems to be an ambivalence within psychoanalysis concerning values and morality. On the one hand, psychoanalysis highly regards value and moral neutrality, does not advocate a single ethical perspective, and lacks normative criteria for comparing competing systems of morality (Gedo, 1986, p. 214). On the other hand, despite its apparent value neutrality moral questions pervade analysis, from lacunae in the values of patients seeking our help (Lytton, 1984) to the implicit and explicit values in our theories and practices. From the metapsychologies underlying our theories to the interpretations we make, values shape psychoanalytic theories and practice. To know what a cure is—to know what recovery would look like—the analyst must already have a vision of what the good life is (Phillips, 1994). The good life, according to classical psychoanalysis, involves rationality, alignment with the Real, self-renunciation, self-control, self-composure, and self-integration. Such a vision places us squarely in the land of values and morality. A person with different values might, for example, aspire to a life of more passion and less renunciation or greater authenticity or aliveness.

A psychoanalytic view of morality underwritten by an individualistic sense of self leads to a morality rooted in the neglect of the other, which does not provide an adequate framework for ethics. Because ethics and tolerance also involve continually questioning the centrality of our own cherished viewpoints so as to take into account those of others (Varela, 1984), psychoanalysis offers a necessary, though insufficient, perspective for thinking about morality. The greater self-acceptance and lessened narcissism that often develop as a result of analytic treatment exists without the larger perspective fostered by less self-preoccupation, wherein one's own experience is viewed as a *part* of a more encompassing reality.

This is not to say that spiritual perspectives are a panacea or that psychoanalysis has no critique to offer them. It is beyond the scope of this chapter to explore what psychoanalysis has to offer to spiritual perspectives. Elsewhere I have explored some of the problems caused by ethical psychologies such as Buddhism that privilege selflessness and neglect the importance of self-centered subjectivity (Rubin, 1996b). Nonpsychoanalytic spiritual conceptions of self and morality tend to neglect the psychological complexity of selfhood and ethics—for example, the multiplicity of conflicting motives that may underlie a particular action. If contemplative traditions temper the traces of egocentricity in psychoanalysis and deabsolutize the self-centered self, then psychoanalytic attention to psychic complexity and the shaping role of unconsciousness in human life might deprovincialize the non-self-centered, contemplative self (Rubin, 1996b).

## Psychoanalysis and Non-Self-Centered Subjectivity

Attention to non-egocentric states of subjectivity can challenge the absolute validity of the self-centered self, help psychoanalysts recognize that there is more in the nature of self-experience than is dreamt of in psychoanalytic psychologies, widen psychoanalysis's conceptions of self, and aid psychoanalysts in conceiving of subjectivity in less excessively narrow and less self-centered ways.[11] A spiritual sense of self teaches us that when we think about action, choice, moral commitment, and relational affiliations, we need to focus on the other as well as the self.

Detaching from an overly egocentric sense of self may free us from the prison of a self-alienating egoism, enhance our capacity for empathy and tolerance, and foster a sense of connection with and compassion for others. Loosening the grip of excessive self-preoccupation—whether by deeply immersing oneself in playing a musical instrument, watching an engrossing cultural event, or creating art—often leads to a heightened sense of living. Such a view of subjectivity opens subjects up to the possibility of greater intimacy, for friendship and love necessitate that we loosen and sometimes transcend our normally more restrictive sense of separateness from others and the world.

Non-self-centered subjectivity might enrich treatment in several ways. A state of non-self-centered subjectivity can foster the analyst's capacity to listen creatively and respond freely to the exigencies of the clinical moment. In a less bounded, non-self-preoccupied, non-self-centric state, the analyst can more easily engage in transient identifications with subtle affective experiences, access somatic knowledge,[12] and challenge habitual and limiting psychological conditioning. In this state, there is sometimes "an easy commerce of the old and the new" (Eliot, 1963, pp. 207–8). This often results in what the Indian philosopher Jiddu Krishnamurti (1969) termed a "freedom from the known," in which we are able to spring from familiar patterns of thinking and relating and experience newness. It is illustrated by the analyst who makes a creative interpretation or intervention—saying something she was not consciously aware that she knew or relating in an unfamiliar manner—instead of reiterating something unoriginal that she already knows.

Analytic change requires the analysand to alternate among what Arnold Modell (1989) terms the "multiple realities" of the analytic setting and process, such as past and present and the transference as "real" *and* illusory. Accessing states of non-self-centricity fosters the analysand's ability to experience these multiple realities and to free associate, allowing refined access to fleeting thoughts, feelings, and fantasies to develop.

## Psychoanalysis and Civic Culture

"[The] danger to democracy," claims historian and social critic Christopher Lasch (1991), "comes less from totalitarian or collectivist movements abroad than from the erosion of its psychological, cultural, and spiritual foundations from within" (p. 24). Reconceiving what it means to be a self in our world may be crucial to addressing this crisis. Historically, tension has existed between rights-based liberal political theory and the republican tradition emphasizing civic engagement (Sandel, 1996). The ascendance of an unencumbered self focused on fulfillment privileges the liberal tradition over the republican tradition, which contributes to the erosion that Lasch pinpoints. Psychoanalysis has an ambivalent relation to this process. The two traditions that have dominated the psychoanalytic accounts of the good life, the Platonically inspired attempt to discover the Real and the Winnicottian search for the uncorrupted, authentic Self (Peter Carnochan, personal communication) both encourage the myth of the isolated self even as they sometimes foster resources for mitigating narcissism (Rubin, 1997a). To return to the irony of my title: to the extent that psychoanalysis remains "self-centered"—centered on the separate, unencumbered self—its capacity to contribute to this topic will be compromised. It will envision self-centeredness and selflessness as polar oppositions, and it will foster a constraining view of ethics. To the extent that psychoanalysis is "self centered" it can exquisitely elucidate multidimensional aspects of self-experience—including non-self-centered subjectivity—and thus contribute something indispensable to contemporary discussions of the role of self in civic culture. For example, it could elucidate barriers to civic engagement. Why is there so much passivity on the part of the citizenry in the face of overt corruption and dehumanizing choices by politicians? Psychoanalysis could also offer nondichotomous views of a self-in-relation—a self that is both connected *and* individuated, capable of attending to the other *and* caring for the self. Psychoanalysis could also present complex views of morality that attend to the needs of both the other and the self.

When the spiritual is no longer delegitimized—as it has been traditionally in psychoanalysis[13]—a "widening scope" of psychoanalysis might encourage psychoanalytically informed investigations of issues that adversely affect the health of individuals as well as cultures: the seductions of materialism and consumerism; the psychology of greed, authoritarianism, racism, sexism, homophobia, ageism, and submissiveness to colonialism and fanaticism. Questions about such things as the nature of creativity, health, and intimacy, constructive and engaged citizenship, and the process of fostering psychological decolonization might then be seen as more germane to our field. In a psychoanalysis that was not *only* self-centered, might psychoanalysts contribute to a civilization with less discontent?

## Theory and the Blindness of the Seeing I

The self is, in Thomas Pynchon's (1976) evocative image in *Gravity's Rainbow*, a "crossroads, a living intersection" (p. 625) of multiple determinants and dimensions. It is complex and dense: composed of conscious and unconscious beliefs, values, desires, memories, fantasies, and associations and a plenitude of condensed, symbolic, and displaced meanings. Given the self's polyvalent nature and open-ended structure, it may not be as strange and startling as it sounds to liken the self, as Christopher Bollas (1992) does, to a dream. Like a dream, the self is complex, multidimensional, and unfinalizable.

"Is it not the characteristic of reality [one might add "the self"]," asks Roland Barthes (1977), "to be *unmasterable*? And is it not the characteristic of any system [or theory] to master it?" (p. 172). Confronting a universe of complexity and uncertainty, skeptical about foundational Truths and the quest for absolute knowledge, we moderns (or postmoderns) are cast adrift, without comforting frameworks of certain meaning and action. It can be enormously unsettling psychologically to realize that there are no authorities who have a God's-eye view of reality and "really know." In the face of this emotional disorientation, it is tempting to make a Faustian choice: embracing totalizing or encompassing explanations or theories that offer solace even as they foster prideful certainty, closure, and even dogmatism. The self is then viewed, for example, as having a definitive nature (such as bipolar) or essence (such as the True Self).

Theories, the models we utilize to understand clinical material, are essential to psychoanalysis. They guide and anchor the clinician, providing a structure to organize disparate data and impressions. But theorizing is always an act of abstraction, by which I mean it literally fails to take account of the world it seeks to comprehend. The theoretical map is never the living terrain. Theories are thus always and inevitably reductive. They can shackle the fluidity of experience by conceptually freeze-framing and "fixing" or cutting off the life of what is fluid, ever-changing, and potentially emergent. Theorizing, like self-development, can also be phobic or perverse, limiting where we can intellectually "travel" or "knowing too exactly what one wants" beforehand, which prefigures and thereby forecloses future possibilities (Phillips, 1993, p. 108). Theories are inevitable and necessary, as well as reductive and distorting.

The moral of the stories I have told about universalistic selves, True Selves, False Selves, preferred selves, multidimensional selves, noninstrumental selves, and spiritual selves in the five chapters in Part 2 is that psychoanalysis needs different kinds of theories: theories that do not reduce the complexity and fluidity of self-experience; theories that have an uncongealed structure and are nomadic and migratory, by which I mean that they are fluid with no fixed, static, a priori limits such as the bipolar or True Self. Psychoanalytic theories of the subject or self need to incorporate into their own structure and language a recognition of the fluid, evolving, and emergent aspects of selfhood—they need, that is, to resist fixity, essentialization, immobilization, premature closure, stagnation, and the last word. Psychoanalytic theories, from the perspective that I am pointing toward, would be self-correcting, capable of transformation and emendation based on feedback. Such theories would be customized rather than Procrustean. When psychoanalysis has theories that are unfinalizable and open-ended, as opposed to finished systems of thought, then we analysts will be more likely to generate stories about selves-in-process—as unfinished works of art—rather than (the fixed and immobile) Truth about a Subject. We would foster the liberation of selfhood, rather than its confinement.

PART 3

# Psychoanalytic Practice

Psychoanalysis began, in Freud's hands, as "virtuoso improvisation" (Phillips, 1993, p. 3). Freud and his more creative collaborators,
like Sandor Ferenczi, might profitably be viewed as jazz musicians who
played without psychological sheet music; creating and improvising as
they went along. Improvisation is notoriously difficult to sustain. It is
safer and easier to forgo the risk and challenge of creativity and retreat
into the path well-traveled (rather than the road not taken). Intellectual
movements, no less than jazz groups or individuals, need a sense of orientation and direction. It can be deeply unsettling to practice psychoanalysis without a map.

Psychoanalysis usually disavows its disciplinary uniqueness by analo-
gizing with things it differs from, including science and mothering, instead
of seeing its uniqueness as a virtue. For psychoanalysis to flourish, its
practices, as well as its theories, need to be reimagined as well as found.
When analytic practices are unquestioningly inherited, rigidity and intellectual sclerosis set in.

In the next three chapters I explore several blind spots in psychoanalytic practice and theory, namely, narcissistic attachments to one's clinical
methods, hidden authoritarianism in the analytic relationship and setting,
and intellectually imperialistic modes of representing patients and the
therapeutic process. I offer a point of view about psychoanalytic practice
that is *posthumanist* (rather than postmodern), evolutionary, and antiauthoritarian. In chapter 9 I argue that one of Freud's seminal contributions to human self-understanding was his *posthumanist* conception of
practice (and self-experience), which he did not theorize and did not always follow. A posthumanist practice draws on certain valuable dimensions of the Cartesian, humanist and antihumanist, poststructuralist
traditions while avoiding crucial difficulties with each. The humanist tradition encourages an affirmative skepticism—a willingness to question
the foundations of one's own thought and practice and a belief in the

efficacy of reason to provide corrective feedback—which makes it amenable to change and evolution. The poststructuralist tradition encourages us to search for the theoretical unconscious of our own methods and theories and to interrogate all practices and theories—even ones that we identify with. A posthumanist practice is a mode of investigation that challenges and is skeptical of conventional meanings and authorities yet is committed to decisive conclusions, values reason and searches for unconsciousness, and appreciates psychological complexity without becoming nihilistic.

Chapter 10 examines the deep-seated attachments we have to our favored practices (and theories) and recommends a more fluid relationship in which we are committed to them without being enslaved by them. Chapter 11 explores hidden authoritarianism in psychoanalytic practice. Here I recommend a more egalitarian therapeutic stance and relationship and a more collaborative way of thinking about and representing the treatment. Cultivating forms of psychoanalytic practice that are self-reflective and self-correcting, and types of therapeutic relatedness that are egalitarian and nonauthoritarian, could foster the development of a psychoanalytic practice that resists closure and constriction and interminably questions and expands its own foundations. This would foster new images of the analyst's role and the therapeutic relationship, process, and cure. My hope is that this could reanimate how psychoanalysis is conceived and practiced and help us liberate our patients.

# 9

# Freud's Legacy
## Toward a Posthumanist Practice and a Multidimensional Self

For psychoanalysis as a discipline to reach its developmental potential, it needs to actualize its emancipatory possibilities as well as detect and work-through its clinical and theoretical blind spots. Discovering neglected resources within psychoanalysis, such as Sandor Ferenczi's writings on technique or cure, as well as pinpointing hidden tensions and gaps in its theories and practices, is a crucial facet of this enterprise. In this chapter I reflect on overlooked gems in Sigmund Freud's work. Arguably the most important and enduring of Freud's multiple legacies[1] was his development of a radical methodology for investigating psychological life and his exemplary conception of human selfhood. Psychoanalysis, according to Freud (1923a), was three things: (1) a method of investigation; (2) a mode of treatment; and (3) a theory of human development and mental life. The methodological revolution that Freud initiated has been inadequately appreciated because most commentators have tended to focus on psychoanalysis as simply a *theory* while neglecting its other two dimensions.[2]

The liberating possibilities in Freud's method and his conception of self have not been fully assimilated by psychoanalysis. This chapter explores methodological and theoretical possibilities opened up by Freud's *posthumanist* practice and multidimensional self. Posthumanist refers to a practice developed by Freud (who was unaware of its implications) that embodies the best qualities of the humanist, Cartesian tradition of self-transformation through the exercise of reason and insight, and the contemporary antihumanist, poststructuralist tradition of relentless, skeptical critique. Such a practice also avoids many of the excesses and blind spots of each tradition, such as the overemphasis on reason and the neglect of the shaping role of unconsciousness in the former, and the attention to critique and the evasion of positive reconstruction in the latter. A posthumanist practice is self-questioning and committed yet not nihilistic, affirmative as well as deconstructive, attuned to psychological complexity and subjectivity without eschewing causality or ushering in a disabling indeterminacy.

Freud offers a multidimensional view of the origins, nature, and determinants of human selfhood that contains an exemplary sense of self-complexity and self-fluidity missing from most contemporary analytic and nonanalytic accounts of self. He conceives of people as embodied, fantasizing, partially unconscious, desiring, self-judging, guilt-ridden, conflicted beings who are shaped by history, culture, the family, the body, relationships, and ideals. He recognizes that they are capable of self-deception, self-awareness, and self-transformation. Freud's posthumanist theory of self offers a less reified, essentialized, and teleological view of the self than the postclassical formulations discussed in chapters 6 and 7.

Freud's multidimensional self also offers resources for escaping the intellectual logjams generated by humanist and social science discourses on self, and this can aid us in responding to the challenges and difficulties of contemporary life in the West. Besieged by the heterogeneous and often conflicting demands in our complex, fast-paced, ever-changing world, we need to address these gaps in theories of the self and provide tools for transforming selfhood.

Because Freud's novel conception of the self coexists with and is sometimes only tacitly or germinally present in his nominal theory, his radical insights have to be distilled from the sometimes antiquated conceptions that surround them, namely, reductionistic and mechanistic notions about self. After presenting Freud's view of the self, I conclude this chapter by briefly reflecting on how Freud's posthumanist method can keep Freudian theory honest.

In the preface to *The Ego and the Id*, perhaps the locus classicus of his conception of selfhood, Freud (1923b) acknowledges that his theory "does not go beyond the roughest outline." To avoid potential misunderstanding, one point needs to be underscored at the outset. Psychoanalytic listening and theorizing, in my view, involve the fluid utilization of a variety of explanatory narratives rather than the single-minded adoption of a singular framework or model of the mind. Most conceptions of what humans are and explanations of how they came to be that way fall victim to the *pars pro toto* fallacy—claiming that one superordinate cause (biology, family, distorted cognition, environment, etc.) determines what we have become. Freud himself sometimes engaged in such reductionistic theorizing. In dividing the self into three parts, reason (the ego), wishes, desires and instincts (the id), and conscience (the super-ego)—an apparently simplistic schema—Freud's conception appears to illustrate such reductionistic thinking. But when we defamiliarize the concepts of id, ego, and super-ego and consider them afresh, without the distorting lens of either knee-jerk devaluation or uncritical deification, an exemplary, multidimensional model of human development and self-structionalization emerges. Freud presents a variegated account of the development, nature, and determinants of human selfhood.

One does not have to subscribe to Freud's specific concepts or descriptions (I do not) to recognize that a theory of selfhood cannot afford to neglect, as most contemporary conceptions do, the determinants and aspects of subjectivity mentioned earlier. Each of these facets of selfhood must be addressed (even if one sees them differently from Freud) in order to comprehend the complexity of a person.

Freud's investigative method consists of a transformative context and a special methodology for investigating and illuminating conscious and unconscious aspects of human subjectivity. The context is the self-reflexive dialogue of analyst and analysand; the methodology is the special way of speaking and listening in which the analysand and the analyst engage. The analysand "free associates" or says whatever comes to mind without concern for social propriety or logical coherence.[3] The analyst listens to the analysand with a special quality of heightened attentiveness that Freud (1912a) termed "evenly-hovering attention."

The analytic situation and the methodological principle of speaking and listening with a minimum of constraints and preconceptions create an altered state of consciousness for both analyst and analysand, one akin to an imaginative, dreamlike state. This encourages the optimal emergence of the patient's characteristic patterns of seeing and relating to herself and others as well as the analyst's capacity for creative listening. Although this process is literally unpredictable, it often has a similar result —optimally disclosing hidden facets of the analysand's subjective world.

Because the analysand is less concerned with logical consistency, social decorum, self-judgments, pride, and shame, her thinking and speech take on a more spontaneous and unfettered form. This opens up the possibility of experiencing previously hidden aspects of herself. The patient's discourse is not transparent and lacks a self-evident meaning. The analyst's conception of the analysand is shaped, at least in part, by the analyst's own theoretical models and desires. The Freudian method thus leads not to the Truth about who the patient Really Is but to a variety of ways—including formerly unconscious ones—of conceiving of her life. The recurrent unconscious principles and patterns of relating to self and other from the patient's past that shape and delimit her, or her *transference*, then appear with greater clarity.

In recommending that the analyst listen afresh to the patient and her associations—and, as it were, dream along with the analysand—the Freudian method can destabilize "fixed" theories, including Freudian ones. When the analyst's understandings of the patient's material emerge out of the mutual dialogue between analyst and analysand, rather than the therapist's a priori knowledge and authority, a nonauthoritarian psychoanalytic climate is promoted and the analyst is encouraged to have a less narcissistic relationship to his or her theories and practices.[4]

Contradictions, gaps, inconsistencies, and displacements in the taken-for-granted narrative that the analysand brings to analysis are more readily recognized when the analyst listens in this way to the analysand's free associations. As alternative conceptions of one's life become possible, one's sense of one's self becomes more complex and less rigid and one-sided (Schafer, 1992). This alters the analysand's sense of her past as well as enriching the possibilities for her present and future. When excessive and inappropriate guilt or shame are, for example, analytically questioned and ultimately mitigated, one may exchange a life lived under an oppressive cloud for an undreamt of sense of freedom. Or, as the unconscious apathy or passivity resulting from disclaimed responsibility for one's life becomes more conscious, a greater sense of personal responsibility and agency may flourish.

The psychoanalytic situation and method I have briefly described led to Freud's second great legacy—a novel and radical conception of human selfhood. That Freud offers us a unique and profound way of thinking about human beings might initially appear to be a strange claim. His famous "anatomy of the soul" (Freud 1923b)—the structural model of the mind—in which processes such as desiring/wishing, perceiving/adapting, and self-judging/self-punishing are made into tangible, spatially localized entities (id, ego, and super-ego), has been severely criticized for its mechanism and reductionism (Schafer, 1976; Stolorow & Atwood, 1979). A main thrust of Freudian theorizing, notes Robert Holt (1975), is Freud's *"mechanistic image"* of persons, in which each person is "best understood as a machine or *apparatus*, composed of ingenious *mecha-*

*nisms*, operating according to Newton's laws of motion, and understandable without residue in terms of physics and chemistry" (p. 19).[5]

But when Freud's often maligned conception of the self is approached in a Freudian manner, that is, with an interest in what is unconsciously conveyed, then what emerges is a radical and multidimensional perspective on the development and structuralization of human subjectivity. This may become clearer when we reexamine and defamiliarize Freud's concepts of id, ego, and super-ego. It is worth reiterating what I mentioned in the introduction, namely, that the *implications* of Freud's work on selfhood often exceed the particular *intentions* he had in formulating specific ideas about it.

Freud (1923b) stated that "we are 'lived' by unknown and uncontrollable forces" (p. 23). He termed this facet of mental life *das Es*, or "the It," which English translators have rendered as the "id." "The It" may better convey Freud's attempt to depict the impersonal, inherited, somatically based, and irrational parts of our experience—the "dark, inaccessible part of our personality" (1933d, p. 23), which "contains everything that is present at birth, that is fixed in the constitution . . . which originate[s] from the somatic organization and which find[s] a first expression here [in the id] in forms unknown to us" (1940, p. 145). The concept of the id signifies that for Freud, the body, desires, wishes, and self-unconsciousness play a central role in the development and functioning of the self. The subjective meaning these facets of self-experience have in a particular human life tend to be insufficiently attended to in contemporary discourse on selfhood.[6]

*Das Ich*, which English translators have rendered as the "ego," is used in two senses in Freud's corpus: it designates the person as a whole, including her body, and a "particular part of the mind characterized by special attributes and functions" (1923b, p. 7). The ego is the "coherent organization of mental processes" (p. 17) within each individual. It "represents what may be called reason and common sense" (p. 25) and is responsible for supervising "all its constituent processes" (p. 17). It is "essentially the representative of the external world, of reality" (p. 36), and "tries to mediate between the world and the id, to make the id pliable to the world" (p. 56). It is like a "constitutional monarch without whose sanction no law can be passed but who hesitates long before imposing his veto on any measure put forward by Parliament" (p. 55). The ego is that dimension of persons capable of adapting to or coping with internal and external phenomena. In relation to the id, Freud likened the ego to "a man on horseback, who has to hold in check the superior strength of the horse" (p. 25).

Unconsciousness flourishes in this realm of experience, as in any other. "It looks, as though his own self were no longer the unity which he had considered it to be," notes Freud (1926b), "as though there were something else as well in him that could confront that self" (p. 188). Freud's (1917b) radical insight that we are not masters of our own mind emerges out of this discovery. We may, for example, be unaware of certain self-protective strategies that we utilize to ward off emotionally painful perceptions or that impede or distort our judgments.

The ego develops from two sources: it is "first and foremost a body-ego" (Freud 1923b, p. 26), derived from bodily sensations, as well as *identifications* with images of significant others. When, for example, we lose someone who is important to us, we internally identify with that person by retaining an image of him or her. The ego is composed in part of such "substitutions" and identifications: the "character of the ego is a precipitate of abandoned object-cathexes and . . . it contains the history of those object-choices" (p. 29).

The importance of reason, adaptation, and the capacity for self-transformation is depicted in the notion of the ego. It allows Freud to posit a self that is capable of modification in mitigating the conscious and unconscious forces that influence it.

What Freud termed *das Über-Ich*, or "super-ego," is our conscience and our inherited standards, ideals, values, and injunctions—some of which are unconscious—which are derived from parental and cultural influences and ideals, including religious teachings, schooling, and readings. It is composed of commandments and prohibitions and provides internal "guidelines for morally acceptable behavior" (Freud 1923b, p. 29). It might be viewed as our "self-guiding" and "self-punishing" tendencies (Stolorow & Atwood, 1979, p. 184).

The origins of the super-ego are both "historical" and "biological"—stemming from, respectively, "the lengthy duration in man of his childhood helplessness and dependence, and the fact of his Oedipus complex" (Freud 1923b, p. 35), and the "phylogenetic acquisition of each individual—his archaic heritage" (p. 36).

The super-ego is heir to the Oedipus complex. As the child renounces affectionate feelings and wishes toward the opposite-sex parent and hostility toward the same-sex one, she or he identifies with the values of the latter. The general outcome of this process is "the forming of a precipitate in the ego . . . an ego-ideal or super-ego" (1923b, p. 34). The concept of the super-ego thus conveys Freud's awareness that selfhood cannot be understand apart from one's history and one's family. The self, in this formulation, is irreducibly historical, social, and familial. Our ideals and fears, hopes and afflictions arise and are perpetuated in specific relational contexts.[7]

Freud's theory of the self is not without certain problems. It has androcentric biases (Flax, 1990) and a reductionistic account of desire (subsuming it to biology). It neglects cultural differences in consciences (Roland, 1988). The impact on self-experience of pre-Oedipal mothering, gender, and post-Oedipal identifications not based on fear or danger are also eclipsed. Shorn of its reifications, mechanism, and reductionism, however, it is still of greater complexity and scope than any other contemporary theory of selfhood. It suggests to an exemplary extent some of the crucial ingredients for conceiving of self-experience.

Freud presents a multidimensional view of the origins, nature, and determinants of human selfhood that contains a sense of self-complexity and heterogeneity missing from most humanist and antihumanist accounts (Flax, 1990). His model acknowledges that human motivation is shaped by multiple internal and external forces, including the body, history, the family, culture, relationships, ideals, desires, fantasies, guilt, self-unconsciousness, internal conflicts, and reason (Flax, 1990). He realizes that we are conflicted beings capable of self-deception and enslavement, self-awareness and freedom.

Freud's view of the self offers a complex and nuanced conception of freedom that takes into account the partial insights about emancipation and determinism of the humanist and antihumanist viewpoints, respectively, while refusing both the illusory belief in self-mastery of the former and the totalistic, nihilistic image of human enslavement in the latter. In illuminating the pervasiveness of unconscious aspects of human subjectivity—the way we are not masters of our own minds—Freud's writings (e.g., 1917b) challenge the naiveté of humanist conceptions of the self-dominion of a unified, rational, free subject and are a testament to the human capacity for self-deception and the delimited nature of human freedom. Here Freud is aligned with antihumanist critiques of humanism's belief in self-unity, self-transparency, and self-awareness.

But in simultaneously acknowledging the human capacity for self-awareness, insight, agency, and self-transformation—which are insufficiently acknowledged in most antihumanist writings—Freud counters potentially nihilistic poststructuralist claims about the essential psychological impotence and enslavement of humans and enlarges the range of human freedom even as he demonstrates that we greatly exaggerate its scope. Freud suggests that we are simultaneously determined by our histories *and* capable of choice and self-modification. Conceiving of the self as both *created* (by the way we live in the present) and *found* (by investigating our past), a *multidimensional self* would offer a less reified, essentialized, and teleological view of the self than the postclassical formulations discussed in chapters 6 and 7.

Freud's theory of the self respects features of subjectivity highlighted by humanists and antihumanists, respectively—such as freedom *and* determinism, psychic agency *and* enslavement—while also avoiding some of the excesses and blind spots of each conception. In perceiving self-disunity without jettisoning agency, affirming psychological overdetermination without falling victim to nihilism, acknowledging determinism and history[8] without eclipsing freedom and responsibility, valuing the body without neglecting the mind, and recognizing rationality without eliminating individuality, Freud's multidimensional self offers resources for escaping the intellectual cul-de-sac that social science and humanist discourses on subjectivity have generated. It can also better help us deal with the enormous complexities and challenges of postmodern life in the West, where we need to be attuned to the self's complexity and fluidity.

As we reflect on the other part of the epoch-making inheritance he left us—his novel *posthumanist* investigative method—we see that Freud's legacy transcended the unique conception of selfhood he offered. Freud's method is *post*humanist because it offers tools to challenge its own foundations, thereby going beyond the humanist tradition it grew out of (and still draws on). In other words, it goes where no self-respecting Cartesian ever goes. But it does not merely provide a way of putting its own conclusions under erasure (*sous rature*)—simultaneously advancing and problematizing its own assertions. Rather, it is post*humanist* or post-poststructuralist because it can demythologize its own favored formulations without devolving into nihilism or narcissism. A posthumanist method retains a belief in rationality and the capacity for self transformation even as it engages in self-deconstruction. The tools Freud bequeathed to us for fostering an exemplary kind of intellectual self-reflexivity and openness facilitate an analyst's capacity to be more open to, and thus more readily hear, clinical data that might destabilize and ultimately usurp any settled psychoanalystic theory—including sacred Freudian ones.

Conceptions of the self are not universal or transhistorical. Each era produces particular configurations of self that can be viewed, in part, as reflections of, and tactics for dealing with, specific historical, psychological, and sociocultural conditions endemic to that age (Levin, 1987). Universalizing *any* conception of selfhood will necessarily eclipse newly emerging facets of self-experience that have not yet entered any theoretical lexicon. The increasing attention in the social sciences to the impact of gender, race, and social class on identity, for example, signals an important lacuna in Freud's view of selfhood. The particular Freudian *theory* of self that I have enumerated in this chapter may thus have great potential for addressing certain thorny issues in contemporary discourse (even as it might itself need revision). Freudian *method*, however, encourages a capacity to be open to conceptions of self that are not yet named or experienced and that may eventually emend or displace even Freud's suggestive formulations. With its openness to the new forms of life that each person potentially presents in psychoanalysis and its capability for on-going theoretical self-transformation, Freud's interrogative method is, in my view, one of the seminal contributions to twentieth-century thought and human self-understanding.

Let us reflect critically on several facets of this chapter. The differentiation between Freud's *theory*, his "theorizing about mind," and his *method*, his "working with mind" (Lothane, 1981, p. 349), may be heuristic; but Freud's theories (his viewpoints and doctrines *about* mind, culture, history, and civilization) and his methods (his operationalizable techniques for investigating mental activity) both are *and* are not separate. The tangible difference between Freud's theories and methods suggests that theory and method should be seen as conceptually distinct. But the fact that changes in analytic theory often foster changes in method and vice versa suggests that they are *also* interrelated. With the ascendancy of various relational *theories* of human development and treatment, for example, the therapeutic setting and relationship, as well free association, "evenly-hovering attention," and the interpretation of unconscious material, have increasingly been viewed as essential facets of psychoanalytic method. This demonstrates that theory can and often does alter method.

Method, like theory, is not a singular thing. My account of Freud's method highlights the special way of speaking and listening that he bequeathed us (rather than a particular sort of relationship) that may be more central to a one-person/body theory of psychoanalysis than to my relational perspective. As countertransference and the analyst's subjectivity take on greater importance in analysis, the analytic relationship and the analyst's participation as a *subject*, rather than an object or receptacle for the patient's projections and distortions, becomes more central to psychoanalytic method. This is neglected in Freud's method.

Let me suggest a promising line of future inquiry in this area, namely, the need for new psychoanalytic methods to address the unique problems patients confront in our postmodern world. In the next chapter I explore another overlooked facet of method—the analyst's creative use of imagination. Every method is designed to solve a particular problem (Dan Inosanto, personal communication). Freud's archaeological method of unburying censored and disavowed psychic contents through free association and "evenly-hovering attention" might have been wonderfully suited to strategically counteract the self-inhibition and repression fostered by nineteenth-century Victorian European culture, a strait-laced, stratified, patriarchal society permeated by hypocracy and moral duplicity, including double standards for men and women, depriving marriages, and sexual inhibition and guilt (Janik & Toulmin, 1973). Detecting the hidden meaning of experience is important in a cultural context pervaded by mystification and inhibitions. But might the different exigencies and problems patients (and analysts) now confront require a revised or at least supplemented psychoanalytic method? The methods of promoting self-delineation, enriching personal subjectivity, and facilitating the aliveness and personal integrity of analytic patients in the work of Sandor Ferenczi, D. W. Winnicott, and Heinz Kohut, as well as various contemporary Freudians, self psychologists, object relations theorists, interpersonalists, and intersubjectivists, might be more useful for besieged, disconnected, impoverished, devitalized analysands in our unsettling world than methods fostering self-disinhibition and self-control that were central to Freud and many of his followers.

I have privileged method over theory in this chapter. One way of deconstructing the hierarchical relationship between method and theory that I have posited is to reverse the relation that exists between them in my discourse and explore how analytic *theory* might enrich analytic method.[9]

Neither psychoanalysis nor postmodern discourse has provided us with fulfilling images of the self after analysis. We are left with incomplete and unsatisfying pictures such as "integration," "adaptation," the genital character, and the "depressive position" (e.g., Bollas, 1997, p. 50). Psychoanalysis needs different theories of self—theories that elude reifying and reductionistic trends; that value emergent and evolving as well as fixed and determinate facets of selfhood; and that are polyphonic or many-sided, rather than monological or one-dimensional. We might then see the self as an orchestra composed of a variety of instruments—consciousness and unconsciousness, self-centeredness and selflessness, rationality and imagination, unity and diversity, authenticity and inauthenticity, ambitiousness and aimlessness—each with its own idiosyncratic sound and application. The self is impoverished if certain instruments are not played. The best music occurs when no instrument dominates or is excluded, and when there is communication and cross-fertilization among them (Rubin, 1996b).

*Posthumanist* methods—critical yet affirmative, dialogic and evolutionary—offer a way of exploring self-experience that encourages us to experience its multidimensionality. This can aid besieged selves-at-risk in addressing the epistemological and moral complexity they confront in a world in which foundational realities and rationalities are challenged, subjects experience multiple and sometimes conflicting self-states, and the claims of otherness coexist with the need to take care of the self.[10]

# 10

## The Psychoanalyst and Freedom

> The patient should be educated to liberate and fulfill his own
> nature, not to resemble ours.
> —Sigmund Freud, "Lines of Advance
> in Psycho-Analytic Therapy"

> To develop, it is necessary to liberate ourselves from our parents,
> our analysts, and our teachers.
> —John Klauber, *Difficulties in the Analytic Encounter*

The analyst's freedom of thought and practice is an essential
and neglected facet of psychoanalytic treatment and cure. It fosters the
analyst's creative participation in the treatment, and this in turn facilitates
the possibility of the patient's freedom. This chapter explores a hidden
enslavement that psychoanalytic practice—even in its contemporary revisionist forms—is prone to, namely, the analyst's narcissistic attachment
to or overinvestment in the validity of his or her own favored theories
and practices. This predilection pervades every school of psychoanalysis.
Each analytic tradition, as I argued in chapter 4, has treated certain methods as sacred, which renders them immune to feedback and critique. We
can neither transcend nor afford to become captive to the practices that
we value. Meditating on this hidden bondage opens up a more fluid relationship to our practice, a freedom-within-structure, in which we continually reflect on the practices that we employ so that they can evolve
based on corrective feedback. Such evolutionary practices foster both the
analyst's and the patient's freedom.

Freedom has an ambivalent position in psychoanalysis. With its recognition of the pervasiveness of human unconsciousness, transference,
and psychological determinism, psychoanalysis is a testament to the circumscribed nature of human freedom. Unconscious processes, as Freud

taught us in may ways, determine our conscious mental life (e.g., 1915b; 1916–17). Yet, psychoanalysis can also enlarge the range of human freedom, even as it demonstrates that we greatly exaggerate its scope. With its simultaneous sensitivity to determinism and the potential for self-transformation, ethical complexity, and moral accountability, Freud's "deterministic psychology of freedom" (Gay, 1990, p. 89) offers the *possibility* of a unique perspective on freedom that avoids the pitfalls pervading both popular and more academic discussions of this topic.

In terms of the latter, psychoanalysis's complex and nuanced conception of freedom refuses, for example, the false and disabling polarities structuring humanistic and social science discourse—namely, the illusory belief in self-mastery of the Cartesian/Sartrean tradition and the nihilistic image of human enslavement authorized in much poststructuralist writings. Psychoanalysis casts grave doubt on the utility of a Sartrean voluntarism that might exaggerate our autonomy and self-control or a poststructuralist pessimism that sees little daylight in the tunnel of human possibility. If the pervasiveness of human unconsciousness renders belief in unbridled freedom suspect, then the profound changes patients and analysts may experience in psychoanalysis challenge the unmitigated enslavement antihumanist, poststructuralist writings too often treat as gospel. Freud manages to neither neglect the determinism pervading human life nor the possibility of rationality, choice, and self-transformation.

Contemporary popular discourse on social issues generally oscillates between two narrow options: a politics of blame or a politics of victimization and irresponsibility. If many conservative politicians and social commentators have demonized the underclass (as if a single African-American woman on welfare is a sign and cause of our collective moral malaise), then many liberal ones have endorsed a culture of complaint that deflects attention from issues of ethical responsibility. Those who emphasize the importance of responsibility tend to be punitive, while those who are alert to the role causes may play in human conduct encourage nonaccountability. In recognizing that we are both responsible *and* determined,[1] psychoanalysis at its best offers a model of compassionate, nonpunitive accountability. In this model, one does not excessively blame the victimized or disregard psychological or sociocultural circumstances that may have played a formative role in their conduct, nor does one disclaim responsibility for behavior and exculpate the accused (e.g., the Menendez brothers killed their parents *because* they were abused by them).

But the radical potential of the psychoanalytic conception of freedom —and the liberation it might engender—often remains unrealized because of an unresolved tension in psychoanalysis between its liberating and constricting tendencies. These are embodied in its emancipatory interrogation of *and* enslaving conformity to its own theories and practices. Too often, the capacity of psychoanalysts to self-correctively expand analytic concepts in light of what they learn from patients, and thus promote self-transformation and expansion, is subverted by their tendency to fit analysands (and themselves) into established psychoanalytic theories and procedures, which can foster self-imprisonment.

The Freudian theory of dream practice illustrates the constricting and liberating dimensions of psychoanalytic practice. It also sheds light on what obstructs and facilitates freedom in the analyst, and it has important implications for the psychoanalyst's relation to his or her own theories and practices. Recognizing the tension between these two facets of dream practice elucidates how the emancipatory possibilities within Freudian practice might be tapped so that the conservative and constricting tendencies within Freudian theory do not enslave us.[2]

## The Freudian Theory of Dream Practice

Dream interpretation is the process by which the latent meaning of dreams is illuminated. According to Freud (1900), previous investigators adopted one of two typical approaches to dream interpretation: they assumed that there was a singular symbolic meaning to a dream as a whole or utilized a fixed key for decoding the meaning of a dream (pp. 96–97). In the latter view, the "decoding method," dreams are treated as "a kind of cryptography in which each sign can be translated into another sign having a known meaning, in accordance with a fixed key" (p. 97). Freud challenges the legitimacy of this approach because it does not realize that "the same piece of content may conceal a different meaning when it occurs in various people or various contexts" (p. 105) and "every element in a dream can, for purposes of interpretation, stand for its opposite just as easily as for itself" (p. 471).

The meaning of a dream, according to Freud, is arrived at not by translating dream material into the a priori meaning and "fixed-key" of a "dream-book," but by eliciting the dreamer's unique associations. Freud's method "imposes the task of interpreting upon the dreamer himself [or herself]. It is not concerned with what occurs to the interpreter in connection with a particular element of the dream, but with what occurs to the dreamer" (1900, p. 98 n. 1).

An important exception to this occurs when the analyst determines that the dream contains what Freud terms *symbols*, by which he means certain elements of the dream that indirectly represent latent dream thoughts, which are not derived from the day residue, are not revealed by free association, and must be decoded by the *analyst*.

> As contrasted with other dream-elements, a fixed meaning may be attributed to them [symbols] . . . since we know how to translate these symbols and the dreamer does not . . . it may happen that the sense of a dream may at once become clear to us as we have heard the text of the dream, even before we have made any effort at interpreting it, while it still remains an enigma to the dreamer himself. (1933d, pp. 12–13)

"The concept of a symbol," Freud (1916–17) admits,

> cannot at present be sharply delimited; it shades off into such notions as those of replacement or representation, and even approaches that of an illusion. . . . You see, then, that a symbolic relation is a comparison of a quite special kind, of which we do not as yet clearly grasp the basis, though perhaps we may later arrive at some indication of it. (P. 152)

Freud recommends a "combined technique" when dealing with "those elements of the dream-content which must be recognized as symbolic" (1900, p. 353). The "combined technique," on the one hand, "rests on the dreamer's associations"; and on the other hand, "it fills the gap from the interpreter's knowledge of symbols" (ibid.).

Freud does not specify *how* the analyst knows that a given portion of the dream is a *symbol*, rather than something that needs to be examined anew using the associative method (Lansky, 1992b, p. 13). He also does not offer any criteria to validate such a decision. That this can open the door to interpretive confusion is suggested by his acknowledgment that "the presence of symbols in dreams not only facilitates their interpretation but also makes it more difficult" (1900, p. 352). One important difficulty is hermeneutical reductionism, by which I mean that the analyst, to use Freud's image in a different but compatible context, "interprets *into*" the analysand's utterances what cannot be interpreted *from* them and thus assimilates the uniqueness of the dream material into the "fixed meaning" of his or her nomothetic lexicon.

Both the analyst and the analysand in Freud's *theory* of dream interpretation illustrate the conflict between a wish-to-know and a wish-*not*-
to-know. The analysand's censorship in the dream work and his or her
resistance to the decoding of the manifest dream imagery illustrate the
reluctance to know, while the analysand's presentation of and associations to the dream illustrate the urge to know.

Freud's dream *practice*—his interpretive work with his own dreams—
also partakes of this simultaneous seeing and *not*-seeing. In his unprecedented openness in revealing and reflecting on his dreams and inner life,
he inaugurates a radical deepening of the centuries-old Augustinian tradition of self-examination—while also concealing important information
and associations from his writings on dreams, as the infamous specimen
dream of Irma illustrates, which forecloses more extensive understanding
of his psychic life. "The celebrated 'specimen dream,' " as Melvin Lansky
(1992b) notes,

> is analyzed only to the point of demonstrating that the associative method
> leads to Freud's preconscious preoccupation concerning the circumstances
> of Irma's mishandled treatment and especially with exculpating himself in
> the eyes of his colleagues in the face of charges of incompetence. Schur
> (1966) has pointed out that even the aspects of the day residue concerning
> Freud's protection of and his competitiveness with Wilhelm Fliess—con-
> vincingly evident from his correspondence to Fliess at the time—have not
> been revealed in the text of *The Interpretation of Dreams* at all. (P. 5)

Describing the difficulty of analyzing Goethe, in words that I believe are
autobiographical, Freud (1930) remarked: "This is because Goethe was
not only, as a poet, a great self-revealer, but also, in spite of the abundance
of autobiographical records, a careful concealer" (p. 212). Freud, like his
beloved Goethe, was a "careful concealer" who hid the import of his
dreams both by failing to associate to crucial elements and periodically
translating dreams into the "fixed-key" of formulaic symbols.

The Freudian theory of dream practice—with its clashing conceptions
of the associational and symbolic approach to the ideographic dream
material—both illustrates and provides resources for transforming the
tension between the constricting and liberating dimensions of psychoanalysis. The presumption that the analyst can ascertain that particular
material in a dream is *symbolic*, and therefore can be interpreted without
the dreamer's associations, funnels the radically novel content of the
dream into the preexisting categories of the *analyst's* dream meanings—

the "fixed key" of his or her personal "dream book"—and thus prevents the uniqueness of the analysand's subjectivity from fully emerging. It also reinstitutes the very lexical method of dream interpretation that Freud elsewhere eschews (e.g. Lansky, 1992b, p. 13) and thus paves the way for an authoritarian analytic ambience in which the analyst possesses the Truth, to be dispensed to the passive patient. This sort of approach usually promotes a narcissistic and imprisoning investment in one's own theories; when we believe we possess the Truth, we tend to aggrandize and excessively identify with our own beliefs and to discount the potential value of alternative ways of thinking. Our privileged notions then become immunized from questions or challenges.

"Free-association," according to Adam Phillips (1993), in a view that seems to have a consensual acceptance in psychoanalysis, is "the heart of psychoanalytic treatment" (p. 3). In recommending that the analyst listen afresh to the dreamer's associations, the associational approach helps the unique meanings of the analysand's dream material emerge and opens up the possibility of experiencing previously hidden aspects of the patient's subjectivity.

Is it any wonder that many analysts—myself included—agree with Freud's (1931b) claim that the patient's free associating, as well as its complement, the analyst's evenly-hovering attention, is "the methodological key" (pp. 402–3) to psychoanalysis? But if free association and evenly-hovering attention can encourage the expression of disavowed and neglected thoughts, feelings, and fantasies and can challenge our familiar and narrow narratives about ourselves and thereby open up unforeseen possibilities in living, then why do our ideological preferences seem to be left intact so much of the time? Why, in other words, do Jungians see archetypes rather than interpersonal reenactments? Why do self psychologists tend to find self-defects or missing selfobjects functions rather than compromise formations? The fact that the ideological preferences analysts start with are so tenacious and self-revision is so difficult suggests that it might be prudent to reexamine whether free association or evenly-hovering attention offer an infallible, unmediated contact with ourselves or others.

Let us consider the treatment of a woman I shall call Arlene, a kind, highly intelligent, depressed, lonely single woman in her early fifties, who experienced profound emptiness and meaninglessness in her life. She likened herself to an "empty space" and "void" and indicated that she did not feel that she had a life that was her own. Her life was permeated by compliance and submission to the needs of others. What *she* wanted lacked significance for her, and often for those she became involved with. She felt deeply unfulfilled and adrift, damaged and "inherently unfixable." Arlene not only did not have a life, she did not even feel entitled to having one.

This was not surprising, given what we knew about her family background and childhood. Her family was a parent-centered home in which she felt invisible. Arlene was a twin who felt that she had no independent emotional life. She experienced a "twinship" with her mother as well as her sister. In her relationship with her competent, highly self-absorbed, and unintrospective mother, she felt a mandate to be the sort of person her mother wanted her to be. Arlene felt that with her mother everything but her came first and that she was not important or special in her mother's eyes. The price of connectedness to her mother was to lose herself. To not conform to what her mother wanted was to jeopardize the relationship.

Her father was a highly competent, stern, and inaccessible executive who was much more interested in work than in his family. Arlene experienced her father as a self-absorbed presence who was rude and abrasive to others—including his daughter, whom he saw as inferior. He constantly criticized and rebuked Arlene and did not affirm her identity in any way.

Arlene put her parents on a pedestal (which also entailed devaluing herself) so as to retain an emotional tie to them. One salient form that this took was the unquestioned belief that her parents' way of living— denying feelings and treating others as means rather than as ends—was "natural" and correct. "If my parents' way of living didn't work for me," Arlene assumed, "then something must be wrong with *me.*" One of the mystifying aspects of her relationship with her parents was the notion they inculcated in her, and she uncritically accepted, that things "come naturally to people": that one just accomplishes tasks, has relationships, masters avocational pursuits without learning, experimentation, failure, risk, and effort. Her experience of not being able to do things—have relationships, learn new hobbies, and so forth—was doubly difficult for her because her parents (1) did not teach her how to think about these things *and* (2) taught her that it all comes naturally.

Arlene experienced herself as a "force driven by habit out of control." Her life oscillated between self-neglecting and depriving connections with others and painful social isolation, both of which left her feeling deprived, invisible, self-doubting, and directionless. Her relationships were usually stamped by a self-abnegating attention to the needs of the other. Adopting a "negative identity" of being nonjudgmental and nondiscriminating— so as to not be critical and "elitist" like her father—led to her "flowing" with the needs and demands of others rather than considering and respecting what she felt and needed. She habitually got involved with self-centered men who seemed uninterested in her emotional needs. She was left feeling neglected and deprived.

Her unsplendid isolation was what she termed a "survival mechanism," designed to protect her against interpersonal exploitation, self-loss, disappointment, and deprivation. Isolation and hyperindependence enabled her to deny her needs and ensure that she would not be connected to others and nullified. It also resulted in a life of pervasive inhibition, minimal risk, lacunae in experience and skills, and a painful sense of emptiness.

Arlene saw life as one of two deadly options: relatedness to others, which resulted in self-loss; *or* disconnection from others, which generated profound deprivation. Socially withdrawn, emotionally and spiritually unfulfilled, she felt a pervasive hopelessness about ever having a meaningful and fulfilling life. In fact, such a life for her seemed like an impossibility.

Toward the end of a session in which Arlene had begun to realize that neglecting her own needs contributed to her sense of pessimism about having a meaningful life, she expressed appreciation for the changes she had recently experienced in treatment. She indicated that she was definitely learning to listen to and trust her own feelings instead of simply reacting to the needs of others. This gave her more of a sense of "choice." But she felt "slightly self-indulgent" coming to treatment. After all, she continued, in a tone we had come to associate with her father, what good was it to talk about the further changes that she wished to make, such as reacting less to the demands of others and developing more of a direction in her life? She just needed to do it, to *act*. She valued treatment, but what of value, she wondered, had really happened in today's session?

Arlene had said this sort of thing several times in the year or so that we had been working together, especially after she had undergone some important growth or there had been a disruption in the treatment because of either a vacation or some misunderstanding on my part. I had taken different tacks at different times depending on a range of factors including the state of the transference-countertransference and what seemed to have greatest motivational saliency at a particular clinical moment. We had generated various possible meanings and purposes through free association and evenly hovering attention. At certain times, unconscious themes and conflicts regarding fear of psychic growth and individuation seemed most germane. At other times, her pessimism seemed to embody pre-and postlinguistic *moods* of sadness and hopelessness. We had wondered whether she was treating herself the way her father had treated her or unconsciously re-creating frustrating and depriving relations with her parents. Sometimes she seemed to be maintaining a link with her depriving past so as to keep alive the faint hope that she might eventually gain acceptance and love from her distant and self-involved parents. And finally, it sometimes appeared as if I was cast in the role of her father and she was turning the tables on me by maintaining the status quo. Even though we had generated a good deal of insight about the possible sources and function of her pessimism, it had not really impacted on either her pessimism or the possibilities for a meaningful and fulfilling life.

I was intrigued by Arlene's assessment of the session because from my perspective something very important *had* happened on an emotional level, although I was aware that she still felt trapped in a life that felt empty. As I reflected on Arlene's remarks about the insignificance of the session, I asked myself what function it might serve for her self to experience the session in a pessimistic way. I then said to her: "Since it feels impossible to imagine a world in which you are central and your needs are valued by you and those close to you, does it seem that it is irrelevant to even talk about your pessimism let alone work on it?" "I feel," she replied, "that it will never happen. I am just now realizing that I have an investment in my pessimism; in keeping it alive. This is something that I have never thought about."

It was something that neither of us had thought about until I had the freedom to imagine—and then share with Arlene—an image of a mode of being that she (like the Winnicott of chapter 5 with his "incommunicado" core) may never have known, namely, non-self-annihilating connectedness, which opened up another way of being-in-the-world. In non-self-annihilating connectedness, which was different from the two deadly life-denying options that had structured and delimited her life and our work together up until this moment, one is neither related and nullified nor socially isolated and deprived. Rather, one is connected and enriched.

Arlene began the next session with a dream: "I was suddenly pregnant in the hospital having a baby. My sister was also delivering. I was sad that my baby was not alive. My sister's baby was okay—actually, she had twins, a girl and a boy."

After recounting the dream, Arlene began talking again about pessimism. "Pessimism allows me to maintain my lifestyle, which I'm attached to. It allows me to say: 'I'm a hermit/recluse.' " I eventually asked about her associations to pregnancy. "Being pregnant," she indicated, "is giving birth to optimism—it means giving up pessimism. I don't remember any *dead* baby in the dream—they said 'it didn't work out.' I never saw a trace of any dead baby." I asked her if she had experienced a life-long sense from those close to her—such as her parents [the "they" in her associations to the dream who told her "it didn't work out"?]—that things didn't work out for her, were not and could not be generative. Arlene added a pregnant alternative: "Or, I could be pregnant, but not with something of *mine*." I asked her if she experienced the options for her life as being either no pregnancy/generativity or a self-alienating pregnancy—giving "birth" to something that was not of/for her. She answered: "Yes. . . . I had dreams that I have never talked about in which I was trying to scream/communicate but I couldn't. Pessimism is acceptance: this is the ways things are and they won't change. No highs and lows but everything is manageable. This will hold me together. I don't get too low but I self-medicate [food, valium]." I asked if pessimism could be a kind of *mental* self-medication. She got sad and pensive. "I can remember when I looked forward to doing social things; when I felt bad if I was not included. There was a point in my life when I felt more human. It [social isolation] is a way of not rendering my self vulnerable. My parents were strong and dominant. They had no appreciation of differences; how I was different from them. Not to have any one see you as a child. That is so sad. I never realized that I was so deprived. I thought everyone had these feelings. I remember in grade school every night crying myself to bed. There was no outlet for it or talking about it. To fit in with my family you had to destroy it [negative feelings]. Like they are not there. Through talking with you I have come to see the importance of this. I was like a girl in a washing machine with a lot of starch. A starched girl."

She began the next session describing an encounter with a friend from out of town who told Arlene that she had never been listened to so well. "It came after our session where I felt deeply listened to by you. I was never aware that I felt I was never seen or heard by my parents. I just felt deprivation. A large part of that was that I was not seen for who I am by them, but for who they wanted me to be." Arlene ended the session speaking about her growing recognition of her reclusiveness and the way it protected against losing herself, which often happened when she was with others.

In the following session, she spoke about seeking out and talking with an interesting woman she met at a party and engaging in a long and satisfying conversation that felt authentic and interesting. She felt inspired by the woman's commitment to social justice and also felt a "sense of optimism" that she might eventually meet other like-spirited people. They exchanged phone numbers and agreed to keep in touch. It felt to Arlene like the "dawn of a new era."

"Every metapsychology," notes Edgar Levenson (1992), "contains the seeds of an incipient counter-transference" (p. 464). Exploring the roots and meanings of Arlene's pessimism through the methods of free association and evenly-hovering attention made it possible for us to understand various meanings and purposes of her hopelessness, including, for example, the way it gave her a stable identity, normalized her depriving past, and linked her to her parents while keeping alive the hope of finally gaining their acceptance and love. But the void and emptiness that permeated her life still remained. She still had glaring deficits in self-confidence, self-assertion, and relational skills and was unconsciously committed to perpetuating limited modes of being and relating deriving from the past.

The problem with the tendency to valorize free association (or evenly-hovering attention) as a royal (even if not exclusive) road to the patient's or analyst's unconscious, as I and others (e.g., Barratt, 1994) have done, is that it assumes what certain contemporary hermeneutically sympathetic analysts (Atwood & Stolorow, 1984; Goldberg, 1990), psychoanalytic social constructivists (Hoffman, 1991), philosophers (Rorty, 1979; 1982), historians (McNeill, 1986), anthropologists (Geertz, 1973; Clifford, 1988), and feminists (Harding & Hintikka, 1983), among many others, have taught us to be suspicious of, namely, immaculate perception. Observation and theorizing always occur in specific historical, sociocultural, linguistic, and psychological contexts that shape and delimit the methodology that is utilized, the questions that are asked (and not asked), and the conclusions that are drawn. There is thus no impartial or totalizing perspective from which to speak or listen, observe or theorize. Unfettered contact with oneself or another is therefore an illusion.

Free association is not, as I argued in the last chapter, really "free" (e.g., Spence, 1982). "The designation 'free'," notes Roy Schafer (1978), "makes sense only as referring to one's freeing oneself from the usual self-imposed constraints of verbal reasonableness, coherence, and decorum" (p. 70). While saying everything that comes to mind does lessen self-censorship, the diminishing of the patient's restraint is never complete.

Indelibly influenced by the analyst's personality and theories, the analyst's evenly-hovering attention is also not an infallible road to the patient's unconscious experience. If theory is what we *already* know about human experience, then it can actually filter the analyst's evenly-hovering attention and convert the potentially pluralistic universe of the patient into a psychic territory that has already been mapped. When analysts know beforehand what is important developmentally and therapeutically—and theory seems to legislate that the present must play second fiddle to knowledge from the past—then theory might be termed "phobic," that is, delimiting the field of theoretical possibilities by restricting where one can intellectually travel. When analysts endow a less threatening theoretical phenomenon with special significance so as to ward off anticipated danger unconsciously associated with focusing on more dangerous things, then theory might also be "fetishistic."[3] For all these reasons, the analyst's evenly-hovering attention *shapes* rather than simply records the patient's subjectivity.

Meaning is fashioned, not simply found. What we "hear" in the patient's material is not merely a representation of a world "out there" or "in here," but is continually co-created in the dialogue between analyst and analysand and shaped by such things as the analyst's personality and theoretical predilections. Evenly-hovering attention and free association are thereby *necessary* but insufficient aspects of psychoanalytic method. Free association and evenly-hovering attention have the capacity to resist closure and constriction, interminably question the foundation of one's thought and practices, and reveal the unmanifest, even as the theory-laden nature of listening and theorizing draws us toward the past—what we *already* know—and thus preempts the future.

The dawning recognition that there are various versions of the patient's life (Schafer, 1983) and that the analyst does not possess the Truth has generated a "crisis of confidence in psychoanalytic theorizing and a crisis of authority in the psychoanalyst's self-image" (Mitchell, 1993a, pp. 47–48) in contemporary psychoanalysis. There have been at least three responses to this crisis: empiricism, phenomenology, and social constructionism. Science is the final arbiter of truth and validity in the first perspective; the patient's experience is valorized in the second. The third viewpoint acknowledges the importance of the analyst's knowledge but recommends a reconceptualization of that knowledge. While empirical studies may challenge outmoded theories or suggest possible lines of future inquiry, they cannot serve as a court of final appeal to solve the crisis of confidence in analytic knowledge. Reversing the naive realism of Freud's day, phenomenologists point to the patient's subjective experience as a way of handling the crisis concerning the analyst's knowledge, granting the *analysand* rather than the analyst a privileged vantage point on the patient's experience. Phenomenologists such as Evelyn Schwaber have usefully highlighted the importance of understanding the patient's experience from within his or her own perspective. The analyst's theory, in this perspective, is often viewed as an impediment to understanding the patient's experience, which is presumed to be knowable directly. While the analyst's theory can be a huge barrier to understanding the patient, unmediated contact with the latter seems illusory. In the hermeneutical, constructivist, and constructionist perspective, apprehending experience involves organizing it rather than discovering it; analysts construct knowledge in terms of their ideas, beliefs, observations, and wishes. The analyst's shaping hand is thus a central and inevitable aspect of the treatment as well as a powerful tool for understanding the patient.

But it may not be sufficient to acknowledge one's shaping impact on psychoanalytic data. The issue of one's own *relation* to one's constructivist activities may need to be further elucidated in the constructivist perspective. Some years ago I attended a conference in which analysts representing a variety of schools of analytic thought, including classical psychoanalysis, ego psychology, object relations theory, interpersonal psychoanalysis, and self psychology, discussed the "same" clinical material, an excerpt from Paul Dewald's nearly verbatim account of an analysis. Evaluations of his work ranged from excellent to disastrous! It is not simply that each analyst presented a different version of Dewald's work, but that each perspective tended to naturalize and universalize itself, that is, present itself as corresponding to an independent reality that the analyst merely directly apprehended and reported.[4]

Given the unfortunate aspects of psychoanalytic history and politics discussed in previous chapters—such as orthodoxy and intolerance, the idolatry of certain figures and theories, the castigation of dissenting viewpoints, and the absence of self-reflectiveness about the validity of one's own theories—it is not surprising that the narcissism underlying psychoanalytic conceptions of self may also exist in our relation to our own theories. Undetected narcissism in a constructivist perspective could compromise its efficacy by generating an overinflated view of one's own constructions.

It is difficult to have an "analytic attitude" toward our own guiding frameworks when we overvalue them and underestimate (and often denigrate) the formulations of those from different perspectives. With its notion of *nonattactment*, or commitment with the capacity for continual dis-identification and self-transformation, Eastern meditative disciplines offers a less egocentric way of relating to our theories (Rubin, 1996b). There are intimations of this stance toward practices and theories in psychoanalysis at its self-reflexive best (e.g., Ferenczi, 1955; Winnicott, 1971; Kohut, 1984, pp. 202–3; Phillips, 1993; 1994).

A nonattached relation to our own formulations would foster recognition of the necessity *and* the inevitable contingency and partiality of our theories and practices. Our favored models and methods are no more final and uncontestable than they are dispensable. We can neither afford to overidentify with them and thereby imprison our capacity for self-modification and transformation, nor eschew them in a quixotic dream of a theory-free contact with our patients, ourselves, or the world. We cannot transcend our favored models and practices, but hopefully we are not blithely immersed in them either.

Acknowledging both the necessity and the provisionality of our concepts and methods fosters a never-ending reexamination and transformation of them that promotes a fluid awareness—what I would term a freedom-within-structure—which helps the analyst de-center from the frameworks of understanding she or he habitually utilizes. Freedom, in this perspective, always occur within a context of constraint. When we have a nongrasping commitment to, and a nonpossessive and nondefensive delight in, the concepts and methods that we value, we may develop a nonauthoritarian, nonnarcissistic, and unfettered relationship to our own theories.

A sense of freedom-within-structure can help the analyst utilize the neglected and liberatory logic of psychoanalysis—and that, in turn, can be freeing for both the analyst and the patient. When the analyst is liberated from the constraint of a suffocating relationship to his or her theories and practices, the patient is able to participate in the analysis in a freer way. When truth is neither the special province of the analyst nor an endpoint or static possession, the analysand is neither the handmaiden to the analyst's theoretical perspective nor a passive vessel waiting to have the (analyst's) truth poured in. Rather, the analysand becomes a partner engaged in a process of searching and self-creating. Such a therapeutic environment can encourage the analysand to be more self-trusting and playful; indeed, it can be empowering.

Of course, the analysand, like the analyst, is never so free. A patient's life, like all our lives, is, from a certain perspective, the compromised, unfree embodiment of an unconscious attempt at self-cure for the difficulties and strains of being a member of a particular family in a particular culture. If pathology is, in Stephen Mitchell's (1993a) evocative notion, a "failure of imagination," a "life that is stuck because old constraints foreclose the possibility of new experiences, new states of mind" (p. 222), then the analyst's freedom of imagination may be an essential—although not exclusive—facet of facilitating the patient's freedom. The analytic relationship might then be, as D. W. Winnicott, Hans Loewald, and Arnold Modell, among others, have suggested, a playground in which new ways of being might be generated.[5]

The stories I have told about psychoanalysis in earlier chapters highlight at least three restrictive habits of mind—perhaps even afflictions—in our field that curtail the analyst's imagination and thus inhibit the possibilities of treatment: (1) reified views of self such as the True Self and the bipolar self; (2) linear, noncomplex[6] views of causation that place most of the explanatory weight of pathology on formative experiences from the distant past and neglect the way pathology is often perpetuated and health is averted by the patient in the present;[7] and (3) a narcissistic relationship to our own theories.

As I became less attached to free association and evenly-hovering attention as privileged methodological principles and tools in my work with Arlene, I recognized that my own freedom of thought and responsiveness as an analyst had been constrained by the very methodology that had initially facilitated freedom. Something a martial artist and teacher once said to me—which I alluded to in the conclusion of the previous chapter—then became clearer: systems of thought and practice and the methods they utilize are designed to solve particular problems. A particular method may be quite useful, for example, in revealing buried experience in a culture that encourages inhibition. But when they are treated as idols (as I may have done with free association and evenly hovering attention) and their validity is universalized, then their value is compromised. Treating a method—even a heuristic method such as free association—that is applicable in a particular therapeutic context as a kind of Procrustean bed into which all experience is fitted fosters closed, congealed systems of thought and practice.

The idea of *open* and fluid systems of practice and thought—while perhaps enticing—seems like a psychoanalytic oxymoron. We have trouble conceiving of—let alone creating—systems that recognize their own essential contestability and contain the possibility of error-detection and self-modification. Such models recognize that the methods that one utilizes—no matter how cherished—are provisional and need to be open to, and deeply value, the potentially enriching facets of alternative, foreign practices. This spirit can help us recognize what is idiosyncratic and partial about our own preferred notions (Bernstein, 1992, p. 328), which encourages continuous reexamination and modification of the methods we employ. When we treat our favored theories and methods as provisional, we are less locked into any theory or practice and freer to creatively transform our training and our theoretical preferences. We might then practice a psychoanalytic art that was "open to all ways [yet] . . . bound by none" (Lee, 1986).

Psychoanalysis has identified two crucial kinds of self-pathology: an insufficiently structuralized self and a pathologically structuralized self (Atwood & Stolorow, 1984). For Freud, pathological structures such as hysteria were a recurrent problem. Because of its focus on pathological structures, psychoanalysis, as I suggested in chapters 6 and 7, has often neglected and insufficiently elaborated the building of self-structure and the development of an identity. Recognizing that one has lived an inauthentic or empty life does not automatically foster a life of authenticity or meaning. In fact, a great deal of therapeutic work such as learning new modes of self-care, experiencing new ways of relating to affect and others, and developing new skills, capacities, and views of oneself may be necessary before such a person feels alive or vital.

Because Arlene did not have a sense of self and felt empty and directionless, she needed to construct an identity, not simply discover a buried self or resume aborted development. The method of free association and evenly-hovering attention—which seems better suited to working with a pathologically structured self rather than an insufficiently structured self—provided necessary but insufficient tools for addressing her difficulties in living. Empathizing with or interpreting the self-defects would not build a new self-structure. Something else was needed, namely, the analyst's *imagination*. If it is true that methods are designed to solve particular problems—and I suspect that it is—then the question becomes: "What problems need to be solved in a particular therapeutic context and what is the best tool for the job at hand?"

The analyst's own freedom, according to Christopher Bollas (1989), is central to successful psychoanalytic treatment. It is one of the "multiple functions" he or she plays. As I lived with Arlene's hopelessness about a life that she could call her own, it was clear to me that engaging her life differently—which was crucial if she was to construct a personally meaningful identity—depended in part on my own freedom of being.

In the clinical discussions of constructing an identity in the chapters on Winnicott's True Self and Kohut's nuclear program, the emphasis I placed on such things as the analyst's self-delineating self-object function and the patient's self-creative efforts illuminated certain crucial aspects of this process. But they eclipsed other important facets, such as the analyst's use of his or her imagination. The constraining grip of Arlene's self-annulling past and present was loosened and the treatment opened up in new and productive ways as I was freer to utilize my imagination in my work with her.[8]

"There are some things," notes Aristotle, "about which it is not possible to pronounce rightly in general terms." A comprehensive discussion of the complex topic of the analyst's use of his or her imagination is beyond the scope of this chapter. Since questions about how analysts might draw on their imagination or when facets of the analyst's imaginative life—images, daydreams, fantasies, dreams, and so forth—might be shared are context-dependent and therefore do not admit of a standardized answer, it will perhaps clash with the spirit of what I am pointing toward in this chapter to offer any generalized recommendations. Let me offer a few brief reflections.

Psychoanalysis has tended to oscillate between two perspectives regarding the analyst's use of his or her own imaginative phenomena. Classical psychoanalysis has tended to inhibit the therapist's use of his or her own experience out of an alertness to the dangers of countertransference.[9] Self psychology, with its heuristic focus on the patient's experience from within his or her frame of reference, has privileged the patient's self-understanding, which may also compromise the analyst's capacity to draw on his or her imagination. Strains of interpersonally oriented approaches have suggestively illuminated the value of the analyst's own experience but have sometimes treated their own experience as if it is "oracular" (Mitchell, 1993a, p. 62). The patient's experience can be eclipsed when the analyst's perspective is valorized, which may set the stage for the patient's inauthentic compliance with the analyst's perspective. The pendulum swings in psychoanalytic history between the restrictive poles of either foreclosing or excessively identifying with one's own imaginative life could be viewed as a cautionary tale about some of the potential pitfalls in the analyst's relation to his or her imagination. With imagination, as with our relation to preferred theories, attending to our experience without being attached to it, sailing an ever-changing course between fearing or overvaluing our experience, and being neither phobic nor narcissistic about what we imagine, think, fantasize, or feel may get us the most therapeutic yield.

Analysts working within every school of thought have undoubtedly made therapeutically disciplined and creative use of their own subjectivity. Paula Heimann, Margaret Little, Harold Searles, Loewald, Bollas, Thomas Ogden, and Mitchell, among others, seem to have felt most comfortable drawing on the potential resources of their own imaginative life.

Judicious and selective use of one's imagination—based on an understanding of the transference-countertransference matrix shaping the treatment—is crucial, as is the analyst's motivation for doing so. Other considerations might include the patient's readiness to use, and freedom to play with, the material that is shared. There may be some patients for whom one could not ever usefully express one's subjective life (Bollas, 1987, p. 211). In situations where this is not the case and it may be generative for the analyst to share what she or he has imagined, then the analyst needs to present it in a provisional as opposed to authoritative way (Winnicott, 1971; Bollas, 1987). The patient needs to feel free to use or reject whatever is suggested by the analyst.

When I began writing this chapter, I hoped to illuminate something that I felt psychoanalysis had to offer discussions about freedom, particularly its "deterministic psychology of freedom" and its ability to foster the expression of the patient's unique subjectivity. I end this chapter months later with the sneaking suspicion—which may not be unrelated to the topic—that I have moved in an unexpected direction, away from the territory that I started from and was familiar with. The analyst's fluid, evolving, nonnarcissistic relationship to his or her own guiding framework *and* his or her capacity for imagination are crucial to the topic of psychoanalysis and freedom.

Because what is imaginative in the present may be imprisoning in the future, the possibilities for freedom that Arlene and I generate in the present will probably need to be overcome in the future in order to preserve our freedom. Arlene and I may need to imagine what is currently unimaginable for us in order to keep alive her fragile hope for a life that might feel like her own.

# 11

## The Analyst's Authority

This is doubtless an uncomfortable region. To explore it we must
renounce the convenience of terminal truths, and never let ourselves be guided by what we may know.
— Michel Foucault, *Madness and Civilization*

The analyst's authority is less authoritative in contemporary
psychoanalysis. In a psychoanalytic universe permeated by the subjectivity of knowledge, the contextual nature of meaning, the multiplicity of
interpretive possibilities, and the fallibility of the analyst's knowledge, the
analyst's sovereign authority—as what Jacques Lacan terms the one-
who-knows—is increasingly suspect.

The subversion of the analyst's claims to epistemological omniscience
has benefited contemporary analytic thinking and practice. More sophis-
ticated and nuanced views of the analytic process and relationship have
emerged from the increased appreciation of the complexity, ambiguity,
and subjectivity of analytic knowledge. When the analyst is no longer
viewed as possessing absolute truth or authority, her relationship to her
own theories may become less narcissistic and the patient may become
more actively involved in the analytic process.

Hidden authoritarianism operates in subtle and unconscious ways in
our increasingly democratic contemporary psychoanalysis. In this chapter
I explore a tension at the heart of the movement in psychoanalysis to
challenge the analyst's privileged authority. I examine two instances of
the analyst's unchallenged authority in the analytic relationship and process: the ground rules and the ways that analysts represent the complexity
of the therapeutic process in case reports.

By locating hidden domains of authoritarianism in analysts' thinking
about the analytic framework and the way they represent patients and
their work, we can challenge unconscious exercise of the analyst's au-

thority, open up the treatment, and empower the patient. Freed from the constraining grip of authoritarianism, patient and analyst might in turn be freer to create a different, more liberatory process of treatment. Greater freedom for the patient might then be possible.

## Frame Up: Whose Treatment Is It Anyway?

I began this chapter after I could not answer a patient's intriguing question. She had just finished reading Robert Stolorow and George Atwood's *Contexts of Being* (1992) and Stephen Mitchell's *Hope and Dread in Psychoanalysis* (1993a), two esteemed works in the burgeoning literature in contemporary psychoanalysis on the relational perspective. My patient learned a great deal from both books and was inspired by relational perspectives. But she was struck by a contradiction that neither of us had heard voiced before—namely, that cases were always written from the vantage point of only one person, the analyst, even in contemporary relationally oriented theories that stress the *relational* nature of treatment. Why is it, she wondered, that analytic case reports completely omit the *patient's* point of view except as it is viewed by someone else, namely, the analyst?

At about the same time my patient was raising these thought-provoking questions, I was reading several works of postmodernist anthropology, including George Marcus and Michael Fischer's *Anthropology as Cultural Critique* (1986) and Margery Wolf's *A Thrice-Told Tale* (1992). Acutely aware of the "crisis of representation" (Marcus & Fischer, 1986, p. 6) afflicting the humanities and social sciences—the fact that the act of representing a person, a foreign culture, or a social phenomenon is never objective and is always mediated by human interests, values, and power—many contemporary anthropologists were asking how an ethnographer might present the other in a nonexploitative, noncolonialistic manner.

Psychoanalysis is not ethnography. There is a significant difference between providing a "thick description" of a Balinese cockfight, as anthropologist Clifford Geertz (1973) did, and addressing a troubling symptom or healing a developmental arrest, as a psychoanalyst does. But psychoanalysts do write about, as well as attempt to heal, the other. Given the "crisis of representation" throughout the social sciences and humanities, I began to wonder why the question of representing the other seems rarely even to have been *raised*, let alone addressed, in psychoanalysis?[1] Was this an accidental lacuna—perhaps an artifact of psychoanalysis's relative historical isolation from academia—or was it a symptomatic omission?

As I began to reflect on my patient's suggestive questions in light of the work being done in contemporary anthropology, I wondered about the deeper implications of the psychoanalytic convention of writing about the two-person process of treatment from only one person's perspective. Was the relational perspective truly relational? Was it relational enough? Were there other areas in which the analyst's authority, unacknowledged asymmetries, and perhaps subtle authoritarianism covertly appeared in our predominantly antiauthoritarian contemporary psychoanalytic climate? What might be warded off and/or preserved by not thinking about issues of representation and power in psychoanalysis?

A psychoanalytic candidate concludes his report of a creative intervention involving a self-revelation in which he found a way to connect with a fearful, detached, inhibited patient with the plaintive question/apology "But was it analytic?" This is a question I have heard countless times in the classroom and in supervision. Let us consider another similar situation in which a "supervisee" sheepishly tells his supervisor that he acted spontaneously, openly, and affably with a patient without any untoward results. The supervisee indicates that at various moments in the treatment he had made realistic clarifications of distortions on the patient's part about important matters of fact, answered a patient's question, aided a patient in a practical way, made some noninterpretive interventions, and so forth. In such cases, it is likely that the supervisor and the supervisee might feel that the latter was behaving in an "unanalytic" manner. The supervisee might well feel guilt and shame.

"Psychoanalysts," notes Robert Gardner (1983), "try to prove themselves and psychoanalysis 'classical' or prove themselves and psychoanalysis 'not classical.' What is 'classical'? Pure? What is 'not classical.' Impure" (p. 3). Gardner continues: "Psychoanalysts say 'I know this sounds classical, but . . . ' They say: 'I know this does not sound classical, but . . . ' What is all this concern for how things sound? What are all these buts?" (ibid.).

In the course of investigating psychoanalytic technique, Freud (1912a, 1912b, 1913a, 1914a, 1915a) delineated what has become the normative outline of the ground rules and framework of psychoanalysis. Freud, as well as many subsequent psychoanalysts, found that certain consistent and stable conditions of treatment—set time, frequency, fee, and location, the patient's use of free association, the analyst's neutrality, anonymity, and evenly hovering attention, and so forth—safeguarded the transference and facilitated the unfolding of the therapeutic work. The "analytic" became synonymous with this framework as well as certain theoretical postulates such as the importance of infant sexuality, the Oedipal drama, transference, resistance, and so forth. Freud (1912a) noted that this framework was what suited him and might not be applicable to everyone. He suggested that analysts with different dispositions and temperament might practice differently. He admitted, for example, that he sat out of the patient's sight behind the couch because he could not stand to be stared at for eight (or more) hours a day.

Freud did not always follow his own recommendations in practice. In fact, he often deviated from them. Given the fact that he made realistic clarifications of what he felt were distortions on the patient's part about important matters of fact, answered patients' questions, aided patients in practical ways, gave a patient a gift of a book he wrote (which his patient had expressed interest in), and made noninterpretive interventions (Lipton, 1977), it may not be surprising that the "supervisee" in the second vignette refers not to someone that I supervised (although I have encountered many supervisees and analytic candidates who have engaged in similar behaviors and have suffered from feeling that they were "unanalytic"), but to Freud himself.

Despite Freud's nonabsolutizing stance toward his own recommendations, the framework he recommended has rarely been openly questioned in the psychoanalytic literature and seems to be the foundation for most subsequent analytic treatment.[2] Since few analysts disagree in theory, if not in practice, with the analytic framework that Freud adumbrated, it subsequently became an explicit or at least implicit frame of reference for most analytically oriented therapists. Its foundational status emerges in the fact that analysts (1) treat it like analytic common sense, which is rarely, if ever, questioned; (2) feel guilty—like my student—when they do not conform to it, even if it has a positive effect on the treatment; and (3) rarely challenge the standard guidelines in public even when they clinically disagree with them. The fact that the traditional framework exercises a formative, if silent, influence, even in cases where analysts do not fully subscribe to Freud's guidelines, is illustrated by the concern so many analysts have with the question "But is it analytic?"

The " 'maintenance of the frame' of psychoanalysis," suggests Thomas Ogden (1994), "is not simply a reflection of rigid obsessionality on the part of the analyst, but a very important arena for communication between patient and analyst" (p. 189). But what exactly is it that is communicated? It is taken for granted that the frame provides stability, safety, and security and that analytic work is optionally facilitated by the generative environment that it fosters. Nearly a century of analytic history does nothing to challenge this claim.

My experiences with a man I shall call Teddy suggest that the issues may be more complex. Teddy, a single man in his early thirties, sought treatment because of a vague sense of malaise, social isolation, and directionlessness. He periodically alluded to stealing library books and eating at restaurants without paying. He seemed to disregard the feelings of others and to be unaware of his impact on them. He also communicated an unwillingness to explore his stealing or his feelings about others, both of which he found intolerable. He would either attack me, remain silent, or try to change the subject if I tried to explore the brief remarks he offered.

In the early stages of treatment, Teddy demanded a "Langsian" framework. Robert Langs (1982b) maintained that there is "a single ideal therapeutic environment" defined by a set fee and time; confidentiality; the analyst's abstinence, anonymity, and use of evenly hovering attention; the patient's commitment to free associate, financial responsibility for all sessions, and so forth (pp. 305–7). Freud's periodic violation of the ground rules, in Langs's (1978) view, created "misalliances" between analyst and analysand based on "transference gratifications and acts of shared collusion and defensiveness" (p. 234).

At first, Teddy's wish for this sort of analytic environment was exempt from critical scrutiny because it seemed to embody analytic common sense, just the ways things should be done. Since my training had convinced me of the value of the Freudian ground rules and the Langsian framework, they were a taken-for-granted aspect of my relationship with Teddy. Teddy reacted with hostility and contempt when he felt that I deviated from this framework—when, for example, he heard the ring of a phone or the din of a subway (a subway line ran outside my office) and saw another patient leave my office while he sat in the waiting room fifteen minutes before our session.

I focused on rectifying the framework, which enabled me to attend selectively to feeling attacked and bullied by Teddy. As my curiosity about the meaning and function of Teddy's wish for this sort of framework replaced a desire to establish such an analytic environment, I came to feel that my *striving* for such a framework—not my initial failure to perfectly provide it—expressed my own countertransference. It embodied what Atwood and Stolorow (1984) have termed "countertransference conjunction," which occurs when the correspondence between the patient and analyst's view of something hinders full exploration of its significance for the patient. Teddy and I did not explore the meaning and aetiological significance of the analytic framework for him as long as we accepted its naturalness and reasonableness. My own freedom of inquiry had become restricted by the analytic framework that Teddy sought and that I attempted to provide.

As I became more interested in understanding the meaning and function of Teddy's wish for a hermetically sealed environment, new material about him and his family emerged. Returning home from school as a young boy, he would retreat to his room, where he would be joined by his father and barricade the door against his inebriated mother, who terrorized them both. Bullied by his wife, Teddy's father did not protect his son against her. Teddy felt terrified by his mother and unprotected by his father. In this context, one salient meaning of his wish for a Langsian framework emerged: such an environment offered the promise of protecting him from feeling defenseless and endangered. The analytic framework might offer safety that he had never known.

It is often assumed in analysis that (1) the frame is unequivocally positive; (2) we know a priori—before treatment begins—what it should be for every person we work with; (3) it should be identical[3] for each person; and (4) alterations are universally negative and inevitably experienced as harmful for each patient (e.g., Gill, 1984, p. 401).

So why did Freud recommend a specific sort of analytic environment and often diverge from it? There are at least three possible explanations for the apparent contradiction between Freud's theoretical recommendations concerning the ideal analytic framework and his *practice*: (1) he contradicted himself; (2) he altered his practice without updating his *theory* of practice (which he often did with his theories); or (3) he experienced countertransference.

Once analysts no longer find it an analytically useful enterprise to prove themselves "classical" or "not classical"—once the failure to be the former is no longer hurled as an epithet by true believers and the capacity to embody the latter is not a badge of honor for revisionists—then a fourth interpretation emerges. This option seems rarely, if ever, to have been raised within our field, namely, that the tension embodied in Freud's practice is *instructive*. It is instructive not because it pinpoints a contradiction in Freud that can be deconstructed (and then used to undermine or jettison his genuine contributions to human knowledge and self-understanding), that he said *x* but did *y*, but rather because it unwittingly reveals something novel about analytic theory and practice in general and novel ways of relating to one's own theory and practice in particular.

The first thing that the tension in Freud's practice reveals is the problematic nature of fixed and rigid demarcations of what is analytic and unanalytic. At first glance, the distinction between the frame of psychoanalysis and what is exterior to it appears clear. But the line between the two is blurred. Asserting the primacy of the traditional framework, Ogden (1994), for example, tells one patient who continues to talk at the end of the session, "Our time is up," yet allows other patients to make use of the waiting room apart from sessions (pp. 189–90).[4] Mitchell's (1988) critique of the "developmental tilt" approach to psychoanalytic theory construction renders suspect the assumption that parameters or alterations in the framework are only applicable to more seriously disturbed patients. The developmental tilt viewpoint is the belief that relational needs—in this context, attunement and flexibility—are applicable to early phases of development and to more ill patients, while healthier patients should be treated and responded to according to the perspectives generated by traditional analytic theories of drives and defenses.

Ordinarily we treat such terms as "analytic" and "unanalytic" as binary oppositions, of the same kind as good/evil, health/illness, and purity/contamination. In such binaries, one term, usually the first one, is seen as independent, self-sufficient, and superior. It signifies the privileged entity, the better and "purer" state. That purity is associated with the term "analytic" and impurity and danger with "unanalytic" is illustrated by Freud's remark to Ernest Jones about those members of the International Psychoanalytic Association who were not completely loyal to the party line: " 'Your intention to purge the London Society of the Jungian members is excellent' " (Jones, 1955, p. 254). However, binary oppositions or divisions usually thought to be antithetical and opposed are not dichotomous and conceptually independent, but rather interrelated and mutually interdependent. The first term inevitably ends up relying on the second term, which serves as what Jacques Derrida (1976) terms the *supplement*, an apparent accessory that is actually essential to the privileged term. "Freedom" means nothing without "fate," and to speak of what is "pure" presupposes notions of what is "impure."

Freud's apparently "unanalytic" behavior—his deviation from the standard analytic framework—suggests that the belief in the categories analytic and unanalytic should be more suspect. On closer inspection, such oppositions are more apparent than real. The problem, from this perspective, is not so much that Freud was periodically "impure"—moving outside the analytic frame—but that the attempt to construct a "pure" analytic realm and cordon it off from what is impure is problematic. In this reading, Freud's example might teach us that we become enslaved not by the failure to hold the fort against threats to analytic purity, but by the quixotic attempt to divide and separate what is interrelated. The awareness that no clear and final demarcation is possible between what is inside and outside analysis, what is analytic and nonanalytic, and that they are, in fact, irreducibly entangled, may generate a sense of unease. It may challenge the sense of clear context, and definitional and theoretical clarity and mastery that our identity and practice relies on.

The second thing that the tension between Freud's theory and practice offers us is a vision of a different sort of relation to our theories and practices. We tend to either become attached to our own preferred theories or strive to jettison or transcend them in our concern for the way theory distorts. While "theories, new or old, can . . . interfere with a truly open-minded approach to the configurations of meaning unique to each patient" (Lindon, 1991, p. 15), there is no theory-free listening or conceptualizing. If attachment to a theory or a framework is enslaving, then jettisoning it in the hope of encountering the patient directly "without memory, desire, or understanding" (Bion, 1970, pp. 51–52) is quixotic and invites chaos and even narcissism.

Freud enacted a relation to theory that he never theorized, but that we, in our postpositivistic and postclassical milieu, can. Let us, as Lacan would say, "return to Freud"—but with a difference. Freud offered a different relation to theory—neither the *analyst-as-customs-official* who makes sure that the rules are followed and that nothing foreign/illegal is smuggled in, nor the *analyst-as-independent-operative* who seems to dispense with conventional guidelines and operate (like Lacan) outside extant strictures, but the analyst as *jazz improvisor*[5] who plays with, improvises upon, and extends what she or he inherits. The analyst knows and respects the basic notes but is also able to create new and generative combinations. At its best, Freud's *example*, if not always his theory or even his practice, avoids the stifling rigidity[6] of many of his colleagues, successors, and critics, as well as the narcissism of those who alter the frame without retaining an "analytic attitude."

By pointing toward the need to exceed boundaries without eradicating them, Freud is an unwitting precursor of contemporary complexity theory, as well as of Derrida. Complex adaptive systems—entities such as people and organizations—that have various dimensions, an intricate structure, and a capacity to change and adapt, need to exist in a region between the overly ordered and the chaotic. Too little flexibility renders a person, an organization, or a method of treatment, rigid and unresponsive; too much change and instability is anarchic. From this perspective, the orthodoxy of the traditionalist *or* revisionist, with its potential for a one-size-fits-all attitude toward patients, and a ruleless mode, such as the infamous shortened Lacanian hour, embody two opposite poles, respectively, the too ordered and the too flexible.

The psychoanalytic framework and ground rules may enslave the analyst and subjugate the patient even as they safeguard the treatment and invite the analysand's creation and potentiation. Unquestioningly adopting the standard ground rules may limit, if not profoundly compromise, the analyst's own freedom to respond to the complex exigencies of the psychoanalytic moment—as I now suspect happened in my work with Teddy—as the analyst becomes a captive of the structure she or he is employing to facilitate the patient's freedom. For example, the frame seemed to communicate stability and security for Teddy, but did it communicate anything else? Did it, for example, enable Teddy and me to reenact his relationship with his abusive mother (and turn the tables on her) with Teddy in the role of the bully (mother) and me in the role of the one who was coerced (young Teddy/his father)? Did he bully the proxy for his mother (me) so that he would not be terrorized? Did the protected analytic environment ward off—and enable him to "lock out" and avoid rather than work through—his own terror, narcissism, and rage, which he found shameful and intolerable?

Preset ideas—even about the guiding framework—are actually antianalytic because they hamper the analyst's freedom of inquiry and thought in two ways. First, rigid adherence to prearranged theory and practice renders one intellectually *phobic:* unable to travel in certain directions in the treatment, such as investigating the impact on the patient's transference of the specific framework that the analyst has chosen to structure the treatment. Such topics are off limits when the framework is presumed to be "natural" and unworthy of being questioned. But can the power that the analyst may covertly yield in setting up the rules of the game beforehand and fitting the patient into them influence the patient? Can it, to cite one possibility, render the patient interpersonally impactless? When the shaping influence of the framework that the analyst utilizes is problematic (and eclipsed), any resultant obstacles to the treatment are more likely to be attributed to the patient or to other aspects of the therapeutic interaction. This makes it nearly impossible to explore whether in a specific case the framework the analyst established and the patient seamlessly complied with has any *negative* consequences. Do any patients ever experience such a framework as a sign of withholding, "uncompromising rigidity" (Gill, 1984, p. 401), rationalized deprivation, or fear of intimacy on the analyst's part? Is the silent conformity of certain patients with the framework their analyst has established ever a reenactment of the passivity and compliance they experienced with a parental figure who was, for them, powerful and unchallengeable?

"The problem with the principle of standing firm," notes Mitchell (1993a), "is the assumption that it must mean to the patient what the analyst wants it to mean. Sometimes it does, and the patient feels encouraged by the analyst's ability to set limits, stand by his faith in the analytic process, resist allowing himself into dangerous departures. However, while the analyst thinks she is standing firm, the patient may feel he is being brutalized in a very familiar fashion. Many patients are lost because they feel utterly abandoned or betrayed by analysts who think they are maintaining the purity of the analytic frame" (p. 194).

The second way that a rigid framework may compromise analytic work is that it can inhibit the patient's self-expression and the analyst's freedom, creativity, and optimal responsiveness. Set roles legislated and limited by the frame may foreclose the expression of relational configurations and the patient's modes of self-care (or self-neglect) that could illuminate the patient's life and deepen analytic inquiry. For example, Otto Kernberg (1995) assumes that if a suicidal patient breaks the frame by telephoning the therapist between sessions, then it is "a manifestation of the transference . . . because I assume that this frame is inherently logical" (p. 335). Kernberg then terminates the treatment. He interprets the patient's behavior to mean either that the patient experiences the frame as "an attack" or is engaged in an act of "self-destruction." It is not obvious that this patient is attempting to destroy treatment or himself.

He may, in fact, be attempting to connect with the analyst in order to save his life. But that is not my main point. Perhaps the patient's attempt to connect with Kernberg was necessary as well as a reenactment of a helpless, dependent relationship. The treatment would arguably be enriched if the patient's helpless, dependent stance could be reenacted, understood, and worked through in the therapeutic relationship rather than discouraged from emerging in the treatment. The potential therapeutic value of actively participating in enactments rather than attempting to avoid them is neglected when the therapeutic ground rules too rigidly preclude their emergence (Levenson, 1983; Bromberg, 1993).

I hope it is clear that I am not advocating setting aside ground rules or taking a stance of "anything goes." Certain things in treatment are harmful and even irreparable. But I am suggesting that it may be as erroneous to assume that the frame has a universal meaning and impact, and that to alter it is always negative, as it is to claim that something in a dream has a singular and universal meaning.

The meaning of a dream, according to Freud, is arrived at *not* by translating dream material into the a priori meaning and "fixed-key" of what he termed a "dream-book" (1900) of already existing meanings, but rather, by eliciting the *dreamer's* unique associations. The meaning of the ground rules, in my view, is arrived at not by translating it, as so many analysts since Freud—including myself—have done, into the "fixed-key" of the analysts "dream book" and assuming that they are either indispensable *or* disposable, but by elucidating their unique meaning and impact on those we work with. Maintaining the frame or changing it, like all psychic events, has multiple meanings and functions. Since the meaning of the ground rules and their impact on patients is *variable*, neither holding firm to the frame nor changing it is inherently constructive *or* pathological. There may be situations in which automatically employing all of the features of the standard psychoanalytic framework may *itself* embody the analyst's *countertransference* and impede the psychoanalytic process. In a particular case, holding firm to the frame may, for example, express unconscious fear, hostility, or revenge on the analyst's part. The expression and transformation of the analysand's subjective world may, in such cases, be facilitated by altering the traditional framework to meet the needs of the patient, rather than forcing the patient and the analyst into a preordained, constricting mold. But in other cases, altering the frame may be an expression on the analyst's part of such things as unconscious fear or guilt and may be detrimental to the treatment. Listening afresh to the unique meaning of the ground rules for a particular analysand—rather than assuming that they have an a priori validity or meaning—can heighten our sensitivity to their impact on the analysand and help us find the format that works best with each particular patient. If the birth and modernization of psychoanalysis demanded that Freud transform the medical and psychiatric theories and practices of his age so that they were attuned to the unique conditions of his age, then its postmodernization may occur when contemporary analysts from a variety of theoretical perspectives do the same. Individualizing each treatment, I suspect, may be crucial in this process.

Approaching the psychoanalytic framework not as an idol to be worshiped, but rather as a tool to explore the complexity of psychic life, may not authorize a new form of psychoanalytic practice—which could itself become ossified. But it can point to a more fluid and free way of thinking about the psychoanalytic framework in particular, and psychoanalysis in general, that might transform, reanimate, and enrich the way we practice. Respecting rather than revering the ground rules allow us to recognize simultaneously the necessity for structure in the treatment and the importance of a never-ending playing with and transformation of structure. The analyst's freedom-within-structure facilitates the co-creation of analytic frameworks that may be more responsive to the needs of each unique analytic dyad.

## Psychoanalytic Ventriloquism, or I Speak (for the other) Therefore I Am (and the other is not)

> They have the power of description, and we succumb to the pictures they construct. —Salman Rushdie, *Satanic Verses*

Let's return to my patient's question that initiated this chapter: Why do relational theorists stress that treatment is a two-person process and that it is essential to bring in the perspective of both participants, yet present one person's account of the process? At first glance this accepted analytic convention seems quite natural, inevitable, and unworthy of questioning. Since case reports are, after all, the culmination of many years of deep immersion in and reflection on the psychological world of the patient, one might reasonably ask why it even matters that only the analyst represents the treatment. Who, after all, is in a better position to do so?

With such an arrangement the analyst might be likened—in Lawrence Josephs's (1995) felicitous image—to a ghostwriter of the patient's autobiography (e.g., p. 46). The validity of a text that is written without the subject's direct input is so taken for granted that it is difficult to see it freshly or question it. The Russian literary theorist Victor Shklovsky (1917) claimed that one of the important functions of art was to challenge taken-for-granted ways of seeing and being through a process he termed "defamiliarization," that is, making the familiar *unfamiliar* or strange so that it might be experienced afresh. We need to defamiliarize the topic of how analytic cases are written so that we might consider how to think about it differently.

One way of defamiliarizing this topic might be to engage momentarily in a brief thought experiment. Let us imagine for a moment that from now on sociologists did not write about inmates, anthropologists did not write about natives, and psychoanalysts did not write about patients. How would we know about conditions in prisons, indigenous cultures, and consulting rooms? Let us imagine, to continue the thought experiment, that from now on prisoners, natives, and patients were the only ones who wrote about their experiences. Would any new perspectives, insights, or questions emerge?

In a world without *The Diary of Anne Frank*, or the description of alienation and anomie in Ralph Ellison's *The Invisible Man*, or the depiction of the descent into madness in Sylvia Plath's *The Bell Jar*, we would, I suspect, know less about the holocaust, the African-American experience, and women and madness than we would if all we had read were the accounts of European historians, sociologists, and psychiatrists. It is not only that the inclusion of neglected voices is instructive, it is that the voices of those with power who usually narrate such stories may be less omniscient and infallible than we ordinarily assume.

While many contemporary analysts might agree with Evelyn Schwaber's (1983) claim that what the analyst "knows" about treatment is no more "real" than what the patient "knows," analysts rarely—if ever— *write* as if this were so. Why do analysts speak of the collaborative nature of analytic treatment yet write one-person accounts of it?

At the beginning of this chapter I alluded to the "crisis in representation" in the humanities and social science, by which I meant the recognition that the act of representing anything or anyone, from an ethnographic experience to a therapeutic encounter, a member of an indigenous village or a psychoanalytic patient, is never presuppositionless and objective. While the vast majority of contemporary analysts no longer believe that the analyst listens or theorizes from an Archimedean point of objectivity and authority, analysts *write* as if they do.

Skepticism about the analyst's epistemological authority is belied—even among analysts sensitive to their inevitable role in shaping the treatment (e.g., hermeneuticists, constructionists, and constructivists)—by the total control the analyst exercises over the narrative form of case reports and the complete omission of the patient's point of view. While the subjectivity of patient and analyst is of much greater concern in contemporary psychoanalysis, *descriptions* of treatment are univocal accounts of the analytic process organized from the perspective of only one participant, the analyst. Case reports are generally insensitive to the omissions and evasions on which the narrative rests, and they coexist with a recognition among an increasing number of contemporary analysts of the complexity and ambiguity of analytic knowledge and the inevitable partiality of the analyst's (and the patient's) perspective. Freud was aware of the fictional quality of his work. He called his study of Leonardo da Vinci "partly fiction." *Moses and Monotheism* had the working title *The Man Moses: An Historical Novel.* The unquestioned faith analysts have in the standard textual modes they employ in representing analytic treatments is symptomatic of an unconscious adherence to a correspondence theory of truth—in which it is assumed that the analyst's picture of what is occurring corresponds to an independent objective reality either "out there" or "in here"—which is held in increasing suspicion in other domains of contemporary analysis. Given the theory-laden nature of perception and theorizing, the fact that knowledge is mediated by human desires, goals, and presuppositions rather than simply revealed or discovered, it is significant that analysts employ standard, naive realist narrative modes of representation—the view that psychic life is as it appears to an observer—without greater skepticism.

The faith analysts have in the accuracy of their representations of treatment gives their account of what happens in therapy an implicit if not explicit authority and legitimacy. But the analyst is not a neutral, disinterested party. The authorial authority exercised by psychoanalysts creates a context of asymmetry, power, and domination in which authors (analysts) are active and the subjects represented by such discursive practices (analysands) are passive and spoken for. This fosters a kind of *psychological ventriloquism* in which the analyst speaks for the patient, who is thereby rendered "dumb." The analyst's knowledge is privileged over the patient's and analysands are denied the opportunity to express alternative views of themselves and the analytic relationship and process.

In this format, incongruent viewpoints to the author/analyst are silenced and the *analyst's* unconsciousness and desires are evaded—which is problematic given the fact that no analyst is "fully analyzed" and self-unconsciousness and self-blindness are thus inevitable. What is excluded from the narrative—including the analyst's presuppositions, blind spots, and doubts, and the patient's alternative constructions of him or herself and the treatment—is repressed. The patient's discourse becomes what Michel Foucault (1980) termed "subjugated knowledges," "knowledges that have been . . . directly disqualified knowledges (such as that of the psychiatric patient, of the ill person, of the nurse . . . of the delinquent" (p. 82).

Self-consciousness is absent about both the validity of the analyst's rendering of the data and the impact on analytic knowledge of the analyst's exclusive control over the transmission of analytic knowledge. The absence of self-reflectiveness about the conventional analytic modes of representing analysands also precludes crucial questions relating to such a format: Would patients' accounts of what they need or what makes the analytic process work challenge or enrich the analyst's viewpoint? Does the naive realist narrative mode underpinning the existing form of representing analytic knowledge offer the best way of conveying the intersubjective complexities of our postscientistic psychoanalysis? What narrative strategies would be most useful in communicating the multiple subjectivities comprising the analytic process?

In the face of the crisis of representation that plagues the humanities and social sciences, two responses are often discernible: the naive realism of psychoanalysts; and the antirealist, epistemological pessimism of "skeptical" poststructuralists,[7] who speak of "the demise of the subject, the end of the author, the impossibility of truth, and the abrogation of the Order of Representation" (Rosenau, 1993, p. 13). If psychoanalysts are often too confident about their capacity to represent the other, assuming that their accounts of treatment are transparent windows through which their patient's nature is revealed, poststructuralists may be too pessimistic. Various postmodernists have usefully highlighted the constructed, nonveridical, political nature of representing others—the way, for example, that representation can be an exercise in intellectual colonization. But they often assume an indeterminacy of meaning and a skepticism about the possibility of representing the other that compromises their capacity to assert anything definite about others, which ironically may perpetuate the others' invisibility. If psychoanalysts tend to have too much faith in their capacity to represent the other, poststructuralists may have too little.

From my perspective, we need to think and write about psychoanalytic treatment from a *third* space, perhaps an experimental one, that avoids the unsatisfactory options of either naive realism or epistemological pessimism. We need, I suspect, what Pauline Rosenau (1993) terms an "affirmative" as opposed to a pessimistic postmodernism: theories and practices that are constructive and visionary rather than "eliminative" and "reactive" (p. 16 n. 11). This means we need to challenge the notion of Truth in our case reports but still pursue *meanings*; recognize the complexity of the self but try to embody its *heterogeneity*; and confront the ever-present danger of intellectual *colonialism* yet still struggle to fashion creative and self-reflexive ways of representing others.

Various feminists have usefully warned against two dangers in the movement to experiment with alternative modes of representing the other: (1) its narcissism and (2) its evasion of ethical responsibility. If postmodernists often throw out the baby of representing the other in the act of eliminating the bath water of objectivity, then they often refill the tub, so to speak, with *textuality*, with a greater concern with the nature of their own novel *text*, which may result in a self-absorption in which one loses contact with the other (e.g., Wolf, 1992).

The posthumanist praxis I am pointing to would be nondogmatic, self-critical, open to feedback and alteration, and willing to commit to particular conclusions even as it recognized that they are provisional and always contestable. It is beyond the scope of this chapter to attempt a full-scale delineation of alternative ways of presenting analytic case material. Let me, however, offer some suggestions.

Self-reflexiveness is the first ingredient in the alternative perspective I am recommending. Psychoanalytic case material is notoriously complex. In *Narrative Truth and Historical Truth*, Donald Spence (1982) has illuminated the inherent hermeneutical difficulties of the analytic encounter. The apparently "self-evident" data of psychoanalytic treatments are, in actuality, enormously complex and indissolubly connected to the theoretical frame of reference and clinical orientation of both patient and analyst. Reconstruction may often be a contemporary construction, based on acts of discovery, moments of creation, historical truths, and narrative fit. Roy Schafer (1983) notes that there is no single, comprehensive psychoanalytic life history of an analysand. Rather, there are various histories of the patient's past shaped by the therapeutic environment, including the intersubjective context of the therapeutic relationship, the personal dynamics of both analyst and analysand, and the theoretical orientation and treatment approach employed by the analyst. Thus we need to replace the notion of *the* history of the analysand with *multiple* histories. Joseph Weiss and Harold Sampson (1986), among others, have recommended that psychoanalysts collect more raw data from actual psychoanalytic treatments in order to gain a more nuanced account of the analytic process. Analysts also need to reflect more actively on and pose questions about the theoretical presuppositions and interpretive practices that the incomplete text they construct utilizes. Highlighting (rather than denying or evading) alternative perspectives and potential disagreements with the viewpoints in our text would undermine the author's position as the one-who-knows. Jean-François Lyotard's *The Postmodern Condition* (1984) articulates the logic of this perspective.

Psychoanalytic case histories, as Schafer (1992) notes, are stories: stories about conflicted selves, imprisoned selves, depleted selves, authentic selves, and so forth. These stories are mediated through written language and are thus expressed in existing linguistic genres. Reflecting on the tropes upon which one's stories are based can reveal important possibilities and omissions. Whether the "clever [classical] analyst/detective" solves the mystery; or the flexible and intrepid interpersonalist boldly travels where no previous analyst has gone before—doing something "unconventional and self-revealing" that is transformative; or the persistent self psychologist reaches the developmentally arrested patient by virtue of his or her devotion and empathy (Mitchell, 1992, pp. 444–45), there are at least two underlying commonalities to analytic case reports. First, the analyst and the analytic experience are portrayed in a *positive* light. With its unflinching investigation of the complexities, mysteries, ambiguities, ambivalences, dilemmas, and losses inherent in human existence, psychoanalysis embodies a primarily tragic vision of the world (e.g., Schafer, 1976). Yet even if the protagonist in a psychoanalytic case—the patient—is presented as a conflicted being, struggling against unavoidable conflict, who seeks success and love ambivalently, she usually *triumphs* over obstacles and experiences a "happy ending" as she creates or at least participates in a new and better world. This embodies what the literary theorist Northrop Frye (1957) terms a *comic* mode, by which I mean not that analysis is necessarily humorous or full of laughter or gaiety, but that patients experience progress, integration, and reconciliation by the conclusion of most case reports. This is the second common factor to most accounts of treatment. Reflecting on the possibilities and liabilities that are authorized by the literary modes we utilize in our case reports will facilitate more nuanced and self-reflective accounts of treatment. We need to ask, for example, "What do comic modes omit?"

If psychoanalytic cases are usually tales told by the successful with nary a hitch, then the kind of cases that might be more edifying would (1) reflect on their central assumptions and (2) admit—rather than evade— ambiguity, doubt, even *failure*. Failures in psychoanalysis tend to be denied or finessed rather than explored. Psychoanalysts more readily speak of the patient's resistance, envy, or negative therapeutic reaction than of their own fatigue, preoccupation, rigidity, or lack of imagination.

"The critical reexamination by a therapist of a previously treated case," as Theodore Jacobs (1993) notes, "is an unusual occurrence in our field" (p. 123). Morris Eagle's (1993) reexamination and critique from a different perspective of a treatment he conducted many years earlier offers us one useful example of how we might do this. Serving as a kind of discussant of his own earlier paper, he reanalyzed his data, rather than the patient, and focused on what he initially overlooked and the new ways that he now understood what had transpired in his previous work (e.g., Shapiro, 1993, p. 129).

Writing about our clinical failures as well as our successes could be quite instructive. Freud (1905a) initiated a literature of failure in his description of the Dora case, where he maintained that the case was "broken off prematurely" because he "did not succeed in mastering the transference in good time." "The transference," he admitted, "took me unawares" (pp. 116–19). Would our case reports be enriched if we wrote more about the countertransferences, as well as the transferences, that catch most of us unawares? When we have a literature of countertransference and failure as well as self-congratulation, then questions such as Why did a treatment *not* work? What could I do differently next time? What are the general lessons to be learned? will more readily arise.

It is a "tempting mistake," notes Daniel Dennett (1991), to suppose "that there must be a single narrative (the 'final' or 'published' draft, you might say) that is canonical—that is the actual stream of consciousness of the subject" (p. 113). Because there is no single, authoritative version of a life or a treatment, there are numerous tales *two* could tell about a particular treatment. J.-B. Pontalis's remarks about autobiography apply, with the appropriate changes, to case histories: "One shouldn't write one autobiography," suggests Pontalis, "but ten of them, or a hundred because, while we have only one life we have innumerable ways of recounting that life to ourselves" (quoted in Phillips, 1994, p. 73). A more self-reflexive psychoanalytic author might acknowledge, with the narrator of Salman Rushdie's *Shame* (1983), that "I am forced to reflect that world in fragments of broken mirrors . . . I must reconcile myself to the inevitability of the missing bits" (p. 69). Writing about the "missing bits" in our own stories—like the failures in our treatments—could also be quite instructive.

This approach might also lead to a more ironic tone in analytic case reports. In more ironic texts, the author(s) might offer multiple representations of the treatment and reflections on the possible strengths and limitations of each perspective (e.g., Denzin, 1995). James Agee and Walker Evans's *Let Us Now Praise Famous Men* (1941), which consists of multiple rather than single representations of three white tenant farmers, illustrates what I am pointing toward.

Psychoanalytic case histories embody what the Russian cultural and literary theorist Mikhail Bakhtin termed "monological" discourses in that they offer only one perspective or voice, the analyst's. Since the small literature written by patients about their experiences in analysis (e.g., the Wolf Man [Gardiner, 1971]; Doolittle, 1956; Wortis, 1954; Guntrip, 1977; Little, 1985) is minimally cited and noncanonical,[8] most analytic cases are stories about patients from the analyst's point of view. Readers of analytic cases are only privy to the patient's voice as mediated through the analyst.

Psychoanalysts need to struggle to find ways of bringing what Foucault (1977) terms "counter-discourses" *of* patients rather than *about* them (e.g., p. 209) into analytic cases. The "subjugated knowledges" of patients have the potential to challenge dominant discourses and offer alternative points of view (Foucault, 1980).[9]

What Bakhtin terms *dialogical* discourses, which offer two or more viewpoints, are one alternative to the monological discourses of psychoanalytic texts. The works of Dostoevsky, with their celebration of *polyphony*—that is, multiple voices or perspectives, what Bakhtin terms a "plurality of independent and unmerged voices and consciousnesses, a genuine polyphony of fully valid voices" (1984, p. 6)—offer a suggestive alternative. I have not come across any examples of this in the psychoanalytic literature. The only example that I am aware of outside the psychoanalytic literature is the joint diary of a treatment coauthored by Irving Yalom, an existentially oriented therapist, and a patient of his (Yalom & Elkin, 1974).

Various writers in the contemporary ethnological literature have tried to fashion nonmonological, collaborative texts, in which the indigenous peoples being studied, as well as the ethnologists that study them, speak (e.g., Crapanzano, 1980; Walker, 1982). But as Bakhtin's (1984) discussion of polyphony in Dostoevsky's work inadvertently illustrates, this is easier said than done. In what I would term the Bakhtinian fallacy, one conflates the author's inclusion of a multiplicity of perspectives with true multiple authorship. A joint process singularly inscribed—the dialogue of patient and analyst ghostwritten by the analyst without the subject's direct input—does not a polyphonic text make. Such texts are not truly collaborative because the writer/ethnographer (1) occupies a position of greater power than those being studied (2) usually introduces the project, and (3) controls what is included and excluded.

Let me briefly discuss two suggestive examples of polyphonic texts outside anthropology and psychoanalysis and then propose two ways that psychoanalysis might fashion more multidimensional and collaborative texts. Geoffrey Bennington and Jacques Derrida's *Jacques Derrida* (1993) offers an alternative to the monological perspective underlying the vast majority of psychoanalytic texts. *Jacques Derrida* is two texts in one: Derrida's response—at the bottom of each page—to Bennington's explication of key themes in Derrida's work at the top of the page. Derrida's text, which includes excerpts from his life and thought, resists the closure to which Bennington's systematic account of Derrida's thought aspires. Together these texts are *dialogic* rather than *dialectic*; that is, the jointly constructed text is devoid of synthesizing, harmonizing, or homogenizing impulses and neither of the differing perspectives supersedes or cancels out the other. The two texts within this *stereophonic* text probe, disagree, and sometimes diverge.

Another example of a dialogic text is *Polylogue*, a dialogue between two heterogeneous discourses, Philippe Sollers's novel *H* and Julia Kristeva's commentary on the novel, called "Polylogue." In *Polylogue*, Kristeva's reflections in a different column and register are juxtaposed and interpenetrate with Sollers's novel. The polyphonic discourse occurs neither in the beginning of *Polylogue*, where Kristeva offers theoretical reflections on Sollers, nor at the conclusion, which includes three uninterrupted pages of *H* without Kristeva's commentary, but in the middle, where the two discourses interpenetrate yet are separate. In this section—especially a passage spanning pages 210 and 211—there is suggestive talk of a "new love," a heterosexual marriage that would not be a fusion of two into one. By "heterosexual" Kristeva seems to mean not the relation we conventionally call heterosexual, which may support the heterosexism of our culture and the pathologization of homosexuals, but any relation between two people—whether two men, two women, or a man and a women—which demonstrates a fundamental openness and love for the *heteros*, the other (Gallop, 1982, p. 127). "The passage on that marriage" of two discourses, as Jane Gallop (1982) aptly notes, "*is* that marriage" (p. 125).

There are at least two ways in which psychoanalytic texts might be authored more collaboratively. Patients and analysts could write joint accounts, as Yalom and Elkin did, or they each could offer their impressions and glosses of jointly selected material. The way that the patient's and analyst's involvement in this unorthodox project shapes transference and countertransference and impacts the treatment would, of course, need to be made part of joint analytic scrutiny.

The inclusion of two perspectives, as opposed to one, does not provide a window into the Real. Multiply inscribed texts still offer inevitably incomplete segments of the treatment. Psychoanalytic texts that strive to be more collaborative need to make their psychological, ideological, and political assumptions, functions, and effects, as well as their omissions and reductions, transparent not opaque. They also need to examine the implicit and explicit asymmetries and inequalities in power and position between analyst and patient and their influence on treatment and the fashioning of the text. The word "power" rarely appears in psychoanalytic discourse. Power and inequality, as Sandor Ferenczi's (1932) radical experiments with mutuality in analysis demonstrate, can no more be eliminated from psychoanalysis than from life itself. Asymmetry, power, and inequality will probably always be a feature of human relationships and seem built into the psychoanalytic process, in which one participant, the patient, pays the other, the analyst, because of his or her psychological expertise (e.g., Burke, 1992, p. 241) to help the patient with problems in living. Not all asymmetries are negative, and not all authority is necessarily authoritarian. Authoritarianism has at least two elements: the people in power are not amenable to feedback and those without power cannot impact on the powerful. There is a vast difference between using authority to perpetuate power and employing it in order to empower the person with less authority. Erich Fromm (1947) distinguished between "rational authority" and "irrational authority." The former is authority exercised by an individual with superior knowledge (and expertise) for the purpose of aiding the less powerful one in the relationship. Irrational authority, in Fromm's view, is authority employed for the purpose of perpetuating inequality.

Analysts, as well as patients, need to struggle against forms of authority and power that are *malignant*, that silence the patient or fit her into pre-established molds and interfere with the kind of mutuality that seems to be transformative in psychoanalysis. Each school of psychoanalysis has handled the question of authority and the power deriving from asymmetries differently. For purposes of mapping a complex and diverse terrain—but recognizing that the map is never the territory—I shall briefly note three trends in the history of psychoanalysis regarding this topic. If authority, in a typical classical analysis, resides in the *analyst*, who is often viewed as an objective, rational, omniscient observer with direct assess to Truth, then in self psychology it may lie in the *patient*, whose experience is granted a sovereign authority. "If there is one lesson I have learned during my life as an analyst," notes Heinz Kohut (1984), "it is the lesson that what my patients tell me is likely to be true—that many times when I believed that I was right and my patients were wrong, it turned out, though often only after a prolonged search, that my rightness was superficial whereas *their* rightness was profound" (pp. 83–84). If the patient is usually wrong in classical analysis, she is always right in self psychology.

Analysts within the interpersonal, object relations, and intersubjective traditions suggest a third alternative. Authority for many interpersonalists and intersubjectivists lies in what occurs *between* analyst and patient as perceived by both. Authority for many object relations theorists resides in what is *both* found and discovered by patient and analyst (Winnicott, 1971). One of the implications of these views, I suspect, is that asymmetry, power, and authority cannot be eliminated or transcended but should not be indulged. Analysts need to strive for mutuality and egalitarianism even as we realize the inevitability of authority, power, and asymmetry. When we neither indulge the power we inevitably wield nor attempt to deny it, we might more readily ascertain its impact on the analysand and the treatment.

If the analyst's authority is less authoritative in contemporary psychoanalysis than what analysts traditionally thought—if it is fallible, not absolute—then what does the analyst's expertise consist of? The analyst is highly skilled at fostering a collaborative, self-reflective relationship devoted to illuminating and enriching the patient's life (Mitchell, 1997), rather than revealing the absolute Truth about the patient's psyche. The analyst also teaches the patient a particular method of self-analytical investigation—cultivating in patients the capacity for self-observation and self-analysis (e.g., Gray, 1973)—which is essential to the patient's freedom.[10]

But the patient's ability to develop this capacity and become the author of her own existence is compromised when the analyst's authority remains sovereign and is not subjected to critical scrutiny and eventually subverted. Self-authorization cannot occur when there are pockets of unanalyzed idealization, compliance, or submissiveness in the therapeutic relationship. The reverence many analysts exhibit toward analytic founders such as Freud, Harry Stack Sullivan, D. W. Winnicott, Lacan, and Kohut suggests, as I discussed in chapter 4, that idealization and submissiveness are all too often not resolved in the analysis of many analysts. When idealization and deferentiality are unanalyzed, then the analyst's capacity to find his or her own voice may be compromised. It is difficult for an analyst who has remained deferentially linked to his or her own analyst to appreciate and foster an analysand's possibilities. Such self-subjugation is passed down from incompletely analyzed analysts to analysands, patients, and supervisees. The subversion of the analyst's authority opens up deeper levels of therapeutic safety, intimacy, and equality and thereby contributes to empowering the patient.

There are at least three things analysts can do to address hidden authoritarianism in psychoanalysis: They can pinpoint other examples of covert power and authoritarianism within the practice of analysis; they can struggle to use the power they wield therapeutically (and institutionally) with greater self-awareness, sensitivity, and flexibility; and they can aid patients (and analytic students) in constructively impacting on those in power.

In a psychoanalysis of "non-coercive power" (Clastres, 1989, p. 24), in which the analyst's authority was less sovereign, authoritarianism was lessened, and the patient's needs and wishes were taken more seriously, the ground rules might be more flexible and our descriptions of cases more provisional and collaborative. The analytic process might be less shaped by power and compliance, which could help our patients feel empowered. When the analyst is a jazz improvisor, not a customs official; a collaborator, not a ventriloquist speaking for silenced others, then we may have a psychoanalysis that is more truly relational. If I had to put the moral of the story I have tried to tell in this chapter into a slogan, I might put it thus: Where authoritarianism and hidden modes of domination were, collaboration and emancipation might be.[11]

# Conclusion

I do not wish to arouse conviction; I only wish to stimulate
thought and to upset prejudices. . . . The attitude we find most
desirable is a benevolent skepticism.
—Sigmund Freud, *Introductory Lectures on Psycho-Analysis*

"We are all somewhat hysterical," claimed Freud (1905a,
p. 171), by which I suspect he meant that we all wish to know and wish
*not* to know. Blindness and insight interweave in every human life. The
blindness of the seeing I has played a prominent role in psychoanalytic
history and institutions, theories and practices. It created a fault-line in
Freud's vision and the psychoanalytic edifice. As we have seen, visionary
thinkers like Sandor Ferenczi were marginalized and innovative ideas
about the shaping role of caregivers on emotional development were neglected by Freud and many of his successors.

Yet, psychoanalysis has endured, challenging conventional and taken-
for-granted assumptions and beliefs about rationality, truth, self, freedom, and determinism, and inspiring generations of thinkers, both within
and outside of the world of psychology. Psychoanalysis's influence grows
among philosophers, anthropologists, literary critics, feminists, and the
nonprofessional educated public, among others, even as its public image
suffers. Since I began this book several years ago, reports of psychoanalysis's demise have been increasing. *Time Magazine,* to cite one of various
examples, asked in 1993: "Is Freud Dead?" Psychoanalysis is not
"dead"—witness the proliferating number of journals, books, and
conferences—although it is not experiencing optimal health.

The greatest danger to psychoanalysis is its own blind spots and the
absence of greater disciplinary self-awareness. Psychoanalysis's fear of
knowing has compromised its capacity to fulfill its latent potential.

Psychoanalysis has undergone a modernization in its theories and practices since Freud. Thinkers representing a range of post-Freudian schools of thought have revised and updated Freud's fundamental conceptualizations about human nature, psychological development, and the therapeutic process. Many analysts no longer believe that the patient is an isolated, autonomous being whom they neutrally observe and objectively treat. Analysts are now more attuned to the relational nature of human development and the treatment process and the shaping role of their own theories and personal history on the therapeutic relationship. There is a widening scope of psychoanalysis in which clinical procedures are applied to a greater range of patients than in Freud's day. There has also been a proliferation of interest in neglected topics such as the role of gender in self-development.

Where do we go from here? As psychoanalysis enters its second century, it is worth reflecting, even if only in a provisional way, on its future.

Psychoanalysis does not have a future if it fails to come to terms with or remains bound by its past. Psychoanalysis has to do with itself what it recommends for patients, namely, assimilate its past so that it can understand its present and enliven its future. What psychoanalysis needs to focus on more thoroughly now is its own blind spots and hidden resources. Psychoanalysis's emancipatory potential only emerges when we approach it with what Freud termed "benevolent skepticism"—simultaneously appreciating its virtues and acknowledging its limitations. A compassionate critique makes it easiest to explore in *tandem* the secrets and insights, evasions and discoveries in its history, institutions, theories, and practices. Only then will the hidden pockets of censorship, narcissism, sectarianism, reductionism, and authoritarianism emerge. And only then will its capacity to question inherited motives, meanings, and authorities and provide a sanctuary to illuminate and enrich human individuality and forge new and more humane ways of understanding and connecting with others become possible.

To the extent that psychoanalysis denies or minimizes its difficulties and does not draw on Freud's legacy of continual questioning, self-transformation, and evolution, its future may be limited. Psychoanalysis will become out of step with the world in which patients and analysts are embedded. It will then generate stories about human nature and strategies for addressing human suffering that are constraining rather than enlightening and people will seek other ways of making sense of their experience and deepening self-understanding. To the extent that psychoanalysis acknowledges its need for further and ongoing theoretical and clinical self-reflectiveness, turns its formidable resources upon itself, and subjects its own histories, theories, organizations, and practices to analytic scrutiny and critique, we might justifiably conclude that its future is open and worthy of our continued attention. We might then have a postmodernization of psychoanalysis. The *posthumanist* psychoanalysis I briefly discussed in chapter 9 is one form it might take. A posthumanist analysis would be self-reflective and nonauthoritarian, pluralistic and evolving. Postmodernistic discourse all too often absolutizes its own negative theology—critiquing everything except itself. If deconstructionism rarely, if ever, deconstructs itself, a posthumanist psychoanalysis would seek to deepen self-reflection, question its own foundations, and attempt to discover its own blind spots. It would be affirmative no less than deconstructive, revising as well as critiquing its own favored concepts when the data called for it. Theories would be held more lightly and the therapeutic relationship would be more collaborative and less authoritarian. The psychoanalyst's presence in the treatment would be polymorphous: at once rationalistic and affectively attuned, devoted and empathetic, healing and creative. She would be a tireless detective, an intuitive improvisor, and a gentle midwife. A posthumanist psychoanalysis would be an intellectual hothouse encouraging diversity and creativity, rather than a clerisy propounding dogmas and excommunicating dissidents.

One of the fundamental obstacles to this change is the divisiveness and polarization that have permeated psychoanalysis. The history of psychoanalysis has often been a story of intolerance and Byzantine politics rather than tolerance and creativity. Polarities and apparent oppositions have divided psychoanalysts. They argue whether psychopathology is caused by interpersonal traumas and parental malattunements and inadequacies or intrapsychic fantasies, or whether psychoanalytic cure involves gaining psychological insight or having new interpersonal experiences. Psychoanalysts have traditionally "resolved" these apparent dualities through splitting: seeing one side as good and the other as bad. They then favor one pole of the opposition and neglect the other. A psychoanalyst then places greater explanatory weight on developmental arrests rather than conflicts; or she places greater emphasis on self-care rather than altruism in self-development; or she focuses on transference to the relative neglect of countertransference.

"One of the ironies of the creative process," notes Ernest Becker (1973), "is that it partly cripples itself in order to function" (p. xi). Authors typically exaggerate the importance of their own work and oppose it in a very competitive way with other versions of the truth. They get carried away by the exaggerations in their work, to which their self-esteem is intimately linked. "The problem," concludes Becker, "is to find the truth underneath the exaggeration, to cut away the excess elaboration or distortion and include the truth where it fits" (ibid.). We need, in my view, to create larger theoretical structures that can integrate rather than oppose and segregate disparate insights. The vision underlying a posthumanist psychoanalysis would be complex and integrative rather than monological and divisive. This would make it easier to reconcile some of the apparent polarities in psychoanalytic history, institutions, theories, and practices. Both revisionism and traditionalism in psychoanalytic scholarship would be seen as central to the health of psychoanalysis: analysts would value the histories and traditions that they were embedded in even as they sought to creatively reform psychoanalysis. Both the psychoanalytic mystic and the carriers of the psychoanalytic torch would play a vital role in psychoanalytic organizations. Psychoanalysts would improvise in treatment as well as respect the analytic ground rules. Both self-discovery and self-creation would be crucial in the construction of the patient's identity.

Here are some questions I believe we need to explore in order to create a posthumanist psychoanalysis. Where does censorship still live in analytic history, organizations, concepts, and methods? How can psychoanalytic institutions foster tolerance and creativity rather than sectarianism and stasis? How can we teach psychoanalytically, so that analytic principles of listening, speaking, and relating inform the educational process? Whose dissenting voices are censored or silenced in psychoanalysis? What counterhistories of analytic dissidents still need to be written? What theories or practices are idolized? How does psychoanalytic thinking itself filter awareness? What knowledge in psychoanalysis is taboo? Where is analytic theory phobic or fetishistic—limiting where we might travel intellectually or shielding us from more dangerous knowledge? Where does authoritarianism need to be deconstructed so that we might have freer associations? Are there any Emmy von N's or Ferenczi's among us who could detect what has been buried in the political unconscious of psychoanalysis? What disavowed potentials within psychoanalytic theories or practices are being neglected? How can we nourish the creative and vital frontiers of psychoanalysis?

A successful psychoanalytic treatment not only involves working through repression and self-unconsciousness so that one can gain increased knowledge about and integrate one's disavowed and troubling past. It also entails, as I suggested in the chapters on Winnicott and Kohut, self-creation in the present: forging new meanings, relationships, and ways of being now. For psychoanalysis to do this, it must venture into new territory as well as illuminate well-trammeled land. Organizationally, psychoanalysis is beset by a troubling paradox: the transmission of psychoanalytic knowledge and the training of psychoanalysts requires its institutionalization, yet psychoanalytic societies all too often undermine its vitality as an urge for self-perpetuation clashes with the pursuit of truth. Psychoanalytic organizations are both necessary and stifling. We thus need to create more humanistic kinds of institutions that fear dogma and political correctness and coercion more than freedom of inquiry. The emancipation rather than the socialization of students needs to be a higher priority. Psychoanalysts need to investigate topics that have been neglected in its past, such as the psychology of love and creativity, the politics of analytic knowledge, the moral dimensions of the analytic process, and the role of race, gender, and spirituality on identity.

Psychoanalysts cannot do this alone. Dialogues with allied disciplines such as literature, history, science, anthropology, sociology, philosophy, and feminism will enrich psychoanalysis and enhance its ability to explore new and foreign terrain. Each discipline offers different "observation points" (Braudel, 1980, p. 55), or perspectives on and questions about, the human condition. Psychoanalysis has traditionally tended to have an intellectually imperialistic relationship with other disciplines, focusing on what it could teach these disciplines rather than on how they might enrich psychoanalysis. Intellectual commerce between psychoanalysis and allied disciplines needs to be mutually respectful, so that each discipline can reflect upon what it might learn from the other (Rubin, 1997c). For example, psychoanalysis might explore what light the science of complexity or contemplative meditative disciplines might shed on its own European/ North American–derived conceptions of self-experience. Or literary theorists and anthropologists could heighten psychoanalytic sensitivity to issues of representation.

Exploring symptomatic tensions and inconsistencies within psychoanalysis and cultivating greater theoretical and clinical self-awareness will not lead to the eradication of psychoanalytic unconsciousness, nor will it give us access to the unadorned Truth. But it may uncover and lessen psychoanalysis's blind spots and foster greater theoretical and methodological self-awareness. Blindness will always be part of both the analytic enterprise and life itself. But by developing a more self-reflexive method, we may extend the unique "pathways" Freud opened for us and enrich and reanimate the complex, vastly evocative psychoanalytic enterprise.

How to live with care and responsibility in an age in which individuality is under siege, human life is cheapened, and freedom and dignity are threatened is one of the crucial challenges of late twentieth-century life. In a world in which we are encouraged to pervert our humanity by leading flattened, one-dimensional lives of self-absorption and consumption, it is crucial to have opportunities for reflecting on life and tools for investigating it in all its unsettling complexity. Otherwise, it is too easy to lose track of who we are and who we might be. Psychoanalysis can be a way of getting our bearings. The privacy, quietude, and intimacy of the analytic relationship provide a sanctuary to experience the complexity of a human life and to explore profound questions about how to live. As we learn through the analytic relationship to connect with and befriend our dreams and our demons, and to work through our restrictive ways of caring for and relating to self and others, deeper, more empathetic and nourishing relationships with ourselves and others become possible.

Judging from the negative reception psychoanalysis has received from critics since its inception, Freud's (1914c) remark that "psycho-analysis brings out the worst in everyone" (p. 39) was prophetic. Not only does it illuminate our deepest fears and conflicts, but it also arouses intense antipathy in its antagonists. But psychoanalysis can also bring out the best in us. And that is why it is indispensable for our time.

# Notes

NOTES TO INTRODUCTION

1. Since meaning, as Bakhtin (1986) knew, is the product of an interaction or dialogue between reader and text, rather than a monological essence waiting to be found in a neutral, fixed manuscript, there is no singular, settled, or definitive "Freud" or "psychoanalysis." Both are heterogeneous and evolving—a multitude of beliefs, perspectives, and theories, co-created and transformed by readers from different psychological, historical, sociocultural, and gendered perspectives. The preoccupation with Freud is suggested by the research of Allan Megill, which indicates that Freud is "the most heavily cited author in social science and arts and humanities indices" (quoted in Gelfand, 1992, p. xii n. 1).

2. It would take me too far afield at this point to discuss each of these critiques. In the course of this book it may become clearer why the feminist criticism of Freud's reductionistic and patriarchal account of women is the only one of these anti-Freudian critiques that I find compelling and edifying.

3. As I argue in chapters 9 and 10, these resources were often not actualized in theory or in practice.

4. Despite the variety of attempts, from Karen Horney to contemporary psychoanalysts and feminists, to revise Freud's problematic account of woman as deficient man, psychoanalysis is still riddled with androcentric biases that inhibit its understanding of the experience of women, particularly their enriching complexity. I explore one instance of this in greater detail in chapter 7.

5. The legacy of scientism lives on in psychoanalysis in various guises, including the unproductive debates about whether psychoanalysis is a science. From my perspective, psychoanalysis is not a science. Its purpose, objects of study, and methods are radically different from the traditional conception of science that underwrote Freud's psychoanalysis. To cite three examples: (1) the fact that in psychoanalysis the investigator has an indissoluble influence on what is being investigated clashes with traditional scientific notions of the neutrality and objectivity of the investigator; (2) the possibility of replication is psychoanalysis is deeply compromised by the uniqueness—perhaps the unrepeatability—of the analytic relationship; and (3) psychoanalytic notions do not readily lend themselves to empirical validation as it normally conceived (Stolorow & Atwood, 1986, p. 303). The possibility of validating psychoanalytic hypotheses is profoundly

complicated by the reality of unconscious mentation, motivation, and resistance, which renders data highly complex. Neither the patient's agreement with nor challenge to an analyst's interpretation, for example, is necessarily a sign of validation. Certain crucial facets of psychoanalysis may best be examined, in my view, in the consulting room, not the laboratory. It would be deeply unfortunate if the revolutionary insights about human nature emerging in the unique relationship in the consulting room were thought to be invalid if they had not been or could not be tested in a laboratory.

In claiming that psychoanalysis is not a science, I am not questioning the importance of "consensually validated observation and reason" (Gedo, 1984, p. 159), and I do not mean to devalue or ignore the potential importance of empirical research in psychoanalysis. Psychoanalytic propositions need to be validated consensually by analysts and investigators in allied fields. Research, in the sense of disciplined and systematic examination and evaluation of findings, can be instructive. For example, the work of Joseph Weiss and Harold Sampson, as well as others, on the psychoanalytic process or developmental propositions regarding infant-mother attachment and the impact of early environment on normalcy and pathology has clarified the analytic process by systematically testing the implications of psychoanalytic theory. But science is not the royal road to either the Real or the validation of psychoanalytic propositions.

Not only is psychoanalysis not a science, it should not trouble itself about not being one. Science is not the only way to investigate or illuminate human experience. Given the fact that science cannot answer questions about purposes or meaning, placing all our bets on science when studying human lives may have certain fundamental limitations. Because of this and other issues, I would agree with Flax (1993) that the belief in the scientificity of psychoanalysis or the attempt to make analysis scientific "is a symptom of some of its problems" (p. x), especially the way it is underwritten by the Enlightenment metanarrative of the possibility of objective truth. One of the results of subscribing to such a vision is that it enables analysts to ignore the subjective, power-laden, and political nature of their knowledge and practices. Psychoanalysis would not suffer if the question of its supposed scientificity was no longer posed except in terms of studying the history or sociology of psychoanalysis.

6. I am grateful to Weber's (1987) essay on the blindness of the seeing eye for drawing my attention to this evocative passage in Freud, although he approaches the topic from a somewhat different perspective.

7. There may be many humanisms and antihumanisms. The heterogeneous antihumanist tradition is not an entity with a "common denominator, essential core, or generative first principle" (Bernstein, 1992, p. 8), but a protean mood with some common features. The antihumanist tradition could be viewed as a political strategy, a method of reading, and an approach to discourse. Antihumanist discourses challenge certain conventional viewpoints about knowledge,

self, and world. They assert that inquiry does not disclose a singular monolithic truth, the self is not a transparent essence, and the image of the world is shaped, at least in part, by those apprehending it.

8. Freud's multidimensional self—including its difficulties—is explored in more detail in chapter 9. There are implications in Freud's work and uses to which it can be put in late twentieth-century thought that he did not *intend* and of which he could not have been aware. These implications were foreign to the historical and epistemological context that served as the horizon for Freud's life and thought.

9. Unlike many contemporary writers—Jürgen Habermas is a notable exception—I do not villainize the Enlightenment quest for emancipation even as I realize its imperfections and difficulties. From my perspective, we must avoid both unproblematized faith in reason *and* nihilistic skepticism about its possibility.

10. There is a tension in poststructuralist writings between, on the one hand, an exemplary challenging of authority, a subverting of inequitable hierarchies, and a championing of the subordinated and exiled and, on the other hand, a theorizing that sometimes avoids epistemological accountability (Ellis, 1989) and has had and continues to have quietistic implications (e.g., Bernstein, 1992). Poststructuralist claims about the "undecidability" of meaning and the play of "difference(s)" within a text or theory can serve escapist purposes as well as ethical ends. Such notions can be used to sanction noncommitment and cynical disengagement from life or to challenge relations of dominance (e.g., Flax, 1993, p. xi).

In raising questions about poststructuralism, I need to emphasize that its strategies of uncovering tensions, hierarchies, and gaps in theories and texts have also been of immense help to me in detecting unconsciousness in psychoanalysis and striving toward greater self-reflexivity. My critique of psychoanalysis might have been hampered without the strategies of reading and thinking often available in poststructuralist writings.

11. The work of Ferenczi (e.g., 1928), among others, which exhibits an exemplary sense of its own partiality and a conditional belief in its own validity, is an exception illustrating the rule.

12. Science was central to the self-identity of Freud and psychoanalysis. It was the only viable paradigm available to him. One other reason psychoanalysis might have hitched its star to science was to mitigate the precarious position it was in when it was transplanted to the foreign—and not always hospitable—soil of the United States. Psychoanalysis readily fit into the general and pervasive cultural Zeitgeist valorizing autonomy and individuality. But by demonstrating that humans are not even masters of their own minds, it generated antipathy as well as curiosity. Piggy-backing on the authority and prestige of science, which had replaced religion as our secular god, may have been an attempt to sanction or lessen

in some way the unsettlement analysis generated by the narcissistic blow it dealt human beings in revealing their own inevitable self-blindness. Perhaps having the imprimatur of science was a way of making its disturbing truths palatable.


NOTES TO CHAPTER I

1. I am indebted to Rand and Torok's (1987) examination of secrets in psychoanalysis for this way of looking at it. They highlight various "secrets" in psychoanalysis, for example, the deletions in the case of Emmy von N., the creation of the Secret Committee, and the censorship of the Freud-Fliess letters. They correctly note that the "secrets which permeate the history of psychoanalysis will yield up their meaning once we posit the continuous presence of a secret in Freud himself" (p. 285) and accurately pinpoint both its source (Freud) and the fact of its deleteriousness. They do not, however, offer "content or cause." This chapter attempts to delineate the salient causes of psychoanalytic secrets (or, as I prefer to conceptualize it, psychoanalytic self-censorship), point out additional manifestations. (e.g., Freud's self-analysis and his model of the mind and psychopathology), and explore some crucial theoretical and clinical consequences.

I came across Barron et al.'s (1991) study of Freud's ambivalence regarding "secrets," his simultaneous interest in unveiling and concealing them, as I was putting the final touches on this chapter. They stress that Freud's conflictual relationship with his mother and " 'unspeakable' family secrets" play a central role in this ambivalence and deeply shape Freud's interest in exposing and veiling secrets (e.g., p. 143). In discussing other manifestations of this process, such as Freud's self-analysis and theory of pathogenesis (and, in subsequent chapters, psychoanalytic self-blindness in its theories of selfhood, its institutional politics, and so forth), I am attempting to deepen and broaden the implications of Freud's ambivalence about knowing.

2. It is possible that the presence of a profound and hidden narcissism in Freud's mother may shed light on why in Freud's (1914d) theory he portrays libidinal object cathexis as *diminishing* rather than raising self-regard: "libidinal object-cathexis does not raise the self-regard. The effect of the dependence upon the loved object is to lower that feeling. . . . The re-enrichment of the ego can be effected only by a with-drawal of the libido from its objects" (pp. 98–100). Freud's claims about love, like his remarks about parental narcissism, run counter to the experience of most people, who are *enhanced* rather than depleted by love. While there may be a pervasive element of narcissism in love relations, Freud elevates narcissism to its only constituent. Freud's counterintuitive claim has been validly critiqued by psychoanalysts as an unfortunate remnant of the mental hydraulics of psychoanalytic drive theory (e.g., Stolorow and Lachmann, 1980). Freud's unconscious motivation for this postulate and the subjective truth for him embedded in this fallacious claim are additional reasons. The emotional price of

loving a narcissist *is* depleting, because one has to deny one's own experience of disregard and deprivation in order to maintain the relationship.

3. There are at least two other possible sources of mystification in Freud's early life: "felonious 'financial' activities" in his family (e.g., Gedo, 1986, p. 30) and the "bewildering texture of family relationships" (Gay, 1988, p. 5). Freud's father was twenty years older than Freud's mother; his father's son from a previous marriage, Emanuel, was older than Freud's mother; and Emanuel's son, Freud's nephew, was older than Freud.

4. Classical psychoanalysis is not the only school of psychoanalysis to subscribe to what Stolorow and Atwood (1992) aptly term the "Myth of the Isolated Mind," which ascribes to individuals a mode of being-in-the-world in which they exist as isolated monads estranged from self, others, and nature. Examples of this reductionistic conception of humans appear, in differing degrees, in various schools of psychoanalysis including ego psychology, object relations theory, self psychology, and even interpersonal psychoanalysis (e.g., p. 14).

5. A related point could be made about transference. The concept of transference both illuminates the inner subjective world of the analysand even as it may draw attention away from the interactional determinants of "transference" phenomena. The concept of transference can deny the impact of present reality— including the complex interaction of analysand and analyst—by attributing it to distortions from the past (e.g. Stolorow and Lachmann, 1984–85).

6. Ambivalence about knowing is also reflected in the unresolved tension in the theory of Freudian dream practice between the associational and symbolic approach to the dream material, as I shall discuss in Chapter 10. The former fosters the emergence of the unique meanings of the analysand's dream material and opens up the possibility of experiencing previously hidden aspects of human subjectivity while the latter often funnels the radically novel content of the dream into the pre-existing categories of the *analyst's* dream meanings and thus may prevent the uniqueness of the analysand's subjectivity from fully emerging.

NOTES TO CHAPTER 2

1. Another sign of the "success" of the censorship of Ferenczi was that Anna Freud is universally attributed with discovering the defensive process of "identification with the aggressor" in her *Ego and the Mechanism of Defense* (1936) even though Ferenczi presented this concept in 1932.

2. This was not the first (or last) time this kind of "character assassination" (Gay, 1988, p. 481) of analysts holding different viewpoints than those in power occurred in psychoanalytic history. Jung and Rank had been dismissed as mentally ill after theoretically and personally challenging Freud (Jones, 1957, p. 72).

The impact of politics and Jones's own subjective concerns on psychoanalytic "history" remains to be more fully elucidated. Fromm (1955) has made a suggestive beginning. Let me mention two possible sources of Jones's antipathy towards Ferenczi: Jones was interested both in gaining Freud's acceptance and in undermining others who did—including Ferenczi, whom Freud insisted Jones enter analysis with.

3. One wonders if Freud's pathologizing of Ferenczi and consequent dismissal of his work was due, not simply to the "mistakes and overexaggerations" Ferenczi's friend and literary executor, Michael Balint, pinpoints in his teacher's work, but because Ferenczi elucidates traumatic experiences that Freud wished not to see in his own life and his own clinical work with Ferenczi. As I attempted to demonstrate in chapter 1, Freud's life and thought were deeply influenced by his defensive attempts to deny the emotional traumatization he experienced at the hands of his mother. I wonder if Freud unconsciously needed to suppress Ferenczi's work because the latter was proposing a theory that threatened to decrypt both Freud's own "bad treatment" at the hands of what he once termed, speaking of female development, the "faithless mother," and his own insensitivity to Ferenczi's own childhood traumas.

4. Jones was not the first censor in psychoanalytic history. In 1910, Freud tried to delegate powers of censorship to Jung. At the International Congress in Nuremberg, Freud hoped to make Jung the permanent president of the International Psycho-Analytical Association. His powers would include the "appointment and deposition of analyst and the right to veto their writings before they were published" (Webster, 1995, p. 372). This never actually came to pass.

5. This is not to say that he did not become entangled in sticky and problematic countertransferential situations, as the case of RN in his *Clinical Diaries* suggests.

6. Henry Louis Gates's (1991) similar characterization of Franz Fanon was instrumental in my developing this interpretation of Ferenczi.

7. Menaker (1982) notes the "utter extinction which . . . [Rank] experienced in the literature of psychoanalysis after his break with Freud—much to the detriment of its scientific progress" (p. 145 no. 8).

NOTES TO CHAPTER 3

1. Works such as Leo Rangell's *The Mind of Watergate* (1980) and Joel Kovel's *White Racism* (1984) are exceptions suggesting the generalization.

2. Historian Carl Schorske's (1981) examination of the cultural context shaping Freud's work may illuminate one important facet of this lacuna. The founder of psychoanalysis neutralized and overcame deeply disturbing Austrian sociopolitical realities, according to Schorske, by the "counterpolitical" gesture of psychologizing and thus depoliticizing history—explaining politics in terms of personal psychological categories that undoubtedly influenced them. "Politics is neutralized by a counterpolitical psychology. . . . By reducing his own political past and present to an epiphenomenal status in relation to the primal conflict between father and son, Freud gave his fellow liberals an a-historical theory of

society that could make bearable a political world spun out of orbit and beyond control" (pp. 107, 203). Freud's "flight from politics" (p. 196) may have shaped psychoanalysis's retreat from the political.

3. Not all analysts—including Freud and Ferenczi—dichotomize these issues. Many analysts recognize that each member of the binary pair is essential.

4. There seems to be a dearth of literature, for example, on countertransference during this period. I have only been able to find three references (Hann-Kende, 1933; A. Balint & M. Balint, 1939; Fenichel, 1941).

5. Analysts differ in their tolerance of and support for deviation from whatever they perceive as the mainstream or their favored viewpoints. There is probably a higher tolerance for dissent among those analysts who maintain that there is a "common ground" (Bachant & Richards, 1993, p. 455) among different perspectives on the contemporary analytic scene than those "total composite theorists" (ibid.) who claim that contemporary understandings and innovations about such issues as object relations are already contained within and merely derivative of classical psychoanalysis rather than supplemental or complemental.

6. The writings of Winnicott (1971), Ogden (1986), Phillips (1988), and Bollas (1992) contributed to my conception of potential space. Ogden's (1986) suggestive reflections on the "psychopathology of potential space" might aid attempts to establish a psychoanalytic culture that nourishes dialogue and creativity. It could, for example, alert us to potential difficulties, such as an inhibition of imaginative possibilities due to the absence of a mutual interplay between reality and fantasy. This might occur when there was a dissociation of reality and fantasy; a foreclosure of either fantasy or imagination or a subsumption of reality to fantasy or fantasy to reality. The implications of Ogden's reflections in this area need further elaboration.

7. Mitchell (1988) has convincingly critiqued the "developmental tilt" approach to psychoanalytic theory construction, integration (and deviation) that "postulates that Freud was correct in understanding the mind in terms of conflicts among drives and that object relations are also important, but earlier" (p. 136). In the development tilt strategy of theory construction, relational needs are "integrated" into traditional analytic formulations of drives and defenses by claiming that the former are applicable to early phases of development and to more ill patients, while healthier patients should be treated and responded to according to the perspectives generated by traditional analytic theories of drives and defenses. In analytic theorizing underwritten by developmental tilt perspectives, the tacit assumption is that "young infants have relational needs; older children and adults (those who are healthy or suffer only from neurotic difficulties) struggle with conflicts between instinctual impulses and defenses" (p. 139).

8. Groddeck and Horney, to cite two examples, offered alternatives to the phallocentrism of traditional formulations. Groddeck, for example, admitted to feeling "envy that I am not myself a woman and cannot be a mother . . . that a

man should think of child-bearing is nothing strange, but only that this should be so obstinately denied" (1928, pp. 11–12). And Horney's (1926) experience analyzing men taught her of the "envy of pregnancy, childbirth, and motherhood, as well as of the breasts and the act of suckling."

9. Because of the impossibility of immaculate perception or theorizing and the constructed nature of all knowledge—including introspection—the process of attempting to empathize with clinical material or a theory may be considerably more theory-laden and complex than the literature on empathy sometimes seems to imply. But I do not think that this invalidates the distinction between struggling to understand what something means from within a subject's own frame of reference and from an externally imposed viewpoint. There seem to be readings that stray far from the spirit of what the theorist wrote. Assessing this is always provisional and thereby contestable.

10. I wish to thank the psychoanalytic candidates I taught in a seminar on British Object Relations Theory at Postgraduate Center for Mental Health in the fall of 1994, whose openness to my inchoate reflections on the political unconscious of psychoanalysis spurred me to elaborate further on the implications of this topic, which resulted in this chapter. I am also grateful to the candidates I taught in a seminar on Human Development at Training and Research Institute for Self Psychology, who eagerly collaborated with me in attempting to make the teaching experience a "practice of freedom." The thoughtful reflections of George Atwood, Doris Dlugacz, Bettina Edelstein, James Jones, JoAnn Magdoff, and two anonymous reviewers from the American Academy of Psychoanalysis enriched this chapter, as did the incisive questions from the audience at a presentation I gave at the winter 1995 meeting of the American Academy of Psychoanalysis and the fall 1997 meeting of the International Federation of Psychoanalytic Education. I also wish to thank Matthew Von Unwerth of the New York Psychoanalytic Institute Library, who provided bibliographic assistance, and Ken Eisold, who generously shared with me his own work on intolerance in psychoanalytic institutes.

NOTES TO CHAPTER 4

1. This is not deny the parallel and neglected stream that has run through psychoanalytic history of psychoanalysts such as Silberer (1917), Pfister (1948), Jung (1958), Menninger (1942), Horney (1945; 1987), Fromm et al. (1960), Kelman (1960), Milner (1973), Rizzuto (1979), Meissner (1984), Kohut (1985), Rubin (1985; 1992; 1993; 1996b), Winnicott (1986), Roland (1988), Suler (1993), and Spezzano and Gargiulo (1997) who have embraced psychoanalytic theory and technique while nonreductionistically examining religion. For them, Freud's account of religion's origins in wish fulfillment and its uniformly defensive character are not the last word on religion. They have pointed to various aspects of religion's salutary dimensions, including its "supportive aspect" and "civilizing

influence" (Kohut, 1985, p. 261); its ability to sensitize us to the inner life (Jung, 1958), lessen human anxieties (Pfister, 1948), facilitate "self-integration" (Rizzuto, 1979, p. 182), deepen and amplify the quality of one's life (Meissner, 1984), and "foster life by inspiring love" (Menninger, 1942, p. 191); and its capacity to enrich psychoanalytic practice by cultivating the analyst's capacity for "evenly-hovering attention" and thus refining psychoanalytic listening (Rubin, 1985).

Participating in religion can promote "cultural experience" (Winnicott, 1986, pp. 35–36) and "well-being"—being fully awake and alive—which could expand the psychoanalytic vision of optimal psychological health (Fromm, 1960). Studying Asian patients who are actively involved in spiritual disciplines can reduce psychoanalytic ethnocentrism and expand psychoanalytic conceptions of subjectivity (Roland, 1988; Rubin, 1993; 1996b; Suler, 1993).

2. I find Webster's (1995) claims about the putative "cult like features" of psychoanalysis and the "messianic role adopted by its founder" (p. 315) uncompelling. To my mind Webster does not adequately substantiate his claim and neglects a variety of countervailing facts, such as Freud's committment to an identity as an Enlightenment rationalist, his distaste for religion, the rationalistic and atheistic character of analysis, and the way that the unconscious, as Freud described it, marks "the death of the guru" (Phillips, 1995, p. xvi).

3. Even a religion such as Buddhism, which would appear to be, as Huston Smith (1958) claims, "without authority, without ritual, without theology, without tradition, without grace, and without the supernatural" (p. 158), at one time or another in its variegated history has contained at least five of these elements.

4. Worship of authorities, dogmas, idolatrous relations to doctrines, exclusive organizations, and intolerance of dissent have existed in political systems concerned with oppression, such as Marxism, as well as intellectual, therapeutic, and religious movements. It is thus not the sole province of religion. And there is more to religion, as the psychoanalysts mentioned in note 1 to this chapter have pointed out, than worship of ancestors and doctrines, fundamentalistic attitudes, idolatry, and an intolerance of dissent. Unfortunately, the *spirituality* that may be the spark for, and the core of, authentic religious experiences may often be extinguished or eclipsed as religious experience becomes institutionalized.

5. This was changing toward the end of Kohut's life, although traces of it still appear in his posthumously published *How Does Analysis Cure?* in the notion of disintegration products, which is underwritten by an allegiance to the drive theory he elsewhere eschewed.

6. Since a particular culture is not a homogeneous unity but the site of internal differences, contradictions, and conflicts, even within the "same" culture selfhood may be viewed in multifarious ways.

7. Roland's characterization of the Western self as essentially individualistic is more true of men than women. Male individualism takes for granted and is

indissolubly linked to the support and service of nonautonomous and nonindividualistically oriented women and less privileged men.

8. Journal issues (e.g., *Psychoanalytic Dialogues*, vol. 3, no. 3) and symposiums devoted to psychoanalysis and gender or psychoanalysis and feminism suggest that this is slowly changing, at least in terms of gender. The impact of such issues as race and class seems more neglected, although the small amount of work being done in these areas (e.g., Altman, 1993; Flax, 1993; Javier & Rendon, 1995) suggests the generalization.

9. Derrida, following Heidegger, signifies the simultaneous necessity and inadequacy of a term by putting it "sous rature," or under erasure. Including the term indicates that it is essential, while crossing it out alerts us to its flaws. Strictly speaking, the heterogeneity of cultures and the hybridization of their members problematizes if not invalidates such distinctions as "Western" and "non-Western," since both are categories with permeable and interpenetrating boundaries. I use the term "Western" as a way of pointing to a phenomenon, but I am aware of its essential inadequacy.

10. Other analysts will pinpoint idols that I either worship or do not notice. Two other idols, self-centered subjectivity and the analyst's authority, are discussed in chapters 8 and 11, respectively.

11. I want to thank Peter Hoffer for graciously offering his translation of this unpublished letter from the forthcoming third volume of the Freud-Ferenczi correspondence in a personal communication on December 6, 1996.

12. Phillips's (1994) playful, evocative, and nonidolatrous exploration of psychoanalysis enhanced my reflections on this topic.

NOTES TO CHAPTER 5

1. It is possible that the theoretical sequestering of his two conflicting accounts of subjectivity occurs not because they represent different or evolving reflections on subjectivity, but because it is psychologically disruptive to bring these opposing perspectives together. Did Winnicott's reflections on the endangered "incommunicado" self (1963) represent an update of his earlier (1960a) conception of the frozen True Self that needs to be found? Or was he delineating another facet of subjectivity—the danger of pathological impingements and the importance of privacy and solitude? Was he simply not interested in synthesizing his earlier and later accounts of subjectivity? Since we do not know whether Winnicott discarded, changed, or updated his theory of the True Self when he theorized about the endangered "incommunicado" self, it is unclear whether the inconsistent formulations represent a lack of interest or failure in synthesizing his conceptions or a theoretical splitting symptomatic of his own conflicts about bringing these two formulations together conceptually. In my own reading of Winnicott's life and work, the claim that bringing them together was so unbearable that they were

unconsciously sequestered—his theoretical splitting performatively enacting the psychological danger of bringing them together—makes the most sense.

2. It would take me too far afield to discuss this in detail here. I shall explore the concept of the True Self more extensively in the next chapter, where my claim about reification will be spelled out.

3. I am indebted to Phillips's (1988) work for this insight and a similar way of putting it. There is evidence that taking care of (m)others was reenacted in his unhappy twenty-five-year (first) marriage to Alice Buxton Taylor, an artistic women who "suffered substantial psychiatric difficulties, which included hallucinatory and delusional material" (Kahr, 1996, pp. 43–44). Looking after a needy woman with profound difficulties seems to have replicated his experience with his depressed mother.

4. There is reason to believe that English child-rearing theories and practices in Winnicott's time—as adumbrated by, for example, Truby King—with the emphasis on compliance and meeting social demands, also discouraged authenticity (Gerald Wooster, personal communication).

5. It is conceivable that his father's incapacity to handle affect may have generated a great deal of guilt, which contributed to making Donald eventually feel that the "attainment of a capacity for making reparation in respect of personal guilt is one of the most important steps in the development of the healthy human being" (Winnicott, 1948, p. 91). One wonders whether reparation for guilt would have played so central a role in his sense of a healthy human being if negative affect had been more ably contained in his family.

6. Winnicott's notion of the "use" of the object (e.g., Winnicott, 1971) may have arisen from this kind of soil. Winnicott (1971) distinguished between "relating" to an object and the "use" of an object (p. 88). In object usage, claims Winnicott, the subject "destroys" the object and the object survives. Winnicott is not referring to the "exploitation" of the other, but to the capacity to be comfortable about one's own needs and aggressiveness in relation to others and the other's capacity to endure and psychologically survive the onslaught without crumbling or retaliation. Winnicott's remark about adolescents and their parents provides an apt illustration: the job of the adolescent, according to Winnicott, is to "kill" the parent and the job of the parent is to "survive."

The capacity to use the object, according to Winnicott (1971), "cannot be said to be inborn, nor can its development in an individual be taken for granted. . . . The development of a capacity to use an object is another example of the maturational process as something that depends on a facilitating environment" (p. 89). The object's resilience is crucial. When the other is crushed by the subject's aggression, then the latter has to hold itself back and engage in a delimiting type of self-straitjacketing. The emphasis Winnicott placed on the importance of an aggressive and self-centered "use" of an object (as opposed to a self-denying and self-inhibiting "relating" to an object) may have arisen because of a not-good-enough familial environment in relation to his own aggression. Because Winnicott's parents—especially his father—had great difficulty "surviving" his aggression, he may have been prematurely forced into object relating. This may be why he implictly equated object relating with self-abnegation. Lacking the opportunity to develop the capacity for object usage in his family, and believing that object relating had inherently self-denying facets, Winnicott stressed the importance of the "use" of an object. The "use" of others that Winnicott recommended—and probably lacked in his family—seems like a heuristic alternative to his self-depriving and self-negating experience with his parents, in which he had to forsake his own reactions in the act of fitting into their needs. But it also caused him to neglect another crucial facet of self-development, namely, what the self offers the other. The well-being of others has a place—still to be delineated—in psychoanalytic accounts of self-development.

7. Winnicott used the notions of transitional object, transitional phenomena, and transitional experiencing in various ways. One important way he employed them was to portray a third "intermediate area" contrasted to "inner or personal psychic reality and with the actual world in which the individual lives, which can be objectively perceived" (1971, p. 102). The notion of transitional experiencing deeply enriched psychoanalytic understanding of creativity, mind, cultural phenomena, and "creative living." It also may have provided a segregated region—neither inside nor outside—that protected the self against the twin dangers of being visible and endangered or hidden and depleted. One could then be seen and safe.

8. Another difficulty with the notion of the "permanent isolation of the individual" is that it partakes of what Stolorow and Atwood (1992) term the "myth of the isolated mind" (p. 7), a mode of being-in-the-world in which "the individual exists separately from the world of physical nature and also from engagement with others" (ibid.). Much of Winnicott's work, of course, highlights the opposite view, the inherently *relational* nature of human life. The myth of the isolated mind wards off a variety of psychological dangers, including mortality, alienation, and anguish.

NOTES TO CHAPTER 6

1. Here Winnicott speaks of the True Self as if it is inherited and seemingly neglects the fact that he emphasizes elsewhere that it is alive and ever-changing and cannot be distinguished as a singular essence. Given Winnicott's unique emphasis on and sensitivity to the sacredness of human individuality, aliveness, creativity, and spontaneity, it might at first appear that I am making a strange claim. The tension that I am referring to between his two conceptions will hopefully become clearer later in this chapter.

2. As I suggested in chapter 5, there is compelling evidence that in Winnicott's own family he was simultaneously unseen by his critical and absent puritanical

father and swallowed up by the neediness of his profoundly depressed and emotionally unavailable mother, which generated a fault line in his personality and resulted in unresolved conflicts over authenticity and relatedness. The theoretical tension between Winnicott's two contradictory characterizations of subjectivity depict his attempt to resolve his conflict about authenticity and relatedness and thus heal the rupture in his personality. His wish to embody subjectivity so that it could be seen and mirrored, and his urge not to fix subjectivity and thus allow it to be imprisoned or swallowed up, stem from his own wish to be seen and dread of being found in his family.

3. Rorty's (1989) recommendation that we replace the metaphor of self-discovery of our essence with the project of self-creation of our identity alerted me to an important difficulty with Winnicott's theory and was of crucial importance in the genesis of this chapter, although my experience as a practicing psychoanalyst of the importance of the past for the present encouraged me to place greater emphasis on the former than Rorty perhaps does. Self-creation has genetic, intrapsychic, and interpersonal constraints. In a different body, family, and treatment, other possibilities for self-creation would be possible or foreclosed.

4. After the work of Langs (e.g., 1982b), analysts have become more attuned to their own contribution to various impingements on patients in analysis.

5. This section draws directly from a previous work (Rubin, 1996b).

NOTES TO CHAPTER 7

1. That this tension lives in self psychology is suggested by (if not enacted in) "The Two Analyses of Mr. Z.," the case Kohut himself regarded as the seminal case of self psychology, in which the identity of the subject (and founder) is revealed *and* concealed. It is likely that this essay is autobiographical. Kohut's wife and son, as well as various colleagues, were convinced, for example, that it was (e.g., Cocks, 1994). The central document of self psychology may then be a self-analysis that is presented as if it is a story about someone in analysis with Kohut.

2. Stolorow, Brandchaft, and Atwood (1987) have argued that this concept conceives of self-experience in an overly mechanistic, reified, and restrictive way. One example of this is the conception of the self as bipolar, which is a reification: "the poles of self become ossified entities that belie the organic fluidity of human experience" (p. 20). The complexity of human experience that Kohut elsewhere acknowledges and provides perspectives to investigate and fortify is eclipsed in such formulations. Another example is the conception of a "tension arc" as a motivational prime-mover, which is mechanistic, not unlike the libidinal hydraulics of classical drive theory. Tension arcs are constructs without any experiential or clinical referent.

3. There is, in a certain sense, no such thing as a woman, by which I mean that women are not one *essential* thing. While it can obviously be reductive to essentialize the complexity of anyone's experience, it can be disempowering to

only offer "local," nongeneralizable observations about the world. Generalizations may have a particular strategic use, such as highlighting problematic trends or practices—for example, systematic and systemic inequities arising from androcentric theories. That is why I am not refraining from generalizing about the eclipsing of "women's" experience in androcentric theories out of a quixotic quest for theoretical purity.

4. Cultures that are not individualistically oriented can, of course, foster ambitions and ideals such as loyalty to community. The concept of ambition may be more inextricably tied to individualism than to ideals.

5. Discussions with Joel Kramer and Alan Roland opened up and illuminated different facets of this neglected topic.

6. Ambitions and ideals—such as the wish to be empathic and/or related—*may* obviously partake of a more non-self-centered mode of living.

7. With its exemplary tools for investigating self-experience, self psychology could illuminate a self organized around the value of non-self-centeredness as might occur, for example, in a person pursuing a spiritual practice in which self-nullifying altruism is a central motivational priority.

8. My account of non-self-centered subjectivity is taken from previous works (Rubin 1993; 1996b) and has been enriched by Karen Peoples's (1991) unpublished paper, "The Paradox of Surrender: Constructing and Transcending the Self."

9. Horney (1939), among others (e.g., Rank), struggled to remedy what she felt was the predilection for a genetic fallacy in traditional psychoanalytic formulations. While acknowledging that childhood experiences "exert a decisive influence on development" (p. 152), she also notes that this sort of viewpoint is too mechanistic and unidimensional, neglecting the influence of character structure in the present on conduct and interpersonal relationships. My critique of the genetic perspective emphasizes the way it may, at times, foster the patient's disclaimed responsibility for both perpetuating and transforming problems in living in the present. Wachtel (1977) has illuminated this topic.

10. The emphasis on transference and countertransference suggests that a focus on the here and now has always been part of psychoanalysis. But the emphasis has often been on how the present is an emanation of the *past*. I mean to emphasize both the traditional psychoanalytic emphasis on the shaping role of the past and the importance of the present. I differ from what might be termed "existential analysis" in its uncritical importation into psychoanalytic theory of concepts and categories that are not always derived from clinical encounters. The introduction of Heidegger's ontology of *Dasein*, for example, into psychoanalysis seems of questionable value (e.g., Atwood & Stolorow, 1984, p. 31).

11. Freud presented a dual-track model of mind in which both the past and the present are formative in his concept of "deferred action"—that is, the past is active in the present and the present can alter and "retranscribe" memories from the past (Freud 1985, p. 356). He also presented a dual-track model in his meta-

phor of the "mystic writing pad," in which the mind is likened to a writing tablet composed of traces from both past and present (1925b). The implications of this model seem not to have been fully clarified.

## NOTES TO CHAPTER 8

1. Silverman, Lachmann, and Milich (1982) illuminate the adaptive as well as the pathological possibilities of oneness experiences, although from a slightly different perspective than I adopt in this chapter. They emphasize the way the absorptive union of oneness fantasies can enhance therapeutic success as long as the sense of self is not threatened, while I emphasize the self-expansiveness (and relatedness) of non-self-centered subjectivity. Identity is not "sublated," as Hegel might put it, but extended and enriched. James Jones (1995) has helped me articulate this.

2. Sullivan (1953), Winnicott (1958), Mitchell (1988), Levenson (1991), and Stolorow and Atwood (1992), among others, have alerted us to the limitations of positing an isolated, self-contained self. But because spiritual perspectives are largely absent from most relationally oriented paradigms, individualism still retains a powerful and perhaps unacknowledged impact on views of relationships, intimacy, and morality inspired by relational theories, as I hope to demonstrate later in this chapter.

3. Since Western culture is heterogeneous, the influence of individualism varies. Nonetheless, individualism plays a central role.

4. When Freud (1930) stated in the opening paragraph of *Civilization and Its Discontents* that "people commonly use false standards of measurement—that they seek power, success and wealth for themselves and admire them in others, and that they underestimate what is of true value in life" (p. 64), he was demonstrating that he was troubled by human narcissism and was pointing toward what we might term a more spiritual vision of the world, even if he did not use that language or consciously believe in that category.

5. I came across Cushman's (1995) "cultural history" of American psychotherapy as I was completing this book. Cushman also depicts the costs of "self-contained individualism" (p. 6). His study enriches my focus on the implications for analytic conceptions of self by illuminating the political and economic consequences of this perspective. For example, he portrays the way the psychotherapeutic focus on the individualistic self is the "perfect complement to an economy that must stave off economic stagnation by arranging for the continual purchase and consumption of surplus goods. Psychotherapy is the profession responsible for treating the unfortunate personal effects of the self without disrupting the economic arrangements of consumerism" (p. 6).

6. Atwood and Stolorow (1984) view permeability of self-structure as a sign of a healthy self provided one also is experiencing self-stability.

7. It would take me too far afield to discuss Ogden's (1991) suggestive re-

working of the Kleinian notion of positions. Although I have found this work clinically illuminating, the non-self-centered mode of being I am pointing toward is, among other things, the positing of a *fourth* state of being, a corrective to the emphasis on the regressive and the primitive in the autistic-contiguous, paranoid-schizoid, and the depressive positions.

8. This section has been enriched by Karen Peoples's (1991) unpublished paper, "The Paradox of Surrender: Constructing and Transcending the Self."

9. There seems to be a greater interest in this question in the last decade and a half.

10. I read the suggestive work of Jessica Benjamin (1988) as I was preparing this manuscript for publication. Her emphasis on a psychoanalysis of two subjects, "both empowered and mutually respectful" (p. 8), provides an important direction for a psychoanalytic theory of intimacy.

11. This section draws heavily on and attempts to extend a previous work (Rubin, 1996b).

12. Anyone who cannot remember a PIN number or open a gym lock has experienced a phenomenon in which we "know" more than we know, which may illustrate what I am referring to regarding the notion of somatic knowledge. We punch in the correct number or open the lock—not when we try to think about the number, which only seems to generate more frustration and temporary amnesia—but when we "let our fingers do the walking" (and thinking).

13. The non-Eurocentric work of Horney (1945; 1987), Jung (1958), Kelman (1960), Fromm et al. (1960), Roland (1988), and Rubin (1985; 1991; 1993; 1996b) are, as I suggested in chapter 4, notable exceptions—pointing, for example, to some of Buddhism's salutary dimensions.

NOTES TO CHAPTER 9

1. Freud's work, as I suggested in note 1 in the introduction, is not monolithic or "finished." It is diverse and evolving, composed of numerous theories and practices that take on a different coloration depending on the interests and vantage points of the interpreter.

2. The legacy that Freud bequeathed us was only germinally present in his work. He did not see its full implications or always practice in accordance with it. There are implications in Freud's work and uses to which it can be put that he did not intend and of which he could not have been aware. These implications were foreign to the historical and epistemological context that served as the horizon of Freud's life and thought. There is a tension in Freud's method between its liberating and enslaving possibilities. On the one hand, Freud's view of the analytic relationship and process was often positivistic and authoritarian, with a supposedly neutral, objective analyst standing outside the analysand's discourse and conflicts and serenely interpreting its unconscious meaning. On the other

hand, psychoanalytic method can and often does challenge and subvert psycho-analytic positivism.

3. "Free association," which Freud (1931b) claimed is "considered by many people the most important contribution made by psychoanalysis, the methodo-logical key to its results" (p. 403), is not "free" (Spence, 1982). It is constrained by, among other things, the structure of the language the speaker is utilizing, the speaker's concern with communicating with a particular listener, his or her ana-lyst, the speaker's conscious and unconscious guilt or shame, and so forth. The freedom one experiences when free associating is thus not *unconditional* and does not remove all fetters. Its liberatory potential—its almost Taoist view of life as a kind of journey-without-goal or way-that-is-never-finished—is indicated by Fer-enczi's (1927) suggestive remark that the analysand does not free associate in order to be *cured*, she is cured when she can free associate (p. 79). I take him to mean that one can then live in a playful, authentic, and unconstrained manner that is not permeated by social conformity, blind compliance, or submission to and responsibility for others.

4. Psychoanalysis in general and Freud's theory in particular are haunted by an opposite tendency: too often psychoanalysts' capacity to expand analytic con-cepts self-correctively in light of what they learn from patients, and thus to pro-mote self-transformation, is subverted by their tendency to fit analysand's into the Procrustean conceptual bed of established psychoanalytic theories and pro-cedures, thereby fostering self-imprisonment.

5. Holt also detects a "humanistic" strain in Freud's corpus.

6. The body is obviously of great importance in contemporary human-istic and social science discourse—witness the work of Foucault—but often the emphasis seems to be on the socially constituted and constructed nature of the bodily self, rather than on the meaning of bodily phenomena to a particular person.

7. Freud's (and psychoanalysis's) account of the "social" and its impact on self-experience is incomplete: prohibitions and commandments are only one facet of the way such elements of the social world as the "culture industry," social class, computers, and the self-commodification promoted by capitalism impact on self-experience. Analysts need to develop a more complex picture of the social and its influence on selfhood.

8. Freud's conception of history—that of an individual isolated from broader historical currents—is not without its problems. Suffice it to say that he neglects the influence on identity of the historical and sociocultural surround that people are embedded in. While the genetic point of view—namely, that the adult's past powerfully effects her present—profoundly illuminates selfhood, it neglects the sociocultural matrix in which people develop (Kovel, 1988). This can lead to eternalizing historically specific phenomena (e.g., Timpanaro, 1976).

9. Theory can serve emancipatory or conservative interests—contesting ex-

isting beliefs and practices or justifying them (Eagleton, 1990) as well as clarifying patterns or reifying them.

10. This chapter greatly benefited from the incisive reflections of George Atwood, David Kastan, JoAnn Magdoff, and Steven Reisner. Jane Flax's (1990) suggestive reading of Freud was also enormously useful. Questions raised by Howard Arnette, Alan Rosenberg, and members of the audience—especially Harry Kunneman—at a workshop on "Freud's Legacies" at the International Society for the Study of European Ideas in Graz, Austria, in 1994 helped me clarify my relation to Freud and the stakes of my argument.

NOTES TO CHAPTER 10

1. There is an echo of Karl Marx's claim in *The Eighteenth Brumaire of Louis Bonaparte* (1852) that "men make their own history, but they do not make it under circumstances chosen by themselves, but under circumstances directly found, given and transmitted from the past. The tradition of all dead generations weighs like a nightmare on the brain of the living" (p. 437).

2. Not all conservative tendencies within psychoanalysis in general or Freudian theory in particular are constricting. Tradition, as I argue in the introduction, can enable or constrain or both.

3. This section was enriched by the suggestive reflections of Phillips (1993; 1994).

4. Another problem with the constructivist perspective may be that it can decontextualize and thus deemphasize both the historical context in which the treatment is embedded and the patient's "history," however prone that is to multiple and provisional interpretations that are in part co-constructed by the analyst and the analysand.

5. By highlighting the importance of the analyst's imagination, I do not mean to deny or minimize the importance of the analyst's understanding, insight, interpretations, capacity for mirroring, and availability as a source of identification or idealization, challenger of rigid and punitive conscience, delineator of self and others, metabolizer of affects, and so forth. I just mean to stress a key, neglected dimension of the multiplex therapeutic action of psychoanalysis. In my own pluralistic view of the therapeutic process, a multitude of factors—including the analytic ambience, the analytic relationship, the analyst's provision of a variety of functions, and the analysand's capacity for self-reflection and change—are crucial at different times and in different ways.

6. I am using the word "complex" in its scientific sense, in which it refers to a phenomena with multiple facets, a nonlinear logic, and a "diversity in interactions among the components" (e.g., Pagels, 1988, p. 65).

7. This is not true of the work of Gill, Hoffman, Levenson, Jacobs, Mitchell, Sampson, Weiss, Stolorow, Lachmann, and Atwood, among others, which focuses on the here-and-now, the past, and the complexity of the analytic process.

8. It might be argued that drawing on the analyst's imagination contaminates the treatment and violates "neutrality." Kenneth Frank (1993) has thoughtfully explored the place of action and (nonneutral) directedness in psychoanalysis. From my perspective, neutrality is illusory and not even itself neutral. It is an artifact of psychoanalysis's attempt to be scientific and has a particular impact that is no less formative for often being neglected. For a patient I recently heard about in supervision, for example, a man with a cold and self-preoccupied mother and a highly detached father, the analyst's "neutrality" repeated the glaringly unresponsive familial milieu that had characterized his childhood and left him feeling neglected, lost, and directionless. We would get the most therapeutic mileage, in my view, not in laboring under an anxiety about our therapeutic influence, which results in our trying to eliminate our impact by creating an antiseptic analytic environment, but in illuminating the analyst's inevitable shaping presence—in this case the impact on the patient of the analyst's use of his or her imagination.

9. This is not true of certain analysts within the Freudian fold, such as Jacobs (1988) and Owen Renik (1993).

NOTES TO CHAPTER 11

1. The work of Spence (e.g., 1982) is an exception suggesting the rule.

2. Lindon's (1994) recent critique of the notion of abstinence and advocacy of optimal responsiveness is the exception that suggests the rule.

3. Eissler's notion of "parameters," that is, temporary, necessary, and strategic deviations based on pathology and diagnostic considerations, is an exception to this characterization.

4. Little's (1993) account of a profoundly difficult stage in her treatment with Winnicott suggests a very different way of thinking about the ground rules and the therapeutic ambience. It also indicates why the kind of flexibility I am pointing toward has important clinical consequences and is more than simply a theoretical issue: "At one time I was liable to rush out of his [treatment] room in a fury and drive away dangerously. He [Winnicott] took charge of my car keys until the end of the session, and then allowed me to lie quietly alone in another room, till I could be safe. He emphasized the need to 'come back' (Winnicott, 1954) from the deep regression to ordinary life" (p. 126).

5. I am grateful to Terence Hawkes's *That Shakespeherian Rag* (1986) for the metaphor of *jazz improvisor*, which is the way he characterizes the literary critic.

6. Fromm (1959), as well as many others, has pointed out that Freud was not without rigidity, even authoritarianism.

7. Poststructuralism is not one essential thing. Since it is heterogeneous, it might be more accurate to speak of poststructuralisms.

8. I am indebted to Leslie Wolowitz who reminded me of this literature. Because of this literature we have, for example, Guntrip's (1977) and Little's

(1993) accounts of their treatment with Winnicott. I wonder what we might learn if we also had Winnicott's account.

9. Social constructivist–oriented analysts and analysts grounded in hermeneutics have alerted us to the improbability of either patients *or* analysts having direct, unmediated access to Truth.

10. The relational turn in psychoanalysis has perhaps underemphasized this crucial "one-person" facet of the analytic process.

11. This is a revised and expanded version of an earlier paper (Rubin, 1996a). Conversations with George Atwood, Doris Dlugacz, David Kastan, JoAnn Magdoff, Leslie Wolowitz, Ken Barnes, Bettina Edelstein, James Jones, Eugene Murphy, Paul Kahn, and Karen Smyers were helpful in the development of this chapter. I am also grateful to Paul Kuchynskas for steering me in the direction of complexity theory and the notion of "edge of chaos." The feedback of two anonymous reviewers from the American Academy of Psychoanalysis also enriched this chapter.

# References

Abraham, Ruth. *Freud and 'Mater': The Influence of Sigmund Freud's Mother on his Life and Work*. Davis: University of California Press, 1979.
———. "Freud's Mother and the Formulation of the Oedipal Father." *Psychoanalytic Review* 69, no. 4 (1982–83): 441–53.
Agee, James, and Walker Evans. *Let Us Now Praise Famous Men*. Boston: Houghton Mifflin, 1941.
Altman, Neil. "Psychoanalysis and the Urban Poor." *Psychoanalytic Dialogues* 3 (1993): 29–49.
Anthony, E. James, and Bertram Cohler. *The Invulnerable Child*. New York: Guilford, 1987.
Arlow, Jacob. "Some Dilemmas in Psychoanalytic Education." *Journal of the American Psychoanalytic Association* 20 (1972): 556–66.
Aron, Louis, and Adrienne Harris, eds. *The Legacy of Sandor Ferenczi*. Hillsdale, N.J.: Analytic Press, 1993.
Atwood, George, and Robert Stolorow. *Structures of Subjectivity: Explorations in Psychoanalytic Phenomenology*. Hillsdale, N.J.: Analytic Press, 1984.
Bacal, Howard. "D. W. Winnicott." In *Theories of Object Relations: Bridges to Self Psychology*, ed. Howard Bacal and Kenneth Newman, pp. 185–206. New York: Columbia University Press, 1990.
Bachant, Janet, and Arnold Richards. Review of *Relational Concepts in Psychoanalysis: An Integration*, by Stephen A. Mitchell. *Psychoanalytic Dialogues* 3 (1993): 431–60.
Bakan, David. *The Duality of Human Existence*. Boston: Beacon Press, 1966.
Bakhtin, Mikhail. *Problems of Dostoevsky's Poetics*, ed. and trans. Caryl Emerson. Minneapolis: University of Minnesota Press, 1984.
———. *Speech Genres and Other Late Essays*. Austin: University of Texas Press, 1986.
Balint, Alice & Michael Balint, "On Transference and Counter-transference." *International Journal of Psycho-Analysis* 20 (1939): 223–30.
Balint, Michael. "On the Psycho-Analytic Training System." *International Journal of Psycho-Analysis* 29 (1948): 163–73.
———. "Sandor Ferenczi's Last Years." *International Journal of Psycho-Analysis* 39, no. 5 (1958): 68.

Balint, Michael. *The Basic Fault: Therapeutic Aspects of Regression*. New York: Brunner/Mazel, 1968.

Barlow, Connie, ed. *Evolution Extended: Biological Debates on the Meaning of Life*. Cambridge: MIT Press, 1994.

Barratt, Barnaby. "The Psychoanalyst's Theorizing." *Journal of the American Psychoanalytic Association* 42, no. 3 (1994): 697–723.

Barron, James, Ralph Beaumont, Gary Goldsmith, Michael Good, Robert Pyles, Anna-Marie Rizzuto, and Henry Smith. "Sigmund Freud: The Secrets of Nature and the Nature of Secrets." *International Review of Psycho-Analysis* 18 (1991): 143–63.

Barthes, Roland. *Roland Barthes by Roland Barthes*. Berkeley: University of California Press, 1977.

Bateson, Gregory. *Steps to an Ecology of Mind*. New York: Ballantine Books, 1972.

Baumeister, Roy. "How the Self Became a Problem: A Psychological Review of Historical Research." *Journal of Personality and Social Psychology* 52 (1987): 163–76.

Becker, Ernest. *The Denial of Death*. New York: Free Press, 1973.

Bellah, Robert N., Richard Madsen, William M. Sullivan, Ann Swidler, and Steven M. Tipton. *Habits of the Heart: Individualism and Commitment in American Life*. New York: Harper & Row, 1985.

Benjamin, Jessica. *The Bonds of Love: Psychoanalysis, Feminism and the Problem of Domination*. New York: Pantheon, 1988.

Bennington, Geoffrey, and Jacques Derrida. *Jacques Derrida*. Chicago: University of Chicago Press, 1993.

Bernstein, Richard. *The New Constellation: The Ethical-Political Horizons of Modernity/Postmodernity*. Cambridge: MIT Press, 1992.

Bettelheim, Bruno. *Freud and Man's Soul*. New York: Vintage, 1982.

Bion, Wilfred. *Attention and Interpretation*. New York: Basic Books, 1970.

Bloom, Harold. Introduction to *Sigmund Freud*, ed. Harold Bloom. New York: Chelsea House, 1985.

Bollas, Christopher. *The Shadow of the Object: Psychoanalysis of the Unknown Thought*. New York: Columbia University Press, 1987.

———. *Forces of Destiny: Psychoanalysis and Human Idiom*. London: Free Association Books, 1989.

———. *Being a Character: Psychoanalysis and Self Experience*. New York: Hill & Wang, 1992.

———. Interview. In *Freely Associated: Encounters in Psychoanalysis*. ed. Anthony Molino. London: Free Association Books, 1997, pp. 5–51.

Brandchaft, Bernard. "To Free the Spirit from Its Cell." *Progress in Self Psychology* 9 (1993): 209–30.

Braudel, Fernand. *On History*. Chicago: University of Chicago Press, 1980.

Breger, Louis. *Freud's Unfinished Journey: Conventional and Critical Perspectives.* London: Routledge & Kegan Paul, 1981.

Breuer, Josef, and Sigmund Freud. "Studies on Hysteria" (1895). *Standard Edition* 2:ix–335. London: Hogarth Press, 1955.

Bromberg, Phillip. "Shadow and Substance: Relational Perspectives on Clinical Process." *Psychoanalytic Dialogues* 10 (1993): 147–68.

Buccino, Daniel. "The Commodification of the Object in Object Relations Theory." *Psychoanalytic Review* 80, no. 1 (1993): 123–34.

Burke, Walter. "Countertransference Disclosure and the Asymmetry/Mutuality Dilemma." *Psychoanalytic Dialogues* 2, no. 2 (1992): 241–71.

Chertok, Leon. "The Discovery of the Transference." *International Journal of Psycho-Analysis* 49 (1968): 560–76.

Clancier, Anne, and Jeannine Kalmanovich. *Winnicott and Paradox: From Birth to Creation.* New York: Tavistock Publications, 1987.

Clastres, Pierre. *Society against the State: Essays in Political Anthropology.* New York: Zone Books, 1989.

Clifford, James. *The Predicament of Culture: Twentieth-Century Ethnography, Literature and Art.* Cambridge: Harvard University Press, 1988.

Clifford, James, and George E. Marcus, eds. *Writing Culture: The Poetics and Politics of Ethnography.* Berkeley: University of California Press, 1986.

Cocks, Geoffrey. Introduction to *The Curve of Life: Correspondence of Heinz Kohut (1923–1981)*, ed. Geoffrey Cocks. Chicago: University of Chicago Press, 1994.

Crapanzano, Vincent. *Tuhami: Portrait of a Moroccan.* Chicago: University of Chicago Press, 1980.

Crews, Frederick. "The Unknown Freud." *New York Review of Books,* November 18, 1993.

Culler, Jonathon. *On Deconstruction: Theory and Criticism after Structuralism.* Ithaca: Cornell University Press, 1982.

cummings, e. e. *Complete Poems.* New York: Harcourt Brace Jovanovich, 1972.

Cushman, Philip. *Constructing the Self, Constructing America.* New York: Addison-Wesley, 1995.

Dallmayr, Fred. "Is Critical Theory a Humanism?" In *Polis and Practice: Exercises in Contemporary Political Theory,* pp. 133–65. Cambridge: MIT Press, 1984.

Deleuze, Gilles, and Félix Guattari. *Anti-Oedipus: Capitalism and Schizophrenia.* New York: Viking Press, 1983.

Dennett, Daniel. *Consciousness Explained.* Boston: Little, Brown, 1991.

Denzin, Norman. "The Poststructural Crisis in the Social Sciences: Learning from James Joyce." In *Postmodern Representations: Truth, Power, and Mimesis in the Human Sciences and Public Culture,* ed. Richard Harvey Brown, pp. 38–59. Chicago: University of Illinois Press, 1995.

Derrida, Jacques. *Of Grammatology*, trans. Gayatri Spivak. Baltimore: Johns Hopkins University Press, 1976.

———. *Positions*, trans. Alan Bass. Chicago: University of Chicago Press, 1981.

Dewald, Paul. *The Psychoanalytic Process: A Case Illustration*. New York: Basic Books, 1972.

Doolittle, Hilda. *Tribute to Freud*. New York: Pantheon, 1956.

Eagle, Morris. "Enactments, Transference, and Symptomatic Cures." *Psychoanalytic Dialogues* 3, no. 11 (1993): 93–110.

Eagleton, Terry. *The Significance of Theory*. Cambridge: Blackwell, 1990.

Eckhardt, Marianne H. "Organizational Schisms in American Psychoanalysis. In *American Psychoanalysis: Origins and Development*, ed. Jacques M. Quen and E. J. Carlson. New York: Brunner/Mazel, 1978.

Eisold, Kenneth. "The Intolerance of Diversity in Psychoanalytic Institutes." *International Journal of Psycho-Analysis* 75 (1994): 785–800.

Eissler, Kurt. "The Effect of the Structure of the Ego on Psychoanalytic Technique." *Journal of the American Psychoanalytic Association* 1 (1953): 104–53.

Eliot, T. S. "Little Gidding." In *Collected Poems (1909–1962)*, pp. 207–8. New York: Harcourt, Brace & World, 1963.

Ellis, John M. *Against Deconstruction*. Princeton: Princeton University Press, 1989.

Ellison, Ralph. *The Invisible Man*. New York: Signet Books, 1952.

Emde, Robert. "From Adolescence to Midlife: Remodeling the Structure of Adult Development." *Journal of the American Psychoanalytic Association* 33 (1985 Suppl.): 59–112.

Emerson, Ralph Waldo. "Nature." In *Essays and Journals*, ed. Lewis Mumford, pp. 326–39. Garden City, N.Y.: Doubleday, 1968.

Erikson, Erik. "The Dream Specimen of Psychoanalysis." *Journal of the American Psychoanalytic Association* 2 (1954): 5–56.

Felman, Shoshana. "To Open the Question." In *Literature and Psychoanalysis: The Question of Reading: Otherwise*, ed. Shoshana Felman, pp. 5–10. Baltimore: Johns Hopkins University Press, 1977.

Fenichel, Otto. *Problems in Psychoanalytic Technique*. New York: Psychoanalytic Quarterly, 1941.

Ferenczi, Sandor. "On the Organization of the Psycho-Analytic Movement." (1911) In *Final Contributions to the Problems and Methods of Psycho-Analysis*, pp. 299–307. New York: Brunner/Mazel, 1955.

———. "Discontinuous Analysis." (1914) In *Further Contributions to the Theory of Psycho-Analysis*, pp. 233–35. New York: Brunner/Mazel, 1926.

———. "The Problem of the Termination of the Analysis." (1927) In *Final Con-*

*tributions to the Problems and Methods of Psycho-Analysis*, pp. 77–86. New York: Brunner/Mazel, 1955.

———. "The Elasticity of Psycho-Analytic Technique." (1928) In *Final Contributions to the Problems and Methods of Psycho-Analysis*, pp. 87–101. New York: Brunner/Mazel, 1955.

———. "The Principles of Relaxation and Neo-Catharsis." (1929) In *Final Contributions to the Problems and Methods of Psycho-Analysis*, pp. 108–25. New York: Brunner/Mazel, 1955.

———. "Child Analysis in the Analysis of Adults." (1931) In *Final Contributions to the Problems and Methods of Psycho-Analysis*, pp. 126–42. New York: Brunner/Mazel, 1955.

———. *The Clinical Diary of Sandor Ferenczi* (1932), ed. Judith Dupont, trans. Michael Balint and Nicola Zarday Jackson. Cambridge: Harvard University Press, 1988.

———. "Confusion of Tongues between Adults and the Child." (1933). In *Final Contributions to the Problems and Methods of Psycho-Analysis*, pp. 156–67. New York: Brunner/Mazel, 1955.

———. *Final Contributions to the Problems and Methods of Psycho-analysis*. New York: Brunner/Mazel, 1955.

Fine, Reuben. *A History of Psychoanalysis*. New York: Columbia University Press, 1979.

Flax, Jane. *Thinking Fragments*. Berkeley: University of California Press, 1990.

———. *Disputed Subjects: Essays on Psychoanalysis, Politics and Philosophy*. New York: Routledge, 1993.

Fleming, Joan. "Report of the Ad Hoc Committee on Los Angeles." *Journal of the American Psychoanalytic Association* 24 (1976): 910–15.

Foucault, Michel. "Intellectuals and Power." In *Language, Counter-Memory and Practice: Selected Essays and Interviews*, ed. Donald Boucher, pp. 205–17. Ithaca: Cornell University Press, 1977.

———. "Two Lectures." In *Power/Knowledge: Selected Interviews and Other Writings (1972–1977)*, ed. Colin Gordon, pp. 78–108. New York: Pantheon, 1980.

Frank, Anne. *The Diary of Anne Frank*. New York: Pocket Books, 1953.

Frank, Kenneth. "Action, Insight and Working Through: Outline of an Integrative Approach." *Psychoanalytic Dialogues* 3, no. 4 (1993): 535–77.

Freud, Anna. *Ego and the Mechanisms of Defense*. New York: International Universities Press, 1936.

Freud, Martin. "Who Was Freud?" In *The Jews of Austria*, ed. Josef Fraenkel. London: Vallentine Mitchell, 1967.

Freud, Sigmund. "The Interpretation of Dreams" (1900). *Standard Edition* 4–5: xxiii–627. London: Hogarth Press, 1953.

------. "On Dreams" (1901a). *Standard Edition* 5: 633–86. London: Hogarth Press, 1953.

------. "Psychopathology of Everyday Life" (1901b). *Standard Edition* 6. London: Hogarth Press, 1960.

------. "Fragment of an Analysis of a Case of Hysteria" (1905a). *Standard Edition* 7: 7–122. London: Hogarth Press, 1953.

------. "Three Essays on the Theory of Sexuality" (1905b). *Standard Edition* 7: 125–245. London: Hogarth Press, 1953.

------. "My Views on the Part Played by Sexuality in the Aetiology of Neuroses" (1905c). *Standard Edition* 7: 269–79. London: Hogarth Press, 1953.

------. "Psycho-Analysis and the Establishment of the Facts in Legal Proceedings" (1906). *Standard Edition* 9: 103–14. London: Hogarth Press, 1959.

------. "Analysis of a Phobia in a Five-Year-Old Boy" (1909a). *Standard Edition* 10: 5–149. London: Hogarth Press, 1955.

------. "Notes upon a Case of Obsessional Neurosis" (1909b). *Standard Edition* 10: 153–318. London: Hogarth Press, 1955.

------. "Five Lectures on Psycho-Analysis" (1910a). *Standard Edition* 11: 7–55. London: Hogarth Press, 1957.

------. "Leonardo Da Vinci and a Memory of His Childhood" (1910b). *Standard Edition* 11: 57–137. London: Hogarth Press, 1957.

------. "The Future Prospects of Psycho-Analytic Therapy" (1910c). *Standard Edition* 11: 139–51. London: Hogarth Press, 1957.

------. "Recommendations to Physicians Practising Psycho-Analysis" (1912a). *Standard Edition* 12: 109–20. London: Hogarth Press, 1958.

------. "The Dynamics of Transference" (1912b). *Standard Edition* 12: 97–108. London, Hogarth Press, 1958.

------. "Totem and Taboo" (1912–13). *Standard Edition* 13: 1–162. London: Hogarth Press, 1953.

------. "On Beginning the Treatment (Further Recommendations on the Technique of Psycho-Analysis, I)" (1913a). *Standard Edition* 12: 121–44. London, Hogarth Press, 1958.

------. "The Claims of Psycho-Analysis to Scientific Interest" (1913b). *Standard Edition* 13: 165–90. London: Hogarth Press, 1957.

------. "Remembering, Repeating, and Working Through (Further Recommendations on the Technique of Psycho-Analysis, II)" (1914a). *Standard Edition* 12: 145–56. London: Hogarth Press, 1958.

------. "The *Moses* of Michelangelo" (1914b). *Standard Edition* 13: 211–38. London: Hogarth Press, 1957.

------. "On the History of the Psycho-Analytic Movement" (1914c). *Standard Edition* 14: 7–66. London: Hogarth Press, 1957.

------. "On Narcissism: An Introduction" (1914d). *Standard Edition* 14: 67–102. London: Hogarth Press, 1957.

———. "Observations on Transference-Love (Further Recommendations on the Technique of Psycho-Analysis, III)" (1915a). *Standard Edition* 12: 157–71. London: Hogarth Press, 1958.

———. "The Unconscious" (1915b). *Standard Edition* 14: 166–215. London: Hogarth Press, 1957.

———. "Introductory Lectures on Psycho-Analysis" (1916–17). *Standard Edition* 16: 243–63. London: Hogarth Press, 1963.

———. "Mourning and Melancholia" (1917a). *Standard Edition* 14: 243–58. London: Hogarth Press, 1957.

———. "A Difficulty in the Path of Psycho-Analysis" (1917b). *Standard Edition* 17: 135–44. London: Hogarth Press, 1955.

———. "The Taboo of Virginity" (1918). *Standard Edition* 11: 191–208. London: Hogarth Press, 1957.

———. "Lines of Advance in Psycho-Analytic Therapy" (1919). *Standard Edition* 17: 157–68. London: Hogarth Press, 1955.

———. "Group Psychology and the Analysis of the Ego" (1921). *Standard Edition* 18: 67–143. London: Hogarth Press, 1955.

———. "Two Encyclopaedia Articles" (1923a). *Standard Edition* 18: 235–59. London: Hogarth Press, 1955.

———. "The Ego and the Id" (1923b). *Standard Edition* 19: 3–66. London: Hogarth Press, 1961.

———. "Sandor Ferenczi" (1923c). *Standard Edition* 19: 265–69. London: Hogarth Press, 1961.

———. "Some Additional Notes on Dream-Interpretation as a Whole" (1925a) *Standard Edition* 19: 127–38. London: Hogarth Press, 1961.

———. "A Note upon the 'Mystic Writing Pad' " (1925b). *Standard Edition* 19: 227–32. London: Hogarth Press, 1961.

———. "Some Psychical Consequences of the Anatomical Distinction between the Sexes" (1925c). *Standard Edition* 19: 241–58. London: Hogarth Press, 1961.

———. "An Autobiographical Study" (1925d). *Standard Edition* 20: 7–70. London: Hogarth Press, 1959.

———. "Inhibitions, Symptoms and Anxiety" (1926a). *Standard Edition* 20: 75–174. London: Hogarth Press, 1959.

———. "The Question of Lay Analysis" (1926b). *Standard Edition* 20: 177–258. London: Hogarth Press, 1959.

———. "The Future of an Illusion" (1927). *Standard Edition* 21: 5–56. London: Hogarth Press, 1961.

———. "Civilization and Its Discontents" (1930). *Standard Edition* 21: 64–145. London: Hogarth Press, 1961.

———. "Female Sexuality" (1931a). *Standard Edition* 21: 225–43. London: Hogarth Press, 1961.

———. "Letter # 258, February 7, 1931, to Stefan Zweig" (1931b). In *The Letters of Sigmund Freud*, ed. Ernst Freud, pp. 402–3. New York: Basic Books, 1960.

———. "Revision of the Theory of Dreams" (1933a). *Standard Edition* 22: 5–30. London: Hogarth Press, 1964.

———. "On Femininity" (1933b). *Standard Edition* 22: 112–35. London: Hogarth Press, 1964.

———. "Sandor Ferenczi" (1933c). *Standard Edition* 22: 226–29. London: Hogarth Press, 1964.

———. "New Introductory Lectures on Psycho-Analysis" (1933d). *Standard Edition* 22: 3–182. London: Hogarth Press, 1964.

———. "Subtleties of a Faulty Action" (1936a). *Standard Edition* 22: 233–35. London: Hogarth Press, 1964.

———. "A Disturbance of Memory on the Acropolis" (1936b). *Standard Edition* 22: 239–48. London: Hogarth Press, 1964.

———. "Analysis Terminable and Interminable" (1937). *Standard Edition* 23: 209–53. London: Hogarth Press, 1964.

———. "An Outline of Psycho-Analysis" (1940). *Standard Edition* 23: 144–207. London: Hogarth Press, 1964.

———. *The Origins of Psycho-Analysis: Letters to Wilhelm Fliess, Drafts and Notes*, eds. Marie Bonaparte, Anna Freud, and Ernest Kris, trans. Eric Mosbacher and James Strachey. New York: Basic Books, 1950.

———. *The Letters of Sigmund Freud*, ed. Ernest Freud, trans. Tania Stein and James Stein. New York: Basic Books, 1960.

———. *Psychoanalysis and Faith: Dialogues with the Reverend Oskar Pfister*, eds. Heinrich Meng and Ernst Freud. New York: Basic Books, 1963.

———. *The Complete Letters of Sigmund Freud to Wilhelm Fliess*, ed. Jeffrey Masson. Cambridge: Harvard University Press, 1985.

Freud, Sigmund, and Sandor Ferenczi. *The Correspondence of Sigmund Freud and Sandor Ferenczi*, vol. 1, eds. Eva Brabant, Ernst Falzeder, and Patrizia Giampieri-Deutsch. Cambridge: Harvard University Press, 1993.

———. *The Correspondence of Sigmund Freud and Sandor Ferenczi*, vol. 3, eds. Eva Brabant, Ernst Falzeder, and Patrizia Giampieri-Deutsch. Cambridge: Harvard University Press, forthcoming.

Freud, Sigmund, and Carl Jung. *The Freud/Jung Letters*, ed. William McGuire. Princeton: Princeton University Press, 1974.

Friedman, Lawrence. *The Anatomy of Psychotherapy*. Hillsdale, N.J.: Analytic Press, 1988.

Fromm, Erich. *Escape from Freedom*. New York: Avon Books, 1941.

———. *Man for Himself*. New York: Rinehart & Co., 1947.

———. "Psychoanalysis—Science or Party Line?" In *The Dogma of Christ and*

*Other Essays on Religion, Psychology and Culture*, pp. 125–36. Greenwich, Conn.: Fawcett Press, 1955.

———. "Freud's Authoritarianism." In *Sigmund Freud's Mission: An Analysis of His Personality and Influence*, pp. 62–67. New York: Harper & Row, 1959.

Fromm, Erich, Daisetz T. Suzuki, and Richard DeMartino, eds. *Zen Buddhism and Psychoanalysis*. New York: Harper & Row, 1960.

Frye, Northrop. *Anatomy of Criticism: Four Essays*. Princeton: Princeton University Press, 1957.

Gadamer, Hans-Georg. *Philosophical Hermeneutics*, trans and ed. David E. Linge. Berkeley: University of California Press, 1976.

Gallop, Jane. *The Daughter's Seduction: Feminism and Psychoanalysis*. Ithaca: Cornell University Press, 1982.

Gardiner, Jill K. "Self Psychology as Feminist Theory." *Signs: Journal of Women and Culture* 12, no. 4 (1987): 761–80.

Gardiner, Muriel, ed. *The Wolf-Man by the Wolf-Man*. New York: Basic Books, 1971.

Gardner, Robert. *Self Inquiry*. Boston: Little, Brown, 1983.

Gargiulo, Gerald. "Authority, the Self, and Psychoanalytic Experience." *Psychoanalytic Review* 76, no. 2 (1989): 149–61.

———. "Winnicott's Psychoanalytic Playground." In *Psychoanalytic Versions of the Human Condition: Philosophies of Life and Their Impact on Practice*, ed. Paul Marcus and Allan Rosenberg, pp. 140–60. New York: New York University Press, 1998.

Gates, Henry Louis. "Critical Fanonism." *Critical Inquiry* 17, no. 3 (1991): 457–70.

Gay, Peter. *A Godless Jew: Freud, Atheism, and the Making of Psychoanalysis*. New Haven: Yale University Press, 1987.

———. *Freud: A Life for Our Time*. New York: Norton, 1988.

———. "Freud and Freedom." In *Reading Freud: Explorations and Entertainments*, pp. 74–94. New Haven: Yale University Press, 1990.

Gaylin, Willard. "Love and the Limits of Individualism." In *Passionate Attachments: Thinking about Love*, eds. Willard Gaylin and Ethel Person, pp. 41–62. New York: Free Press, 1988.

Gedo, John. *Psychoanalysis and Its Discontents*. New York: Guilford Press, 1984.

———. *Conceptual Issues in Psychoanalysis: Essays in History and Method*. Hillsdale, N.J.: Analytic Press, 1986.

Geertz, Clifford. *The Interpretation of Culture*. New York: Basic Books, 1973.

Gelfand, Toby. Preface to *Freud and the History of Psychoanalysis*, eds. Toby Gelfand and John Kerr, pp. vii–xii. Hillsdale, N.J.: Analytic Press, 1992.

Gill, Merton. "The Interpersonal Paradigm and the Degree of the Therapist's Involvement." *Contemporary Psychoanalysis* 19, no. 2 (1983): 200–237.

Gill, Merton. "Robert Langs on Technique: A Critique." In *Listening and Interpreting: The Challenge of the Work of Robert Langs*, ed. James Raney. New York: Jason Aronson, 1984.

Gitelson, Frances H. "Identity Crises: Splits or Compromises—Adaptive or Maladaptive?" In *The Identity of the Psychoanalyst*, eds. Edward D. Joseph and Daniel Widlöcher, pp. 157–80. New York: International Universities Press, 1983.

Goldberg, Arnold. *The Prisonhouse of Psychoanalysis*. Hillsdale, N.J.: Analytic Press, 1990.

Gray, Paul. "Psychoanalytic Technique and the Ego's Capacity for Viewing Intrapsychic Activity." *Journal of the American Psychoanalytic Association* 21 (1973): 474–94.

Green, Andre. "Analytic Play and Its Relationship to the Object." In *In One's Bones: The Clinical Genius of Winnicott*, ed. Dodi Goldman, pp. 213–22. N.J.: Jason Aronson, 1993.

Greenson, Ralph. "The Origin and Fate of New Ideas in Psychoanalysis" (1969). In *Explorations in Psychoanalysis*, pp. 333–57. New York: International Universities Press, 1978.

Grinstein, Alexander. *Freud at the Crossroads*. New York: International Universities Press, 1990.

Groddeck, George. *The Book of the It: Psychoanalytic Letters to a Friend*. New York: Nervous and Mental Disease Publishing Co., 1928.

Grolnick, Simon. *The Work and Play of Winnicott*. Northvale, N.J.: Jason Aronson, 1991.

Grolnick, Simon, Leonard Barkin, and Werner Muensterberger, eds. *Between Reality and Fantasy: Winnicott's Concepts of Transitional Objects and Phenomena*. New York: Jason Aronson, 1978.

Grosskurth, Phyllis. *Melanie Klein and Her World*. Cambridge: Harvard University Press, 1987.

———. *The Secret Ring: Freud's Inner Circle and the Politics of Psycho-Analysis*. Reading, Mass.: Addison-Wesley, 1991.

Grubrich-Simitis, I. "Six Letters of Sigmund Freud and Sandor Ferenczi on the Interrelationship of Psychoanalytic Theory and Technique." *International Review of Psycho-Analysis* 13, no. 3 (1986): 259–77.

Guntrip, Harry. *Schizoid Phenomena, Object Relations and the Self*. New York: International Universities Press, 1969.

———. "My Experience of Analysis with Fairbairn and Winnicott (How Complete a Result Does Psychoanalytic Therapy Achieve?)." In *The Human Dimension in Psychoanalytic Practice*, ed. Kenneth Frank, pp. 49–68. New York: Grune & Stratton, 1977.

Haas, William. *Destiny of the Mind, East and West*. New York: Doubleday, 1956.

Habermas, Jürgen. "The Scientistic Self-Misunderstanding of Metapsychology." In *Knowledge and Human Interests*, pp. 246–73. Boston: Beacon Press, 1968.

Hann-Kende, Fanny. "On the Role of Transference and Countertransference in Psychoanalysis." In *Psychoanalysis and the Occult*, ed. George Devereux, pp. 158–67. New York: International Universities Press, 1933.

Harding, Sandra, and Merrill B. Hintikka, eds. *Discovering Reality: Feminist Perspectives on Epistemology, Metaphysics, Methodology, and Philosophy of Science*. Dordrecht: D. Reidel, 1983.

Hartmann, Heinz. *Psychoanalysis and Moral Values*. New York: International Universities Press, 1960.

Hawkes, Terence. *That Shakespeherian Rag: Essays on a Critical Process*. London: Methuen, 1986.

Heimann, Paula. "On Counter-transference." *International Journal of Psycho-Analysis* 31 (1950): 81–84.

Heller, Judith Bernays. "Freud's Mother and Father." In *Freud as We Knew Him*, ed. Hendrik M. Ruitenbeek, pp. 334–40. Detroit: Wayne State University Press, 1973.

Hoffer, Axel. "The Freud-Ferenczi Controversy—A Living Legacy." *International Review of Psycho-Analysis* 18 (1991): 465–72.

Hoffman, Irwin. "Discussion: Towards a Social-Constructivist View of the Psychoanalytic Situation." *Psychoanalytic Dialogues* 1 (1991): 74–105.

Holder, Alex. "The Genetic Point of View." In *Basic Psychoanalytic Concepts on Metapsychology, Conflicts, Anxiety and Other Subjects*, ed. Humberto Nagera, pp. 43–46. London: H. Karnac, 1970.

Holt, Robert. "On Reading Freud." In *Abstracts of the Standard Edition of the Complete Psychological Works of Sigmund Freud*, ed. Carrie L. Rothgeb, pp. 3–71. New York: Jason Aronson, 1975.

———. "Freud's Parental Identifications as a Source of Some Contradictions in Psychoanalysis." In *Freud and the History of Psychoanalysis*, eds. Toby Gelfand and John Kerr, pp. 1–28. Hillsdale, N.J.: Analytic Press, 1992.

———. Review of *Why Freud Was Wrong: Sin, Science, and Psychoanalysis*, by Richard Webster. *Psychoanalytic Books* 7, no. 4 (1996): 511–19.

hooks, bell. *Teaching to Transgress: Education as the Practice of Freedom*. New York: Routledge, 1994.

Horney, Karen. "The Flight from Womanhood." *International Journal of Psycho-Analysis* 7 (1926): 324–39.

———. *New Ways in Psychoanalysis*. New York: Norton, 1939.

———. *Our Inner Conflicts*. New York: Norton, 1945.

———. *Final Lectures*. New York: Norton, 1987.

Houston, Jean. *Life-Force: The Psycho-Historical Recovery of the Self*. New York: Delacorte Press, 1980.

Hutcheon, Linda. *The Politics of Postmodernism*. New York: Routledge, 1989.

Jacobs, Theodore. "Notes on the Therapeutic Process: Working with the Young Adult." In *How Does Treatment Help? On the Modes of Therapeutic Action of Psychoanalytic Psychotherapy*, ed. Arnold Rothstein, pp. 61–80. New York: International Universities Press, 1988.

———. "Insight and Experience: Commentary on Morris Eagle's 'Enactments, Transference, and Symptomatic Cure.' " *Psychoanalytic Dialogues* 3, no. 1 (1993): 123–27.

Jacoby, Russell. *The Repression of Psychoanalysis: Otto Fenichel and the Political Freudians*. New York: Basic Books, 1983.

Janik, Allan, and Stephen Toulmin. *Wittgenstein's Vienna*. New York: Simon & Schuster, 1973.

Javier, Rafael Art, and Mario Rendon. "The Ethnic Unconscious and Its Role in Transference, Resistance, and Countertransference: An Introduction." *Psychoanalytic Psychology* 12, no. 4 (1995): 513–20.

Jones, Ernest. *The Life and Work of Sigmund Freud*. Vol. 1. New York: Basic Books, 1953.

———. *The Life and Work of Sigmund Freud*. Vol. 2. New York: Basic Books, 1955.

———. *The Life and Work of Sigmund Freud*. Vol. 3. New York: Basic Books, 1957.

Jones, Ernest, and Sigmund Freud. *The Complete Correspondence of Sigmund Freud and Ernest Jones: 1908–1939*. Cambridge: Harvard University Press, 1993.

Jones, James. *Contemporary Psychoanalysis and Religion: Transference and Transcendence*. New Haven: Yale University Press, 1991.

———. "The Real Is the Relational: Psychoanalysis as a Model of Human Understanding." Unpublished manuscript, 1995.

Josephs, Lawrence. "Countertransference as an Expression of the Analyst's Narrative Strategies." *Contemporary Psychoanalysis* 31, no. 3 (1995): 345–80.

Jung, Carl. *Psychology and Religion: West and East*. Princeton: Princeton University Press, 1958.

———. *Memories, Dreams, Reflections*. New York: Vintage, 1965.

———. *The Portable Jung*, ed. Joseph Campbell. New York: Penguin Books, 1971.

Kahr, Brett. *D. W. Winnicott: A Biographical Portrait*. Madison, Conn.: International Universities Press, 1996.

Keller, Evelyn Fox. *Reflections on Gender and Science*. New Haven: Yale University Press, 1985.

Kelman, Harold. "Psychoanalytic Thought and Eastern Wisdom" (1960) In *The History of Psychotherapy*, ed. Jan Ehrenwald, pp. 328–33. New York: Jason Aronson, 1976.

Kernberg, Otto. "Countertransference." In *Borderline Conditions and Pathological Narcissism*, pp. 49–67. New York: Jason Aronson, 1975.

———. "An Interview with Otto Kernberg." *Psychoanalytic Dialogues* 5, no. 2 (1995): 325–63.

Kestemberg, Evelyne. "A Yeast for Thought" (Interview). In *In One's Bones: The Clinical Genius of Winnicott*, ed. Dodi Goldman, pp. 165–70. Northvale, N.J.: Jason Aronson, 1993.

Khan, Masud. "The Finding and Becoming of Self" (1972). In *The Privacy of the Self*, pp. 294–305. New York: International Universities Press, 1974.

———. "Obituary." In *In One's Bones: The Clinical Genius of Winnicott*, ed. Dodi Goldman pp. 111–13. Northvale, N.J.: Jason Aronson, 1993.

Kierkegaard, Soren. Entry 136, 1843. In *The Diary of Soren Kierkegaard*, ed. Peter P. Rohde. New York: Citadel Press, 1960.

Kirsner, Douglas. "Mystics and Professionals in the Culture of American Psychoanalysis." *Free Associations* 20 (1990): 85–103.

Klauber, John. *Difficulties in the Analytic Encounter*. New York: Jason Aronson, 1981.

Kohut, Heinz. *The Analysis of the Self*. New York: International Universities Press, 1971.

———. "The Psychoanalyst in the Community of Scholars." In *The Search for the Self: Selected Writings of Heinz Kohut: 1950–1978*, ed. Paul H. Ornstein, pp. 685–724. New York: International Universities Press, 1973.

———. *The Restoration of the Self*. New York: International Universities Press, 1977.

———. "Two Analyses of Mr. Z." *International Journal of Psycho-Analysis* 60 (1979): 3–27.

———. *How Does Analysis Cure?* Chicago: University of Chicago Press, 1984.

———. *Self Psychology and the Humanities*. New York: Norton, 1985.

Kovel, Joel. *White Racism*. New York: Columbia University Press, 1984.

———. *The Radical Spirit*. London: Free Association Books, 1988.

———. *History and Spirit: An Inquiry into the Philosophy of Liberation*. Boston: Beacon Press, 1991.

Krishnamurti, Jiddu. *Freedom from the Known*. New York: Harper & Row, 1969.

Kristeva, Julia. *The Powers of Horror: An Essay on Abjection*. New York: Columbia University Press, 1982.

Kuhn, Thomas. *The Structure of Scientific Revolutions*. Chicago: University of Chicago Press, 1970.

———. *The Essential Tension*. Chicago: University of Chicago Press, 1978.

Langs, Robert. *Technique in Transition*. New York: Jason Aronson, 1978.

———. *The Psychotherapeutic Conspiracy*. New York: Jason Aronson, 1982a.

———. *Psychotherapy: A Basic Text*. New York: Jason Aronson, 1982b.

Lansky, Melvin, ed. *Essential Papers on Dreams*. New York: New York University Press, 1992a.

———. "The Legacy of The Interpretation of Dreams." In *Essential Papers on Dreams*, ed. Melvin Lansky, pp. 3–31. New York: New York University Press, 1992b.

Lasch, Christopher. *The True and Only Heaven: Progress and Its Discontents*. New York: Norton, 1991.

Layton, Lynn. "A Deconstruction of Kohut's Concept of the Self." *Contemporary Psychoanalysis* 26, no.3 (1990): 420–29.

Lee, Bruce. *The Tao of Jeet Kune Do*. Burbank, Calif.: Ohara Publications, 1975.

———. "Liberate Yourself from Classical Karate." In *The Legendary Bruce Lee*, eds. Jack Vaughn and Mike Lee, pp. 62–69. Burbank, Calif.: Ohara Publications, 1986.

Levenson, Edgar. *The Ambiguity of Change: An Inquiry into the Nature of Psychoanalytic Reality*. New York: Basic Books, 1983.

———. *The Purloined Self: Interpersonal Perspectives in Psychoanalysis*. New York: Contemporary Psychoanalytic Books, 1991.

———. "Harry Stack Sullivan: From Interpersonal Psychiatry to Interpersonal Psychoanalysis." *Contemporary Psychoanalysis* 28 no. 3 (1992): 450–66.

Levin, David Michael, ed. *Pathologies of the Modern Self: Postmodern Studies on Narcissism, Schizophrenia, and Depression*. New York: New York University Press, 1987.

Levinson, Harry. "The Changing Psychoanalytic Organization and Its Influence on the Ego Ideal of Psychoanalysis." *Psychoanalytic Psychology* 11, no.2 (1994): 233–49.

Lifton, Robert Jay. *The Protean Self: Human Resilience in an Age of Fragmentation*. New York: Basic Books, 1993.

Lindon, John. "Does Technique Require Theory?" *Bulletin of the Menninger Clinic* 55 (1991): 1–21.

———. "Gratification and Provision in Psychoanalysis: Should We Get Rid of 'The Rule of Abstinence'?" *Psychoanalytic Dialogues* 4, no.4 (1994): 549–82.

Lipton, Samuel. "The Advantages of the Freud's Technique as Shown in His Analysis of the Rat Man." *International Journal of Psycho-Analysis* 58, no.3 (1977): 255–72.

Little, Margaret. "Countertransference and the Patient's Response to It." *International Journal of Psycho-Analysis* 32 (1951): 32–40.

———. "Winnicott Working in Areas Where Psychotic Anxieties Predominate." *Free Associations* 3 (1985): 9–42.

———. "Psychotherapy with D. W. W." In *In One's Bones: The Clinical Genius of Winnicott*, ed. Dodi Goldman, pp. 123–38. Northvale, N.J.: Jason Aronson, 1993.

Loewald, Hans. "On Motivation and Instinct Theory." In *Papers on Psycho-Analysis*, pp. 102–37. New Haven: Yale University Press, 1971.

———. *Psychoanalysis and the History of the Individual*. New Haven: Yale University Press, 1978.

———. *Papers on Psychoanalysis*. New Haven: Yale University Press, 1980.

Loewenberg, Peter. *Fantasy and Reality in History*. New York: Oxford University Press, 1995.

Lothane, Zvi. "Perspective on Freud and Psychoanalysis." *Psychoanalytic Review* 68, no.3 (1981): 348–61.

———. "Confrontation: Clinical Application." In *Basic Techniques of Psychodynamic Psychotherapy: Foundations of Clinical Practice*, eds. Michael P. Nichols and Thomas J. Paolino, Jr., pp. 207–35. New York: Gardner Press, 1986.

———. "Love, Seduction and Trauma." *Psychoanalytic Review* 74, no.1 (1987): 83–106.

Lyotard, Jean-François. *The Postmodern Condition: A Report on Knowledge*, trans. Geoffrey Bennington and Brian Massumi. Minneapolis: University of Minnesota Press, 1984.

Lytton, S. (reporter). Value Judgments in Psychoanalytic Theory and Practice. Panel discussion. *Journal of the American Psychoanalytic Association* 32 (1984): 147–56.

Mannheim, Karl. *Ideology and Utopia*. New York: Harcourt, Brace & World, 1936.

Marcus, George, and Michael Fischer. *Anthropology as Cultural Critique: An Experimental Moment in the Human Sciences*. Chicago: University of Chicago Press, 1986.

Marx, Karl. "The Eighteenth Brumaire of Louis Bonaparte" (1852). In *The Marx-Engels Reader*, ed. Robert Tucker, pp. 436–525. New York: Norton, 1972.

Masson, Jeffrey. *The Assault on Truth: Freud's Repression of the Seduction Theory*. New York: Farrar, Straus & Giroux, 1984.

McDougall, Joyce. *The Many Faces of Eros: A Psychoanalytic Exploration of Human Sexuality*. New York: Norton, 1995.

McNeill, William. *Mythistory and Other Essays*. Chicago: University of Chicago Press, 1986.

Meisel, Perry, and Walter Kendrick, eds. *Bloomsbury/Freud: The Letters of James and Alix Strachey*. New York: Basic Books, 1985.

Meissner, William. *Psychoanalysis and Religious Experience*. New Haven: Yale University Press, 1984.

Meltzer, François. "Partitive Plays, Pipe Dreams." *Critical Inquiry* 13, no. 2 (1987): 215–21.

Menaker, Esther. *Otto Rank: A Rediscovered Legacy*. New York: Columbia University Press, 1982.

Menninger, Karl. *Love against Hate*. New York: Harcourt Brace Jovanovich, 1942.

Miller, Alice. *The Drama of the Gifted Child*. New York: Basic Books, 1981.

Milner, Marion. *The Suppressed Madness of Sane Men*. (1973) London: Tavistock, 1987.

Mitchell, Stephen. *Relational Concepts in Psychoanalysis: An Integration*. Cambridge: Harvard University Press, 1988.

———. "Contemporary Perspectives on Self: Toward an Integration." *Psychoanalytic Dialogues* 1, no. 2 (1991): 121–47.

———. Commentary on Trop and Stolorow's "Defense Analysis in Self Psychology." *Psychoanalytic Dialogues* 2, no. 4 (1992): 443–45.

———. *Hope and Dread in Psychoanalysis*. New York: Basic Books, 1993a.

———. "Reply to Bachant." *Psychoanalytic Dialogues* 3, no. 3 (1993b): 461–80.

———. "True Selves, False Selves, and the Ambiguity of Authenticity." In *Relational Perspectives in Psychoanalysis*. eds. Neil Skolnick and Susan Warshaw, pp. 1–20. Hillsdale, N.J.: Analytic Press, 1993c.

———. *Influence and Autonomy in Psychoanalysis*. Hillsdale N.J.: Analytic Press, 1997.

Modell, Arnold. "The Two Contexts of the Self." *Contemporary Psychoanalysis* 21, no. 1 (1985): 70–90.

———. "Object Relations Theory." In *Models of the Mind: Their Relationship to Clinical Work*, ed. Arnold Rothstein, pp. 85–100. New York: International Universities Press, 1985a.

———. "The Works of Winnicott and the Evolution of His Thoughts." *Journal of the American Psychoanalytic Association* 33 (1985b Suppl.): 113–37.

———. "The Missing Elements in Kohut's Cure." *Psychoanalytic Inquiry* 6, no. 3 (1986): 367–85.

———. "The Psychoanalytic Setting as a Container of Multiple Levels of Reality: A Perspective on the Theory of Psychoanalytic Treatment." *Psychoanalytic Inquiry* 9, no. 1 (1989): 67–87.

Molnar, Michael, ed. *The Diary of Sigmund Freud: 1929–39*. New York: Scribner's, 1992.

Nelson, Cary. "Psychoanalysis as an Intervention in Contemporary Theory." In *Psychoanalysis and . . .* , eds. Richard Feldstein and Harry Sussman, pp. 11–20. New York: Routledge, 1990.

Nunberg, Herman, and Ernst Federn, eds. *Minutes of the Vienna Psychoanalytic Society*. New York: International Universities Press, 1975.

Ogden, Thomas. *The Matrix of Mind: Object Relations and the Psychoanalytic Dialogue*. Northvale, N.J.: Jason Aronson, 1986.

———. "An Interview with Thomas Ogden." *Psychoanalytic Dialogues* 1, no. 3 (1991): 361–76.

———. *Subjects of Analysis*. Northvale, N.J.: Jason Aronson, 1994.

Ornstein, Paul. "Is Self Psychology on a Promising Trajectory?" *Progress in Self Psychology* 9 (1993): 1–11.

Pagels, Heinz. *The Dreams of Reason: Computer Systems and the Rise of the Sciences of Complexity*. New York: Bantam, 1988.

Peoples, Karen. "The Paradox of Surrender: Constructing and Transcending the Self." Unpublished Manuscript, 1991.

Pfister, Oskar. *Christianity and Fear*, trans. William H. Johnson. London: Allen and Unwin, 1948.

Phillips, Adam. *Winnicott*. Cambridge: Harvard University Press, 1988.

———. *On Kissing, Tickling and Being Bored: Psychoanalytic Essays on the Unexamined Life*. Cambridge: Harvard University Press, 1993.

———. *On Flirtation: Psychoanalytic Essays on the Uncommitted Life*. Cambridge: Harvard University Press, 1994.

———. *Terrors and Experts*. Cambridge: Harvard University Press, 1995.

Plath, Sylvia. *The Bell Jar*. Cutchoque, N.Y.: Buccaneer Books, 1975.

Pulver, Sydney E., Philip Escoll, and Newell Fischer. "How Theory Shapes Technique: Perspectives on a Clinical Study." *Psychoanalytic Inquiry* 7, no. 2 (1987).

Pynchon, Thomas. *Gravity's Rainbow*. New York: Viking, 1976.

Rachmann, Arnold. "The Rule of Empathy: Sandor Ferenczi's Pioneering Contributions to the Empathic Method in Psychoanalysis." *Journal of the American Academy of Psychoanalysis* 16 (1988): 1–27.

———. "Confusion of Tongues: The Ferenczian Metaphor for Childhood Seduction and Emotional Trauma." *Journal of the American Academy of Psychoanalysis* 17, no. 2 (1989): 181–205.

———. "Ferenczi and Sexuality." In *The Legacy of Sandor Ferenczi*, eds. Adrienne Harris and Louis Aron, pp. 81–100. Hillsdale, N.J.: Analytic Press, 1993.

Racker, Heinrich. "The Meaning and Uses of Countertransference." *Psychoanalytic Quarterly* 26 (1957): 303–57.

Ralston, Peter. *Ancient Wisdom, Modern Spirit: Investigations into the Nature of "Being."* Berkeley: Frog, 1994.

Rand, Nicholas, and Maria Torok. "The Secret of Psychoanalysis: History Reads Theory." *Critical Inquiry* 13 (1987): 278–86.

Rangell, Leo. *The Mind of Watergate: An Exploration of the Compromise of Integrity*. New York: Norton, 1980.

Renik, Owen. "Analytic Interaction: Conceptualizing Technique in Light of the Analyst's Irreducible Subjectivity." *Psychoanalytic Quarterly* 62 (1993): 553–71.

Rice, Emmanuel. *Freud and Moses: The Long Journey Home*. New York: State University of New York Press, 1990.

Ricoeur, Paul. *Freud and Philosophy: An Essay on Interpretation*. New Haven: Yale University Press, 1970.

Rieff, Philip. *Freud: The Mind of the Moralist*. New York: Anchor Books, 1959.

———. Introduction to *Freud: Therapy and Technique*, ed. Phillip Rieff, pp. 7–24. New York: Macmillan, 1963.

Rizzuto, Anna-Marie. *The Birth of the Living God: A Psychoanalytic Study*. Chicago: University of Chicago Press, 1979.

Roazen, Paul. *Freud and His Followers*. New York: Meridian, 1971.

———. *The Freudian Left*. Ithaca: Cornell University Press, 1990.

Rodman, F. R. *The Spontaneous Gesture: Selected Letters of D. W. Winnicott*. Cambridge: Harvard University Press, 1987.

Roland, Alan. *In Search of Self in India and Japan: Towards a Cross-Cultural Psychology*. Princeton: Princeton University Press, 1988.

———. *Cultural Pluralism and Psychoanalysis: The Asian and North American Experience*. New York: Routledge, 1996.

Rorty, Richard. *Philosophy and the Mirror of Nature*. Princeton: Princeton University Press, 1979.

———. *Consequences of Pragmatism*. Minneapolis: University of Minnesota Press, 1982.

———. *Contingency, Irony, and Solidarity*. New York: Cambridge University Press, 1989.

Rosenau, Pauline. *Post-Modernism and the Social Sciences*. Princeton: Princeton University Press, 1993.

Rothstein, Arnold. *The Structural Hypothesis: An Evolutionary Perspective*. New York: International Universities Press, 1983.

———, ed. *Models of the Mind: Their Relationships to Clinical Work*. New York: International University Press, 1985.

Roustang, François. *Dire Mastery: Discipleship from Freud to Lacan*, trans. Neil Lukacher. Baltimore: Johns Hopkins University Press, 1982.

Rubin, Jeffrey B. "Meditation and Psychoanalytic Listening." *Psychoanalytic Review* 72, no. 4 (1985): 599–613.

———. "The Clinical Integration of Buddhist Meditation and Psychoanalysis." *Journal of Integrative and Eclectic Psychotherapy* 10, no. 2 (1991): 173–81.

———. "Psychoanalytic Treatment with a Buddhist Meditator." In *Object Relations Theory and Religion: Clinical Applications*, eds. Mark Finn and John Gartner, pp. 87–107. New York: Praeger, 1992.

———. "Psychoanalysis and Buddhism." In *Comprehensive Handbook of Psychotherapy Integration*, eds. George Stricker and Jerrold Gold, pp. 249–66. New York: Plenum Press, 1993.

———. "The Analyst's Authority." *Journal of the American Academy of Psychoanalysis* 24, no. 3 (1996a): 457–83.

————. *Psychoanalysis and Buddhism: Toward an Integration.* New York: Plenum Press, 1996b.

————. "Reflections on Values and Morality in Psychoanalysis." *Psychologist-Psychoanalyst, Division 39 Newsletter* 18, no. 1 (1997a): 17–21.

————. Review of *D. W. Winnicott* by Brett Kahr. *Psychoanalytic Books* 8, no. 4 (1997b): 472–78.

————. Review of *Psychoanalysis and the Humanities* by Laurie Adams and Jacques Szaluta. *Psychoanalytic Books* 8, no. 3 (1997c): 360–65.

Rudnytsky, Peter. *The Psychoanalytic Vocation: Rank, Winnicott and the Legacy of Freud.* New Haven: Yale University Press, 1991.

Rushdie, Salman. *Shame.* London: Pan Books, 1983.

Rycroft, Charles. *A Dictionary of Psycho-Analysis.* Totowa, N.J.: Littlefield, Adams, 1973.

Said, Edward. *The World, the Text and the Critic.* Cambridge: Harvard University Press, 1983.

Sandel, Michael. *Democracy's Discontent: America in Search of a Public Philosophy.* Cambridge: Harvard University Press, 1996.

Sandler, Anne-Marie. "Comments on Varieties of Psychoanalytic Training in Europe." In *Tradition and Innovation in Psychoanalytic Education*, eds. M. Meisel and E. Shapiro. Hillsdale, N.J.: Lawrence Erlbaum, 1990.

Schafer, Roy. *A New Language for Psychoanalysis.* New Haven: Yale University Press, 1976.

————. *Language and Insight: The Sigmund Freud Memorial Lectures University College London, 1975–1976.* New Haven: Yale University Press, 1978.

————. *The Analytic Attitude.* New York: Basic Books, 1983.

————. "Narratives of the Self." In *Psychoanalysis: Toward the Second Century*, eds. Arnold M. Cooper, Otto F. Kernberg, and Ethel Person, pp. 153–67. New Haven: Yale University Press, 1989.

————. *Retelling a Life: Narration and Dialogue in Psychoanalysis.* New York: Basic Books, 1992.

Schorske, Carl. *Fin-de-Siècle Vienna: Politics and Culture.* New York: Random House, 1981.

Schwaber, Evelyn. "Psychoanalytic Listening and Psychic Reality." *International Review of Psycho-Analysis* 10 (1983): 379–92.

Searles, Harold. "The Patient as Therapist to His Analyst." In *Countertransference and Related Subjects*, pp. 380–459. New York: International Universities Press, 1975.

————. "Concerning Transference and Countertransference." *International Journal of Psychoanalytic Psychotherapy* (1949) 1977: 165–88.

Sennett, Richard. *The Uses of Disorder: Personal Identity and City Life.* New York: Norton, 1970.

Shapiro, Robert. "Theory and Change: Commentary on Morris Eagle's 'Enactments, Transference, and Symptomatic Cure.' " *Psychoanalytic Dialogues* 3, no. 1 (1993): 129–38.

Shklovsky, Victor. "Art as Device" (1917). In *Russian Formalist Criticism: Four Essays*, ed. Lee T. Lemon and Marion J. Reis, pp. 3–24. Lincoln: University of Nebraska Press, 1965.

Shore, Bradd. *Sala'ilua: A Samoan Mystery*. New York: Columbia University Press, 1982.

Silberer, Herbert. *Problems of Mysticism and Its Symbolism*. New York: Moffat, 1917.

Silverman, Lloyd, Frank Lachmann, and Robert Milich. *The Search for Oneness*. New York: International Universities Press, 1982.

Simmel, Georg. "The Stranger." In *The Sociology of Georg Simmel*. trans. and ed. Kurt Wolff, pp. 402–8. New York: Free Press, 1950.

Smith, Huston. *The Religions of Man*. San Francisco: Harper, 1958.

Spence, Donald. *Narrative Truth and Historical Truth: Meaning and Interpretation in Psychoanalysis*. New York: Norton, 1982.

———. *The Freudian Metaphor: Toward Paradigm Change in Psychoanalysis*. New York: Norton, 1987.

Spezzano, Charles and Gerald Gargiulo, eds. *Soul on the Couch*. Hillsdale, N.J.: Analytic Press, 1997.

Spurling, Laurence, ed. Introduction to *From the Words of My Mouth: Tradition in Psychotherapy*, ed. Laurence Spurling, pp. 1–17. New York: Routledge, 1993.

Stanton, Martin. *Sandor Ferenczi: Reconsidering Active Intervention*. Northvale, N.J.: Jason Aronson, 1991.

Stekel, Wilhelm. *Autobiography of Wilhelm Stekel: The Life Story of a Pioneer Psychoanalyst*. New York: Liveright, 1950.

Stolorow, Robert, and George Atwood. *Faces in a Cloud: Subjectivity in Personality Theory*. New York: Jason Aronson, 1979.

———. "Reply to R. White, M. Basch, and M. Nissim-Sabat." *Psychoanalytic Review* 73, no. 3 (1986): 301–8.

———. *Contexts of Being: The Intersubjective Foundations of Psychological Life*. Hillsdale, N.J.: Analytic Press, 1992.

Stolorow, Robert, George Atwood, and Bernard Brandchaft. "Three Realms of the Unconscious and Their Therapeutic Transformation." *Psychoanalytic Review* 79 (1992): 25–30.

Stolorow, Robert, Bernard Brandchaft, and George Atwood. *Psychoanalytic Treatment: An Intersubjective Approach*. Hillsdale, N.J.: Analytic Press, 1987.

Stolorow, Robert, and Frank Lachmann. *Psychoanalysis of Developmental Arrests*. New York: International Universities Press, 1980.

———. "Transference: The Future of an Illusion." *Annual of Psychoanalysis* 12–13 (1984–85): 19–37.

Stone, Leo. "Some Problems and Potentialities of Present-Day Psychoanalysis." *Psychoanalytic Quarterly* 44 (1975): 331–70.

Strachey, James. "The Nature of the Therapeutic Action of Psychoanalysis." *International Journal of Psycho-Analysis* 15 (1934): 127–59.

Strozier, Charles. "Glimpses of a Life: Heinz Kohut (1913–1981)." *Progress in Self Psychology* 1 (1985): 3–12.

Suler, John. *Contemporary Psychoanalysis and Eastern Thought.* Albany: State University of New York Press, 1993.

Sullivan, Harry Stack. *The Interpersonal Theory of Psychiatry.* New York: Norton, 1953.

Sulloway, Frank. *Freud, Biologist of the Mind: Beyond the Psychoanalytic Legend.* New York: Basic Books, 1979.

———. "Reassessing Freud's Case Histories: The Social Construction of Psychoanalysis." In *Freud and the History of Psychoanalysis,* eds. Toby Gelfand and John Kerr, pp. 153–92. Hillsdale, N.J.: Analytic Press, 1992.

Suzuki, Shunryu. *Zen Mind, Beginner's Mind.* New York: Weatherhill, 1970.

Sylwan, B. "An Untoward Event: Où la Guerre du Trauma De Breuer à Freud de Jones à Ferenczi." *Cahiers Confrontation* 2 (1984): 101–15.

Symington, Neville. *The Analytic Experience.* New York: St. Martin's Press, 1986.

Thompson, Nellie. "Psychoanalysis and History." In *Psychoanalysis and the Humanities,* eds. Laurie Adams and Jacques Szaluta, pp. 149–68. New York: Brunner/Mazel, 1996.

Timpanaro, Sebastiano. *The Freudian Slip: Psychoanalysis and Textual Criticism.* London: Verso, 1976.

Tomkins, Silvan S. *Affect, Imagery, Consciousness,* vol. 2, *The Negative Affects.* New York: Springer, 1963.

Turkle, Sherry. *Psychoanalytic Politics: Freud's French Revolution.* Cambridge: MIT Press, 1981.

Tyson, Phyllis, and Robert Tyson. *Psychoanalytic Theories of Development: An Integration.* New Haven: Yale University Press, 1990.

Varela, Francisco. "The Creative Circle: Sketches on the Natural History of Circularity." In *The Invented Reality,* ed. Paul Watzlawick, pp. 309–23. New York: Norton, 1984.

Wachtel, Paul. *Psychoanalysis and Behavior Therapy: Towards an Integration.* New York: Basic Books, 1977.

Waelder, Robert. "The Principle of Multiple Function: Observations on Over-Determination." *Psychoanalytic Quarterly* 5 (1936): 45–62.

Walker, James R. *Lakota Society,* ed. Raymond J. Demallie. Lincoln: University of Nebraska Press, 1982.

Wallerstein, Robert. "One Psychoanalysis or Many?" *International Journal of Psycho-Analysis* 69 (1988): 5–21.

Wallwork, Ernest. "A Constructive Freudian Alternative to Psychotherapeutic Egoism." In *Community in America: The Challenge of* Habits of the Heart, eds. Charles H. Reynolds and Ralph V. Norman, pp. 202–14. Berkeley: University of California Press, 1988.

Ward, Ivan, ed. *Is Psychoanalysis Another Religion? Contemporary Essays on Spirit, Faith and Morality in Psychoanalysis.* Northampton, England: Printek, 1993.

Waugh, Patricia. *Feminine Fictions: Revisiting the Postmodern.* New York: Routledge, 1989.

Weber, Max. *From Max Weber: Essays in Sociology,* trans. and eds. H. H. Gerth and C. Wright Mills. New York: Oxford University Press, 1946.

Weber, Samuel. "The Blindness of the Seeing Eye: Psychoanalysis, Hermeneutics, *Enstellung.*" In *Institution and Interpretation,* pp. 73–84. Minneapolis: University of Minnesota Press, 1987.

Webster, Richard. *Why Freud Was Wrong: Sin, Science, and Psychoanalysis.* New York: Basic Books, 1995.

Weiss, Joseph, Harold Sampson, and the Mt. Zion Psychotherapy Research Group. *The Psychoanalytic Process.* New York: Guilford Press, 1986.

Widlöcher, Daniel. "Freedom of Thought" (Interview). In *In One's Own Bones: The Clinical Genius of Winnicott,* ed. Dodi Goldman, pp. 177–82. Northvale, N.J.: Jason Aronson, 1993.

Winnicott, Clare. "D. W. W.: 'A Reflection.' " In *Between Reality and Fantasy,* eds. Simon A. Grolnick and Leonard Barkin in collaboration with Werner Muensterberger, pp. 15–33. Northvale, N.J.: Jason Aronson, 1978.

———. "An Interview with Clare Winnicott." In *The Psychoanalytic Vocation: Rank, Winnicott, and the Legacy of Freud,* ed. Peter Rudnytsky, pp. 180–93. New Haven: Yale University Press, 1991.

Winnicott, Donald Woods. "Hate in the Countertransference" (1947). In *Through Paediatrics to Psycho-Analysis,* pp. 194–203. London: Hogarth Press, 1958.

———. "Reparation in Respect of Mother's Organized Defence against Depression" (1948). In *Through Paediatrics to Psycho-Analysis,* pp. 91–96. London: Hogarth Press, 1958.

———. "Birth Memories, Birth Trauma, and Anxiety" (1949a). In: *Through Paediatrics to Psycho-Analysis,* pp. 174–93. London: Hogarth Press, 1958.

———. "Mind and Its Relation to the Psyche-Soma" (1949b). In *Through Paediatrics to Psycho-Analysis,* pp. 243–54. London: Hogarth Press, 1958.

———. "Metapsychological and Clinical Aspects of Regression within the Psycho-Analytical Setup" (1954). In *Through Paediatrics to Psycho-Analysis,* pp. 278–94. London: Hogarth Press, 1958.

———. "The Capacity to Be Alone" (1958a). In *The Maturational Processes and the Facilitating Environment,* pp. 29–36. London: Hogarth Press, 1965.

———. *Through Paediatrics to Psycho-Analysis*. London: Hogarth Press, 1958b.

———. "Ego Distortion in Terms of True and False Self" (1960a). In *The Maturational Processes and the Facilitating Environment*, pp. 140–52. New York: International Universities Press, 1965.

———. "The Theory of the Parent-Infant Relationship" (1960b). In *The Maturational Processes and the Facilitating Environment*, pp. 37–55. New York: International Universities Press, 1965.

———. "Communicating and Not Communicating Leading to a Study of Certain Opposites" (1963). In *The Maturational Processes and the Facilitating Environment*, pp. 179–92. New York: International Universities Press, 1965.

———. *The Child, the Family, and the Outside World*. London: Penguin, 1964.

———. *The Maturational Processes and the Facilitating Environment*. New York: International Universities Press, 1965.

———. "James Strachey: Obituary" (1969). In *Psychoanalytic Explorations*, eds. Clare Winnicott, Ray Shepherd, and Madeleine Davis, pp. 506–10. Cambridge: Harvard University Press, 1989.

———. *Playing and Reality*. London: Tavistock, 1971.

———. "Fear of Breakdown" (1974). In *Psychoanalytic Explorations*, eds. Clare Winnicott, Ray Shepherd, and Madeleine Davis, pp. 87–95. Cambridge: Harvard University Press, 1989.

———. *Holding and Interpretation: Fragment of an Analysis*. London: Hogarth Press, 1986a.

———. *Home Is Where We Start From: Essays by a Psychoanalyst*. New York: Norton, 1986b.

———. *Psychoanalytic Explorations*, eds. Clare Winnicott, Ray Shepherd, and Madeleine Davis. Cambridge: Harvard University Press, 1989.

Wolf, Margery. *A Thrice-Told Tale: Feminism, Postmodernism and Ethnographic Responsibility*. Stanford: Stanford University Press, 1992.

Wortis, Joseph. *Fragments of an Analysis with Freud*. New York: Simon & Schuster, 1954.

Yerushalmi, Yosef Hayim. *Freud's Moses*. New Haven: Yale University Press, 1991.

Yalom, Irvin D., and Elkin, Ginny. *Every Day Gets a Little Closer: A Twice-Told Tale*. New York: Basic Books, 1974.

Zetzel, Elizabeth. "An Obsessional Neurotic: Freud's Rat Man." In *The Capacity for Emotional Growth*, pp. 216–28. New York: International Universities Press, 1966.

# Index

Abraham, Karl, 29, 39
Abraham, Ruth, 16, 20
Adler, Alfred, 70
Agee, James, 191
Altman, Neil, 212
Andreas-Salomé, Lou, 38
Anthony, E. James, 123
anthropology, contribution of, to psychoanalysis, 174–175, 201
Aristotle, 170
Arlow, Jacob, 52
Atwood, George, 18–19, 21, 34, 111, 120, 124, 146, 164, 169, 174, 178, 203, 207, 214–217, 220

Bachant, Janet, 209
Bacon, Francis, 7
Bakan, David, 72
Bakhtin, Mikhail, 191–192; dialogical discourse theory of, 191
Balint, Michael, 39, 42, 50–51, 54, 208–209
Barratt, Barnaby, 164
Barron, James, 206
Barthes, Roland, 139
Bateson, Gregory, 130
Baumeister, Roy, 128
Bellah, Robert N., 129
Benjamin, Jessica, 218
Bennington, Geoffrey, 192
Bernstein, Richard, 61, 169, 204–205
Bettelheim, Bruno, 133
Bion, Wilfred, 56, 180
blindness of the seeing I, 4–5, 8, 13, 27, 29–30, 34–35, 37–39, 47–48, 139, 166–168, 197–198, 201–202, 204–205, 207, 215. See also psychoanalysis, blindness of the seeing I

Bloom, Harold, ix
Bollas, Christopher, 102, 107, 110, 139, 153, 170–171, 209
Bonaparte, Marie, 16, 24
Brandchaft, Bernard, 111–112, 215
Braudel, Fernand, 201
Breger, Louis, 30
Breuer, Josef, 4, 14–15
Bromberg, Phillip, 183
Buccino, Daniel, 134
Buddhist meditative traditions, 167, 201, 211, 218
Burke, Walter, 191

capitalism, harmful psychological and social consequences of, 117
Carnochan, Peter, 138
Cartesian. See humanist tradition
Clancier, Anne, 84
classical psychoanalysis: contributions of, 76, 82, 189; limitations of, 170, 194; taboo knowledge in, 76
Clastres, Pierre, 195
Clifford, James, 9, 164
Cocks, Geoffrey, 215
Cohler, Bertram, 123
complexity theory, 181, 201, 222
constructing an identity, 66–67, 100, 109–113, 122–124, 215; role of agency in, 109–110
contemporary Freudian thought, 221; contributions of, 76, 152
countertransference, 111, 152, 164, 171, 176, 178, 187, 193, 209; Freud's theory of, 29–30; toward psychoanalysis, 35
Crapanzano, Vincent, 192
Crews, Frederick, 2
cultural unconscious, 117, 120

# About the Author

Jeffrey B. Rubin practices psychoanalysis and psychoanalytically informed psychotherapy in New York City and Bedford Hills, New York. He is a graduate of Princeton and Columbia Universities. He has taught at various psychoanalytic institutes and universities including the Postgraduate Center for Mental Health, the Object Relations Institute, the C. G. Jung Foundation, and Yeshiva University and is on the board of the International Federation for Psychoanalytic Education. He is the author of *Psychotherapy and Buddhism: Toward an Integration* (Plenum Press) and is currently working on a manuscript entitled *Love, Ethics, Spirituality, Creativity, and Health in Psychoanalysis.*